AN ANTHOLOGY OF HOPE

SAFE IN HIS ARMS

THE GOODNESS OF GOD

COMPILED BY ANITA SECHESKY

Safe In His Arms - The Goodness of God

Compiled by Anita Sechesky

Copyright © 2025 FAITH-INSPIRED BOOKS. All Rights Reserved.
A Division of LWL PUBLISHING HOUSE.
A Division of Anita Sechesky – Living Without Limitations Inc.

ISBN 978-1-990686-57-3

Book Cover Design: LWL PUBLISHING HOUSE Multimedia Team
Inside Layout: LWL PUBLISHING HOUSE Editorial Team

No part of this publication may be reproduced, distributed, or transmitted in any form or by any means, including photocopying, recording, or other electronic or mechanical methods without prior written permission of the publisher, except in the case of brief quotations embodied in critical reviews and certain other non-commercial uses permitted by copyright law.

Publisher's Note: This book contains a collection of personal experiences written at the discretion of the authors. The word usage and sentence structure have remained unaltered as much as possible to retain the authenticity of the authors' voices. FAITH-INSPIRED BOOKS uses American English as its standard for its international platform.

Copyright Statement for Bible Scriptures identified as NIV: All Scripture quotations, unless otherwise indicated, are taken from the Holy Bible, New International Version®, NIV®. Copyright ©1973, 1978, 1984, 2011 by Biblica, Inc.™ Used by permission of Zondervan. All rights reserved worldwide. www.zondervan.comThe "NIV" and "New International Version" are trademarks registered in the United States Patent and Trademark Office by Biblica, Inc.™

Copyright Statement for Bible Scriptures identified as ESV: "Scripture quotations are from the ESV® Bible (The Holy Bible, English Standard Version®), copyright © 2001 by Crossway, a publishing ministry of Good News Publishers. Used by permission. All rights reserved. The ESV text may not be quoted in any publication made available to the public by a Creative Commons license. The ESV may not be translated in whole or in part into any other language."

Copyright Statement for Bible Scriptures identified as NLT: Scripture quotations marked (NLT) are taken from the Holy Bible, New Living Translation, copyright ©1996, 2004, 2015 by Tyndale House Foundation. Used by permission of Tyndale House Publishers, Carol Stream, Illinois 60188. All rights reserved.

Copyright Statement for Bible Scriptures identified as KJV: Scripture quotations from The Authorized (King James) Version. Rights in the Authorized Version in the United Kingdom are vested in the Crown. Reproduced by permission of the Crown's patentee, Cambridge University Press.

Copyright Statement for Bible Scriptures identified as NKJV: Scriptures marked NKJV are taken from the NEW KING JAMES VERSION (NKJV): Scripture taken from the NEW KING JAMES VERSION®. Copyright© 1982 by Thomas Nelson, Inc. Used by permission. All rights reserved.

Copyright Statement for Bible Scriptures identified as TPT: Scripture quotations marked TPT are from The Passion Translation®. Copyright © 2017, 2018, 2020 by Passion & Fire Ministries, Inc. Used by permission. All rights reserved. ThePassionTranslation.com.

Copyright Statement for Bible Scriptures identified as TM: Scripture quotations from THE MESSAGE Copyright © by Eugene H. Peterson 1993, 2002, 2005, 2018. Used by permission of NavPress, Represented by Tyndale House Publishers, Inc. All rights reserved.

Copyright Statement for Bible Scriptures identified as NCV: Scriptures marked NCV are taken from the NEW CENTURY VERSION (NCV): Scripture taken from the NEW CENTURY VERSION®. Copyright© 2005 by Thomas Nelson, Inc. Used by permission. All rights reserved.

Copyright Statement for Bible Scriptures identified as NRSV: New Revised Standard Version Bible, copyright 1989, Division of Christian Education of the National Council of the Churches of Christ in the United States of America. Used by permission. All rights reserved.

LWL PUBLISHING HOUSE
Email: lwlclienthelp@gmail.com
Website: www.lwlpublishinghouse.com

Table of Contents

LEGAL DISCLAIMER ix

FOREWORD xi

ACKNOWLEDGMENTS xiv

DEDICATION xv

INTRODUCTION xvi

CHAPTER ONE - Anita Sechesky 1
    Understanding God's Goodness

CHAPTER TWO - Abigail Khan 11
    Walking Through the Storm

CHAPTER THREE - Nasha T. Alexis 23
    A Season of Faith

CHAPTER FOUR - Brian David Fuller 33
    A Testimony of Faith, Perseverance, and Purpose

CHAPTER FIVE - Chanroutie Superville 45
    Redeemed by Grace
    – My Journey from Darkness to Divine Freedom

CHAPTER SIX - Anita Sechesky 55
    Exploring the Attributes of God in Scripture

CHAPTER SEVEN - Cheryl Gardner 65
    Redeemed by His Goodness

CHAPTER EIGHT - Cindy Dawkins 77
    Strength, Joy, and Peace

CHAPTER NINE - Nasha T. Alexis 87
    To Be Known by God

CHAPTER TEN - Dhanmatie Persaud 97
    From Palmyra to Purpose
    – The Goodness of God in My Life

CHAPTER ELEVEN - Anita Sechesky 107
    The Goodness of God in Times of Suffering

CHAPTER TWELVE - Harrichand Persaud 117
    Raised Up by Grace
    – The Testimony of Pastor Harry

CHAPTER THIRTEEN - Jasmine E. Clarke 127
    The Steps of The Righteous
    – Getting into Alignment

CHAPTER FOURTEEN - Jean Lawrence-Scotland 137
    Through Loss, Still Good

CHAPTER FIFTEEN - Joan M. Steward 145
    All Things Are Possible With God

CHAPTER SIXTEEN - Anita Sechesky 155
    The Role of Gratitude in
    Recognizing God's Goodness

CHAPTER SEVENTEEN - Joshua Otabor 165
    The Last Bus to Mercy

CHAPTER EIGHTEEN - Nasha T. Alexis 171
    My New Name

CHAPTER NINETEEN - Judy Brown 181
    Planted by Grace, Growing by Faith

CHAPTER TWENTY - Karen Jiron 191
    A Daughter of God

CHAPTER TWENTY-ONE - Anita Sechesky 201
    Stories of Miracles Reflecting
    God's Goodness

CHAPTER TWENTY-TWO - Karleen J. Poyser 211
    From Brokenness to Boldness:
    Discovering Healing and Victory in Christ

CHAPTER TWENTY-THREE - Kayon Watson 221
    With God All Things Are Possible

CHAPTER TWENTY-FOUR - Nasha T. Alexis 233
    Waiting on the Lord

CHAPTER TWENTY-FIVE - Khaimnie Seepersaud 243
    The Arms That Held Me

CHAPTER TWENTY-SIX - Anita Sechesky 253
    The Goodness of God in
    Community and Relationships

CHAPTER TWENTY-SEVEN - Koreen J. Bennett 263
    The Goodness of God
    – God Knows the Plan

CHAPTER TWENTY-EIGHT - Lesa Isaacs 273
    The Goodness That Found Me
    in the Storm

CHAPTER TWENTY-NINE - Lindsay Cesario 283
    From the Pit to His Presence
    – A Journey Redeemed

CHAPTER THIRTY - Nicole Ragguette 291
    Restoration

CHAPTER THIRTY-ONE - Anita Sechesky 303
   Daily Practices for Embracing Gratitude

CHAPTER THIRTY-TWO - Patricia Giron 313
   The Goodness of God — Patty's Story

CHAPTER THIRTY-THREE - Nasha T. Alexis 323
   A Seed of Hope

CHAPTER THIRTY-FOUR - Samantha Mills-O'Brien 333
   Redeemed by Grace — God in My Story

CHAPTER THIRTY-FIVE - Sharon Teklu 343
   God's Goodness Found Me
   When I Let Go

CHAPTER THIRTY-SIX - Anita Sechesky 353
   The Transformative Power of Gratitude

CHAPTER THIRTY-SEVEN - Koreen J. Bennett 363
   When All You Can Do is Pray
   — GOD is GOOD

CHAPTER THIRTY-EIGHT - Nasha T. Alexis 373
   Fighting the Good Fight
   — Lies from the Enemy

CHAPTER THIRTY-NINE - Tricia Marcellin 381
   Forgiving What I Can't Forget

CHAPTER FORTY - Anita Sechesky 389
   Angels Among Us — Safe in His Love

CONCLUSION 400

SINNER'S PRAYER 403

ABOUT THE AUTHORS 404

A SPECIAL INVITATION 418

Legal Disclaimer

Safe In His Arms - The Goodness of God does not substitute any form of professional counsel such as an Apostle, Reverend, Pastor, Prophet, Medical Professional, Legal Counselor, Psychologist, or Life Coach. The contents and information provided do not constitute professional or legal advice in any way, shape, or form.

All chapters are written at the discretion of and with the full accountability of each contributing author, FAITH-INSPIRED BOOKS, LWL PUBLISHING HOUSE, Anita Sechesky, or Anita Sechesky – Living Without Limitations Inc. are not liable or responsible for any of the specific details, descriptions of people, places or things, personal interpretations, stories, and experiences contained within. The Publisher is not liable for any misrepresentations, false or unknown statements, actions, or judgments made by each author in this book, who are responsible for their own material and have shared their information in good faith to encourage others.

Any decisions you make, and the outcomes thereof are entirely your own doing. Under no circumstances can you hold the Compiler (Anita Sechesky), the co-authors, the Publisher (Anita Sechesky), FAITH-INSPIRED BOOKS, LWL PUBLISHING HOUSE, or Anita Sechesky – Living Without Limitations Inc. liable for any actions that you take.

You agree not to hold the Compiler, the co-authors, the Publisher, FAITH-INSPIRED BOOKS, LWL PUBLISHING HOUSE, or

Anita Sechesky – Living Without Limitations Inc. liable for any loss or expense incurred by you, as a result of materials, advice, coaching, or mentoring offered within.

The information offered in this book is intended to be general information with respect to general life issues. Information is offered in good faith; however, you are under no obligation to use this information.

Nothing contained in this book shall be considered legal, financial, or actuarial advice.

The authors and the Publisher assume no liability or responsibility for actual events or stories contained within.

The insights and testimonies shared in this publication – whether from an Apostle, Reverend, Pastor, Prophet, Medical Professional, Legal Counselor, Psychologist, Life Coach, or any other contributor – are based solely on personal reflection, lived experience, and the individual author's interpretation of events.

These accounts are not intended to replace, substitute, or serve as professional medical advice, mental-health counseling, legal guidance, pastoral counseling, or any form of licensed professional care.

Readers are encouraged to seek appropriate professional support for any medical, psychological, legal, or spiritual concerns.

Foreword

When I think about the title of this anthology, *Safe in His Arms – The Goodness of God*, my heart overflows with gratitude. This book is not just a collection of stories; it is a living testimony of God's faithfulness, His protection, and His unfailing love. Each chapter represents a unique journey of grace, healing, and restoration. Together, they remind us that no matter what we face in life, we are never beyond the reach of His arms.

This anthology was birthed from a place of reflection, compassion, and prayer. The Holy Spirit impressed upon my heart that in times like these, when the world feels heavy and uncertain, people need to be reminded that God is still good. His goodness is not dependent on our circumstances; it is the very foundation of who He is. Whether in moments of loss, illness, disappointment, or waiting, His arms remain open, strong, and steady.

What makes this anthology truly remarkable is the diversity of voices and life experiences represented within its pages. The contributing authors are men and women of faith, many of whom serve as Pastors, Evangelists, Ministers, and Faith Leaders across various ministries and communities. Alongside them are believers from all walks of life, age groups, professions, and backgrounds – each one a living witness of God's sustaining power and grace.

Although I may not know each author personally, I believe they share a deep reverence for the Lord and understand the standard of faith required to be counted upon as one who can testify truthfully of the goodness of God. Each contributor exemplifies a Christ-centered life and strives daily to live righteously – a life pleasing to God – because they know Him personally. This reverence, this authenticity, and this love for the Lord are what make their testimonies so powerful and life-giving.

Some of these authors have courageously shared their personal walks and the struggles it took to arrive at this place where they can now lift God up on such a prestigious platform to minister to you, the reader. It is a true blessing to reach those who feel lost, forgotten, or without anyone to lean on in times of uncertainty. I don't take this lightly. If our collective stories can reach just one soul – one heart that needs hope – then all our effort has been worth it. And maybe that soul is you, reading these words right now.

It is an honor to have your trust in these moments of vulnerability and hopelessness. Believe me when I say that God is an on-time God. He always knows when, where, and how to reach us, especially when everything else seems to have fallen away. His timing is perfect, His arms are secure, and His love never fails.

As you read this anthology, take it as a gentle reminder – a loving nudge from the Father's heart – that God has not forgotten you. He sees every tear, hears every prayer, and remembers every promise He has spoken over your life. Even when you cannot trace His hand, you can trust His heart.

Over the years, I have had the honor of working with hundreds of authors through LWL Publishing House, and yet each project brings something deeply unique. *Safe in His Arms – The Goodness of God* holds a special place in my heart because it embodies both vulnerability and victory. Every story in this book shines with the fingerprints of a loving Father who never abandons His children. These pages carry the fragrance of faith, refined through trials, sustained by prayer, and anchored in hope.

As I read through each chapter, I was reminded of Psalm 27:13 (NKJV): *"I would have lost heart, unless I had believed that I would see the goodness of the Lord in the land of the living."* These testimonies echo that same declaration of faith. They remind us that even in moments of deep sorrow or uncertainty, God's goodness still pursues us. His presence remains near, His mercy remains new every morning, and His arms remain open to catch us when we fall.

Some stories will stir your emotions; others will reignite your faith. But all will strengthen your trust in the One who holds you close. Each author opens a window into their soul, allowing the light of God's glory to shine through their words. Their courage to share what they have endured and overcome through Christ will inspire you to reflect on your own journey and see how His goodness has been present all along.

My prayer is that as you turn these pages, you will sense the peace and presence of the Holy Spirit filling your heart. May you be reminded that no matter how dark the night, the arms of God are never too far to reach you. May you rest knowing that His goodness has already gone before you, preparing the way for new beginnings, healing, and restoration.

To every believer who has ever cried out, *"Lord, where are You?"* this book is your gentle reminder that He has been with you all along. He held you through the storm, comforted you in the silence, and carried you when you didn't have the strength to stand.

You are seen. You are loved. And you are forever safe in His arms.

With love and gratitude,

Anita Sechesky

Visionary Compiler & Publisher

Acknowledgments

All glory and thanks to God for placing this vision in my heart and bringing it to life in His perfect timing.

To my Dad. Thank you for your love, wisdom, and constant support. Your faith and quiet strength continue to inspire me. May God bless you with health, peace, and long life.

To my husband Stephen, thank you for your unwavering support. You are a blessing to me, our family, and all we serve. May God continue to guide and prosper you.

To my sons Nathaniel and Sammy, thank you for your patience and love. May God's hand be upon you both as you grow into His purpose for your lives.

To my brother Trevor and his family, I want to thank you for being a blessing in my life and our family. Thank you for always encouraging me to pursue my dreams. I am blessed to have you in my family. I pray for your protection, health, and blessings. May God's love surround you in Jesus' mighty name. Amen.

Dedication

I lovingly dedicate this book to every heart that is seeking God – to those longing for truth, peace, and purpose in the midst of life's uncertainties. May you encounter His presence in ways that are unexpected yet undeniable, profound yet deeply personal.

When you least expect it, may His light break through your darkest night, His voice whisper hope into your weary soul, and His love embrace you in the stillness of your waiting.

> *"And you will seek Me and find Me, when you search for Me with all your heart."* Jeremiah 29:13 (NKJV)

May every page of this book lead you closer to the One who has been pursuing you all along – the God who loves you beyond measure and longs for you to know that you are never alone.

Introduction

My vision for *Safe in His Arms: The Goodness of God* was born out of seasons of loneliness – times when I didn't feel good enough. Even though I often stood strong for others – encouraging, supporting, praying, and keeping the faith for them – there were moments when I felt unseen and alone. That's the reality of being human.

There's a unique kind of loneliness that can exist even when you have family and loved ones around you. There is a sacred place in your heart that holds thoughts and emotions too deep to share with just anyone. For me, that realization came after my mother transitioned to her eternal home in glory.

In late spring of 2023, I experienced a wave of emotions: anger, fear, loneliness, and then, eventually, hope that I would see my mom again one day. But even as that hope grew, I came to understand that no one could ever fill her place. No one could cook like her, talk like her, or even understand me the way she did.

The vision for this book was born from that space of grief, reflection, faith, and God's encompassing love. Though I am blessed with an amazing husband, two wonderful sons, and my dad, I knew life would never be the same without my mother. I began to search my heart more deeply to understand who God truly is.

Not long before my dearest mommy transitioned to her Eternal home in late Spring of 2023, I played CeCe Winans' song *The Goodness of God* for her. It touched her deeply because it reflected the faith journey she had walked her whole life. As one of the first born-again believers in her family, she led many to the Lord. I realized then that God had truly been good to my mom. He had carried her through times of hardships from struggle to strength, seasons of pain and lonliness to times of hope, courage and refreshing. God transformed her through His limitless and unconditional love, and then used my mom's life journey to shape mine.

As a Publisher working with many writers, I had to make some executive decisions concerning other visionary projects that were delayed in their process but remained strong in their purpose. As a result, this incredible collaboration was birthed with other Christain authors becoming the big project for 2025. So, *Safe in His Arms - The Goodness of God* became more than a book about the profound power of a majestic God. It became a collection of testimonies that reveal how God's goodness sustains us through the most painful and uncertain seasons. I decided to make it bigger than me and my original story. Collaborating together we created a work that speaks to the heart of faith, resilience, and divine love. The intention of this book is also to make things right. Although it was originally several separate visions, as the Publisher of each, I made a CEO decision and integrated them under one umbrella, as Holy Spirit confirmed to me it was all about Him anyways. I only pray that God's perfect will be done and everything that was delayed, discouraged, and divided would now be made right in the eyes of God and that what the enemy meant for harm, God will turn it around for His good! As you read this beautiful book declaring the goodness of God, I pray that wherever there may be division, separation, or indifference in your life, things will begin to shift for His Glory! Let's agree now, that there will be unity, peace, healing, and manifold blessings under the blood covenant of Christ!

You will notice that not every story in this book focuses solely on "the goodness of God" in the title, but every testimony reflects His blessings, grace, and favor in the lives of the writers. My prayer is that as you read these pages, you will be inspired, encouraged, and filled with peace, hope, and even joy, no matter what you're facing right now.

I also wanted to share with you that from the moment I was conceived in my mother's womb, God had His hand on my life (Jeremiah 1:5, NKJV). Even though my mother faced a high-risk pregnancy with many challenges, God preserved my life. He had a plan from the very beginning to bless me and give me a future and a hope (Jeremiah 29:11, NKJV). God has a plan and purpose for you as well!

All my life, I have seen the faithfulness of God, and today, I can boldly say that I am safe in His arms. As you read the stories in this book – written by men and women of faith who have endured hardship, loss, and trials – I trust that you will see how God carried them through. When their faith was tested, they held on. And He proved Himself faithful, again and again.

Lastly, I thank God for all my sisters and brothers in Christ who have contributed a special piece of their heart and soul to the making of this beautiful work of literary art for the Glory of God. May He bless each co-author greatly!

May this book bless you and your household. May it remind you that even in your darkest moments, you are not forgotten. You are safe in His arms, where His goodness and mercy will follow you all the days of your life (Psalm 23:6, NKJV).

Opening Prayer

Heavenly Father,

We thank You for every reader who has opened these pages with a seeking heart. May Your presence wrap around them like a warm embrace, reminding them that they are never alone. *"He who dwells in the secret place of the Most High shall abide under the shadow of the Almighty"* Psalm 91:1 (NKJV).

Lord, for those walking through seasons of loss, confusion, or loneliness, let Your peace be their anchor and Your love their constant refuge. Your Word says, *"Fear not, for I am with you; be not dismayed, for I am your God. I will strengthen you, yes, I will help you"* Isaiah 41:10 (NKJV).

Heal every heart that is broken, restore every weary soul, and remind them that You are still good, still faithful, and still near. Let this book be a vessel of Your hope and healing – awakening faith, stirring joy, and birthing new beginnings in every life it touches.

We declare that every reader will experience the tangible goodness of God and find rest, safety, and strength in Your everlasting arms. For *"The eternal God is your refuge, and underneath are the everlasting arms"* Deuteronomy 33:27 (NKJV).

In the precious and powerful name of Jesus Christ, Amen.

Anita Sechesky

Visionary Compiler & Publisher

Safe in His Arms

The Goodness of God

Anita Sechesky

Chapter One

Understanding God's Goodness

When we speak about the goodness of God, we are not describing a passing virtue that shifts with moods or seasons. We are describing His very essence – the unchanging nature of who He is. God's goodness is not something He occasionally reveals; it is who He is. Every act of mercy, every answered prayer, every breath we take is an expression of that goodness. His goodness is permanent, steadfast, and woven into every detail of creation and every moment of our existence.

Spiritually speaking, goodness goes far beyond human morality or kindness. It is higher than behavior, deeper than emotion, and rooted in the very character of our Creator. His goodness is the foundation upon which all His attributes stand. His love, His faithfulness, His justice, His grace, and His mercy are all expressions of His goodness operating in different forms. This is why Scripture tells us in Psalm 34:8 (NKJV):

> *"Oh, taste and see that the Lord is good; Blessed is the man who trusts in Him!"*

To "taste and see" is more than a simple invitation; it is a divine summons to encounter Him personally. It means discovering His goodness through lived experience; feeling it in moments of peace, recognizing it in seasons of struggle, and remembering it when life becomes overwhelming. God's goodness is constant; only our perception shifts depending on the season we're walking through.

When storms rise, His goodness anchors us. When joy floods our hearts, His goodness rejoices with us. His nature remains steady even when our circumstances shake.

And His goodness does not vanish in suffering. In fact, it often becomes most visible in seasons of pain. God comforts the brokenhearted, strengthens the weary, and draws near to those who feel crushed. He uses dreams, Scripture, intercessors, and divine encounters to remind us that He has not left us. His goodness walks with us through valleys just as surely as it leads us beside still waters.

The more we understand His goodness, the more boldly we trust Him. When you truly know God is good, you no longer interpret His character through the lens of your pain. You interpret your pain through the certainty of His character. It changes everything. It transforms fear into faith, heaviness into hope, and uncertainty into surrender.

As a Registered Nurse with over twenty years of experience, I have witnessed both miracles and moments that tested the human spirit beyond comprehension. I have stood beside patients fighting for every breath and families waiting in trembling hope for a miracle. I've seen peace settle inside hospital rooms where fear once reigned, and I've held hands when no human words could offer comfort. I have watched God breathe supernatural calm into situations the world would describe as hopeless. In those moments, I saw with absolute clarity that the goodness of God is not theoretical – it's tangible.

In those sacred spaces, between life and eternity, I witnessed undeniable evidence of God's goodness. It didn't always manifest as physical healing. Sometimes it manifested as a peace so profound that it silenced panic. Sometimes it was the quiet strength that enabled a grieving spouse to stand. Sometimes it appeared as reconciliation between family members who had not spoken in years, yet found unity in the face of loss. And other times, His goodness came as a holy release where the presence of God filled the room so powerfully that everyone knew Heaven had welcomed one of His children home.

As a Professional Life Coach and Mentor, I have walked with hundreds of people through trauma, grief, depression, betrayal, burnout, and identity crises. Again and again, I witnessed lives transform the moment individuals recognized that God had been present with them all along, even in circumstances that seemed unbearable. Many found breakthrough when they realized that His goodness had not left them in their darkest valley; it had carried them through it.

As a prophetic voice, I have seen how a single God-inspired word can reignite courage, restore clarity, and breathe fresh hope into a discouraged heart. One timely prophetic confirmation can open someone's eyes to the fact that God has been pursuing them, speaking to them, and strengthening them quietly behind the scenes. God's goodness finds us in ways we never expect: through dreams, through encounters with strangers, through intercessors on assignment, or through a still, small whisper that touches a part of the heart we didn't know needed healing.

His goodness is woven into every part of our story, and when we look closely, we can trace His fingerprints everywhere.

The Bible overflows with stories of divine goodness. From Genesis to Revelation, we encounter a God who is compassionate, patient, merciful, righteous, and ever faithful. His goodness is woven into every promise, every warning, every act of deliverance, and every moment of restoration.

In the Old Testament, His goodness is demonstrated through His covenant love toward Israel, a people who often struggled, fell, wandered, and doubted. Yet God never abandoned them. He pursued them, corrected them, restored them, and continually called them back to Himself. Even in discipline, His motives were redemptive.

In the New Testament, His goodness takes human form through Jesus Christ – the perfect image of the invisible God. Every miracle, every healing, every deliverance, every word of compassion was rooted in the Father's goodness. Jesus didn't just teach the goodness of God. He demonstrated it through His touch, His voice, His sacrifice, and His resurrection. Scripture reveals a God who is good in every season, faithful in every generation, and near to all who call upon Him.

It is often in our deepest pain that we most clearly recognize God's goodness. Suffering refines our faith, rearranges our priorities, and brings us into deeper dependence on Him. Pain shapes character, deepens compassion, and stretches our understanding of who God is. While we would never choose the valley, it is often in the valley that we encounter the God who never leaves us. Pain exposes our need, but it also reveals His nearness. It strips away every false support until all that remains is the One who promised never to forsake us.

God does not abandon us in our suffering. In fact, He moves closer. He speaks through Scripture, through dreams, through intercessors, through worship, through strangers who carry a timely word, and through the quiet presence of the Holy Spirit. In seasons of grief, loneliness, and unanswered questions, the Lord surrounds us with reminders that we are not walking alone. Pain becomes the doorway through which we experience divine encounters. It sensitizes our spirit to His voice and softens our hearts to His comfort.

He doesn't waste our tears; He turns them into testimonies. Sometimes God allows the storm not to break us, but to build us into who we were always meant to become. Sometimes what feels like delay is actually divine preparation stretching us, anchoring us, and maturing us. And sometimes what feels like loss becomes the very soil where new purpose grows.

God's goodness isn't diminished by our pain. It is revealed through it. The very places where we thought we would collapse are often the places where His strength carries us. The very wounds that once brought us sorrow become the stories that bring healing to others. Pain refines us, but it never defines us. God's goodness does.

Gratitude as a Doorway to Experiencing His Goodness

One of the most powerful ways to encounter God's goodness is through gratitude. Gratitude shifts our focus from what is missing to what remains. It opens our spiritual eyes and allows us to see God's hand even in situations where clarity is hard to find. Gratitude turns ordinary moments into holy encounters. It transforms perspective, softens the heart, and invites revelation. It doesn't deny pain but gives us the strength to see God in the midst of it.

Gratitude is not just a spiritual discipline. It is a supernatural accelerator. When we thank God intentionally, even before the answer manifests, thanksgiving becomes faith in action. Gratitude aligns our mind, body, and spirit with Heaven's frequency. It shifts our atmosphere. It prepares our hearts for answered prayer and positions us to receive what God has already released. A grateful heart moves us from striving into resting, from worrying into worshiping, and from questioning into trusting.

Gratitude unlocks breakthrough because it demonstrates trust, which moves the heart of God. When we thank Him ahead of time, we are declaring, *"I believe You, Lord,"* even when the natural facts haven't changed. Heaven responds to faith-filled gratitude. This posture brings acceleration, because God can pour into a heart that is open, surrendered, and expectant. Gratitude allows us to step into the flow of grace where miracles, clarity, and divine intervention are birthed.

Gratitude also accelerates emotional healing. Our minds respond to thanksgiving the same way flowers respond to sunlight – they open. Gratitude dismantles fear, rewires toxic thought patterns, calms anxiety, and invites peace to reign. It grounds the soul, stabilizes the heart, and restores emotional equilibrium. When our hearts shift into gratitude, heaviness lifts, confusion fades, and hope begins to rise again.

Physically, gratitude sends healing energy throughout the body. When gratitude rises, stress declines. Hormones balance. The body shifts from fight-or-flight into harmony. Even science affirms what Scripture has always said: a grateful heart is good medicine. Gratitude changes cellular patterns and invites the life-giving vibrational frequency of peace, joy, and spiritual alignment with God.

Gratitude also invites the inspiration of the Holy Spirit. A thankful heart is fertile ground for revelation. When we operate through gratitude, the Holy Spirit within us becomes louder, clearer, and more active in our daily walk, ministry, decision-making, and spiritual discernment. Gratitude sharpens our ability to hear God and sensitizes us to the movements of Heaven.

As our hearts surrender, our mindsets shift, and our attitudes align with Heaven, we become vessels of honor fully available for God to use. Gratitude purifies motives, softens attitudes, and cultivates humility. It transforms us into carriers of His presence, His peace, and His glory. Gratitude turns ordinary believers into world-changers because it connects us directly to the heart of God.

Everything begins to shift. Healing takes place at the core. Our roots sink deeper into the Word. Our breath becomes a worshipful reminder of the One who sustains us. We no longer depend on the world for joy, love, or affirmation because Jehovah Jireh, our Provider, is the One who fills every empty place.

Becoming Vessels of His Goodness

God's goodness was never meant to stop with us. It is meant to flow through us. When we walk in kindness, forgiveness, mercy, and compassion, we reflect the nature of God on earth. The world is longing for authenticity, hope, purity, and spiritual integrity. Every act of goodness we show becomes an echo of Heaven, a living testimony that God is still moving through His people.

Goodness is not weakness; it is strength wrapped in humility. It is authority wrapped in compassion. It is truth wrapped in grace. It is choosing to respond like Jesus when everything in us wants to react like the world.

When we walk in the overflow of His goodness, fear loses its power. Hope rises. Faith awakens. Our outlook shifts. We expect God to move because we have seen Him move before. And as we yield to Him daily, in attitude, decision, and character, we become vessels of honor, carriers of His presence, and living expressions of His goodness to a world desperately in need of Him.

Trusting in God's goodness does not mean we understand everything He allows. Faith is not rooted in explanations. It is rooted in surrender. True faith learns to rest in the character of God even when the details make no sense. There were seasons in my healthcare career when outcomes shattered me, moments when I stood by bedsides praying for miracles that didn't unfold the way I hoped. There were prayers in my personal life that lingered for years without answers, leaving me questioning, waiting, and wondering.

Yet every time I looked back, I saw His fingerprints weaving purpose, protection, and preparation into everything. His goodness was working in hidden places long before it became visible. He was strengthening me, maturing me, and aligning my steps with His perfect timing.

He is good even when life is not. He is present even when we feel alone. He is speaking even when the world feels silent. And He is working intricately, intentionally, faithfully even when we cannot perceive it.

Prayer

Heavenly Father,

Thank You for Your constant, unwavering goodness that carries us through every stage of life. You are faithful even when we falter, and Your love never runs out. Open our eyes to see Your hand at work in every detail – the big and the small. Help us to walk in gratitude and faith, so that our lives would become clear reflections of Your heart. Lord, for the one reading this now, let this be their gentle reminder that You have not forgotten them. Remind them that their name is written on the palm of Your hand. Speak peace where there is anxiety, bring healing where there is pain, and surround them with Your unfailing love. Breathe fresh hope into weary souls. Restore joy where it's been stolen. Reignite dreams that have been buried. And help us all to live daily in the overflow of Your goodness.

In the precious and powerful name of Jesus Christ, Amen.

Anita Sechesky - Visionary Compiler & Publisher

Safe in His Arms

The Goodness of God

Abigail Khan

Chapter Two

Walking Through the Storm

Several years ago, I was in a very dark place. I found myself consumed with feelings of fear, pain, and anger after walking through one of the most difficult seasons of my life – the gradual breaking down of my marriage. It wasn't just a single moment or one situation; it was a series of stressful and heartbreaking circumstances that eventually led to our separation and divorce – something I tried so hard to avoid.

I had poured so much into my marriage – time, energy, prayer, love, and commitment – that the thought of losing it all left me paralyzed with fear. I would sit awake at night asking, *"Where do I go from here? How will I raise three children under the age of eight alone? Can I manage the mortgage and bills on one income? How will my children be affected?"* Those questions echoed in my heart like a storm that wouldn't cease. I longed for peace, but peace felt like a distant dream I could no longer reach.

The enemy began to attack my mind, filling it with doubt, worry, and hopelessness. My lonely days soon turned into restless nights, and those nights bled into weary mornings. I was emotionally, mentally, and physically drained. I cried out to God, asking, *"Why would You allow me to experience such pain? What have I done to deserve this heartache?"* At times, I felt like I was drowning beneath the weight of unanswered prayers, silently pleading for God to rescue me from the chaos I couldn't control.

But in time, I came to understand that I was a work in progress… and that God was still writing my story. Through prayer, surrender, and perseverance, I began to find healing in His presence. His love didn't erase my pain overnight, but it gave me the strength to stand each morning when I wanted to give up.

The pain of that season was unbearable at times. I felt betrayed by circumstances, devalued, and abandoned. I couldn't see how anything good could come from it. I had been faithful, loving, and devoted to my home and family. I worked hard, cared for my children, and supported my husband the best I could. Still, my heart broke under the pressure of losing what I had built.

So why me?

It didn't take long for my pain to turn into anger. That pain grew into resentment, bitterness, unforgiveness, and feelings of rejection. I felt imprisoned and bound by the enemy's grip on the downfall of my marriage. I fought desperately to break free from the anxiousness, worry, and distress, but the chains felt unbearably tight. Everything around me was falling apart.

And yet, even in my brokenness, God was near. He never left me, even when I couldn't feel Him. In my tears, He whispered hope. In my silence, He strengthened my spirit. What I once thought was the end of my story was only the beginning of God's restoration.

A Work in Progress

This work in progress all started when a dear friend invited me to attend her Pentecostal church. She told me how deeply rooted the church was in Scripture and how many classes and service opportunities were available to help grow in my walk with Christ.

At that point, I was tired of feeling stuck, weary, and sad. I had no peace in my life and desperately needed the light of God to shine again. My heart was aching for renewal – a place where I could be seen, heard, and loved without judgment. I had tried everything in my own strength, and yet I still felt empty inside. So, I asked myself, *"What do I have to lose?"*

That Sunday morning, my friend picked me up, and we went together. I still remember sitting there as the pastor preached, and it felt as if God Himself was speaking directly to me. Each word carried power and conviction that reached into the depths of my pain. His words pierced through the fog of my confusion, and I felt hope begin to rise again. For the first time in a long while, I felt the presence of God wrapping around me like a gentle embrace, reminding me that I was never truly alone.

From that day forward, I attended services regularly. The 9:00 a.m. service became my sanctuary – a place of peace and renewal. The messages breathed life into my soul and reminded me to let go, to trust that God would handle my battles in His perfect timing. Even as my marriage continued to unravel, I found peace and strength through those sermons.

I started praying earnestly on my knees before bed and again when I woke. I asked God to take control of my life, my emotions, and my family. I made a decision to stop begging for things to change and instead began trusting that God would change me first.

As my healing journey progressed, I joined Bible study, volunteered for community outreach, and surrounded myself with like-minded believers. I discovered the beauty of spiritual sisterhood – women who encouraged me, prayed with me, and reminded me that there was purpose even in pain. The more I filled my mind with God's Word, the more my peace returned.

Slowly, I began to recognize the incredible love and value my Heavenly Father had for me. I stopped worrying about how others saw me and started focusing on how God saw me – His beloved daughter.

Through it all, I learned to surrender completely, knowing that God was walking beside me every step of the way. The shame, blame, and anger began to melt away. My focus shifted toward the greatest blessings in my life – my three beautiful children.

They needed me.

I had to be their strength, their protector, and their spiritual guide. So, I kept them rooted in our home church, ensuring they grew up surrounded by God's Word, and His love held us together stronger than ever before.

As the months turned into years, I began to notice a powerful transformation taking place in my heart and mind. God was shifting me from pain to purpose. He was rebuilding me piece by piece, gently teaching me that my identity was not found in what I had lost but in who I was becoming through Him.

Where I once felt abandoned, I realized He was realigning me for something better. Where I had believed I was being punished, I saw that I was being refined. I stopped blaming myself for the struggles in my marriage and began to see that God was still at work behind the scenes. Even in the silence, He was orchestrating healing that I couldn't yet see.

Eventually, the season led to separation and, in time, divorce – something I had prayed would never happen. Yet through it all, God's peace never left me. His presence became my anchor on the days I felt like giving up. With much prayer and the loving support of family and friends, I began to accept our new reality, learning that acceptance doesn't mean defeat. It means trusting that God's way is higher than ours.

To my surprise, my ex-husband showed support in moments I never expected. There were times when his kindness felt like the Holy Spirit working through him to remind me that peace was possible even in brokenness. I could see God softening both our hearts. We both learned how to communicate better, respect each other's roles, and work together for the sake of our children.

Despite belonging to different faiths, we have built a foundation of mutual respect and grace – something I truly believe only God could have established. What others might see as impossible has become a peaceful coexistence rooted in shared love for our children. There are moments when I still marvel at how God turned tension into teamwork and division into unity for their sake.

Had it not been for my faith and understanding that I am safe in His arms, I know the story could have ended differently. But God, in His infinite wisdom, turned a painful chapter into a testimony of His faithfulness.

He gave me the strength I never thought I had, replacing fear with faith and despair with hope. The same situation that once broke me now reminds me daily that I am carried by His grace. Every time I look at my children's faces and see their peace, I am reminded that God truly can bring beauty from ashes.

Holding On Through the Hardest Process

The process of separation and rebuilding was far from easy. Between the legal steps, the emotional exhaustion, and the financial pressures, I found myself leaning on God more than ever. There were days when I didn't know how I would make it to the next, yet somehow His mercy always met me in the morning.

I prayed without ceasing for His favor, provision, and guidance. Sometimes those prayers were strong and full of faith, and other times they were whispered through tears, with nothing but a fragile hope holding me together. Each time I felt weak, His Word became my anchor. When confusion tried to cloud my mind, His truth brought clarity. When resentment crept in, His Spirit filled me with grace and forgiveness. God was teaching me to release the weight of control and trust in His perfect timing.

I learned that when God closes a door, it's often to protect us from something that would have destroyed us. And when He says, "Be still," He is preparing a better path. I began to understand that the waiting wasn't wasted. It was where He was building my faith.

"For I know the plans I have for you," declares the Lord, "plans to prosper you and not to harm you, plans to give you hope and a future." Jeremiah 29:11 (NIV)

Those words became my anthem. I clung to them when I felt uncertain about tomorrow. I began to see that even though divorce is painful and never part of God's original design, He can still use it for redemption and restoration. His plans are always for our growth and good, even when they come wrapped in heartache.

Through this process, I discovered my worth wasn't tied to marital status, but to my identity in Christ. I was a chosen daughter, loved beyond measure, and entrusted with a divine purpose that could only emerge through surrender. I realized that sometimes God must dismantle the familiar to rebuild us into something far greater than we could have imagined on our own.

What Once Broke Me Now Refines Me

What had once broken me is now being used to refine me into the woman God always intended me to be. I made a conscious decision to live a life centered in Christ and to break every generational curse that tried to follow my family line. I refused to let pain be the end of my story; instead, I chose to let it become the soil from which new strength and faith could grow.

I chose to raise my children in faith, and today, all three have accepted Jesus Christ as their Lord and Savior. Each has been baptized through full water immersion, and their personal relationships with God fill me with gratitude and awe. Watching them walk in truth has been one of the most healing parts of my journey. Their laughter, confidence, and compassion are daily reminders that God can take what was shattered and rebuild it with His perfect hands.

There are moments when I reflect on how far we've come – the tears, the prayers, the nights I stayed awake asking God for direction – and I realize that His grace carried me every step of the way. I've seen how prayer not only transforms situations but transforms hearts. The same woman who once felt broken beyond repair now stands restored, knowing her value comes from the One who redeemed her.

What the enemy meant for harm, God truly turned for good. His timing, though sometimes slow to my human heart, proved to be perfect. He reminded me that delay is not denial, It's preparation for something greater.

Many people say, *"God won't give you more than you can handle."* But I've learned that sometimes He allows more than we can bear so that we learn to depend on Him entirely. In my weakness, He became my strength. In my tears, He became my comfort. When I felt lost, He became my direction.

Because of my spiritual growth and renewed faith in Christ, I've learned to glorify God through every trial. I now see how He was victorious in my life and in the lives of my children. The peace and unity our family experiences today are proof that God's grace is greater than any pain of the past. We've become living testimonies that even in the aftermath of loss, beauty can rise again.

Yes, the journey was hard, but through it all, I became a stronger, wiser, and more faithful woman of God. My ex-husband and I now live in peace, co-parenting with respect and love. I've learned to admire his commitment to our children and to thank God for the transformation that only He could bring about. What once seemed like an ending has become a story of divine restoration – one written by the hand of a faithful God who wastes nothing.

I emerged from that chapter as a confident and fearless single mother of three: a homeowner, a teacher, and most importantly, a cherished daughter of the one true God. I now walk in the fullness of who He created me to be, forever grateful that when I thought I was falling apart, I was actually falling into His arms.

It is time to walk boldly in my God-given purpose and to declare that I am fearfully and wonderfully made.

"I will praise You, for I am fearfully and wonderfully made; marvelous are Your works, and that my soul knows very well." Psalm 139:14 (NKJV)

Prayer

Heavenly Father,

I thank You for being the anchor of my soul through every storm. I lift up every person reading this who may be walking through the pain of marital struggle, separation, or divorce. Lord, wrap them in Your peace. Remind them that their worth is not defined by what was lost but by Your everlasting love.

Give them strength when they are weary, hope when they feel forgotten, and faith when the path ahead seems uncertain. Heal their hearts, Lord, and teach them to forgive as You have forgiven. Restore joy where sorrow has taken root, and let Your presence fill every empty space.

Thank You for turning brokenness into beauty and for using every trial to draw us closer to You. May each of us find comfort, courage, and confidence knowing that we are safe in Your arms, now and forever.

In Jesus' name, Amen.

Abigail Khan - Co-Author

Safe in His Arms
The Goodness of God

Nasha T. Alexis

Chapter Three

A Season of Faith

"I will sing of the Lord's great love forever; with my mouth, I will make your faithfulness known through all generations" Psalms 89:1 (NIV)

The faithfulness of God is something that can't be compared to anything. That's His character; it's who He is. He reveals Himself in spectacular ways. He knows what we need even before we do it ourselves. He is the God who pursues us and brings us to the place He already planned for us.

When God starts something new in our lives, we often don't always recognize it or understand what is happening. In our finite minds, we only see pain, chaos, and disappointments. For some, it may take minutes, for others, days, and yet for others, even years, to realize that God was or is working. He was or is the One carrying us through all the difficulties we have experienced or are experiencing.

He's been there from the beginning. In my case, it took years for me to see or even realize that God was – and is – continually working in my life. He was with me then, and He is with me even today.

That is true for you, too, in whatever season you are in right now. You are never alone. You can take God at His Word:

"He will never leave you nor forsake you." Deuteronomy 31:6 (NIV)

I don't remember the date it happened, but I do remember having a conversation with God as the pastor at church was preaching. He was speaking about how much God loves us and is always there to protect us – you know, feel-good things like that.

What I felt was my blood boiling with anger as hot tears welled up in my eyes. That day, I interrogated God (all in my mind, of course). Before long, I had stopped listening to the pastor and was focused on drilling God. He was in the "hot seat," and I needed answers.

With my eyes closed so that not a tear would drop – because I am not a crier, I don't cry for anyone or anything – the questions in my mind started pouring out. They got louder and more heated as they rolled around in my head.

With fists balled and teeth clenched, so as not to scream out loud, I screamed in my head, *"Where were You when I was a child!? If You love me so much, why did I have to go through all those horrible things!? Why didn't You stop it!? Now, I am an adult, and things still haven't changed. Instead, things are even worse than before. I now have children to think about. What did I do to deserve such a terrible life? The more I give, the less I get in return. All I seem to know is pain. Even when I'm laughing, I don't feel happiness or joy. I am always in fighting mode, and I am tired – I am exhausted of it all. When will this all end?"*

Without warning, the dams in my eyes finally burst as hot tears rolled down my cheeks. Then, I heard, *"I was there with you through it all. You were never alone."*

My response in that moment wasn't, *"Thank You, Lord,"* nor did I show any form of gratitude. Instead, I retorted, *"Prove it! If You were there and if You love me so much, have someone hug me after service."*

That wasn't much to ask for, but I wasn't expecting it to happen by any means. I didn't say it, but I was looking for a "special hug" – and only I would know if or when it happened.

So, as usual, I was making my way out of the sanctuary to get my children from Sunday School when I was stopped by someone who said, *"I need to give you a hug."* Before I could respond, she wrapped her arms around me, and I found myself hugging her too in this long embrace. And even though I am bigger in size and height than her, it felt like she could lift me off my feet and cradle me like a baby (that's the image that popped into my head).

At the end of that embrace, we both looked at each other, and in laughter and tears, we both said in unison, *"Wow, that was a Jesus hug."*

In that moment, I felt like a little child – the weight and burden of life were lifted from me, and more than that, my heart felt light. I was able to take a deep breath for the first time in a long while.

In tears, I said, *"Thank You, Father."* Until that day, it was difficult for me to call God "Father." He was just God.

Also, what you don't know – and I didn't mention before – was that, by that time, I was already baptized for a few years. Don't get me wrong, I had made an honest confession of faith and believed in Jesus – just not God. That was my first personal encounter with God. My first time calling Him "Father."

Before that fateful day, I lived on autopilot. I knew and understood what was expected of me on the job and at home, and so I did those things without really thinking about any of it.

By 1999, I had my first child and was married in April 2000. Married life was supposed to be the beginning of something new – happy memories and the start of a wonderful life. This was, after all, my family, and things would be different – dare I say it, a happier life.

Prior to saying our vows, we had our struggles, but I had hope that things would get better; I'd make sure of that. I told myself that

I would be the best wife and person ever, that he would forsake all else, and we would live happily ever after.

As you can guess, it was not so. Mind you, it wasn't all bad, but as you can imagine, the bad overshadowed the good.

Then, early in 2005, I got pregnant with my second child. Prior to that, in His divine grace and mercy, God had placed me in a church community where I felt at home from the beginning. I remember on my very first visit to Humberlea Worship Centre – before even meeting anyone – I thought to myself, *"I'm home."* I felt a calmness and peace wash over me that I did not understand.

God is the only One who knows your beginning, middle, and end.

"His plans are to prosper you and not to harm you, plans to give you hope and a future." Jeremiah 29:11 (NIV)

That's where the adage "God works in mysterious ways" rang true for me. In His sovereignty, God was preparing me for this journey – a Season of Faith. Mind you, that didn't happen overnight, but it started with God placing me in the right place with the right people surrounding me.

And when the time came, everyone in that army God placed me in took their position – from the lead pastor at that time to the wonderful ladies who came by with gifts, food, and prayers. There were also those who would pick us up for church. These gentlemen went out of their way to help me and my girls get to church each Sunday.

During the time I was pregnant, I had many appointments to go to. There was a special lady who refused to take no for an answer and would drive me and my mother to these appointments, then return to pick us up. I had people calling me on the phone to check on me and pray for me, which I thought was very strange because I didn't know most of these people. But they spoke to me as though they had known me all my life. They were truly God-sent.

Still, with all these people helping me, I felt alone, unwanted, unseen, and abandoned. I only desired one person to be there with me – and he wasn't. The one who vowed "in sickness and in health" was always too busy or had other interests that took his time away from me and our family.

During those months of this difficult pregnancy, even if Jesus Himself had shown up physically, I wouldn't have recognized Him because my focus was only on what I didn't have – or, more accurately, who I thought I needed at the time.

God is a loving and faithful Father, who knows the needs of His children.

A week after getting the news that I was pregnant, I found myself in the emergency room for the first time. I had to wait in line for what seemed like forever just to get to the Intake Nurse, then it was another wait to see the doctor. That visit ended even before it started. Each visit after that was the same – I was dismissed almost immediately and was told it was just morning sickness, even though I was throwing up throughout the day and night. I was not able to keep any food down, not even water. I visited the emergency room a few more times before I was finally admitted.

That visit was different from the beginning. A young man offered to hold my place in line for me as he was also there holding a spot for his mother. I was very grateful because I was very weak. Looking back, I can see God's hand moving, but I didn't recognize it. I was then placed in a room, half expecting to be sent home just as quickly again by the doctor – but grateful to be lying down in the meantime.

Minutes later, this young man walked in and introduced himself, but I forgot his name just as quickly. All I remember thinking was that I'm probably older than him and came very close to asking his age, but a mouthful of saliva and vomit stopped me. Turns out, he was the doctor on call that evening. After looking me over and questioning me, he ordered some blood work and told me that I was not going home, and he had already planned for a bed for me. I spent the next three weeks in the hospital.

And for the rest of my pregnancy, I was in and out of that hospital – one or two weeks in, and maybe one week out. At the same time, while going through this difficult pregnancy, my marriage hit rock bottom.

Those were the longest nine months of my life. During that time, what I had failed to see was that God Himself was there, helping me. He was my strength when I felt weak. And like Apostle Paul, who pleaded with God to take away the thorn in his flesh, so many nights I wept and pleaded with God to take my life. Each morning, I woke up and became angrier with Him. I refused to pray or even mention His name.

Even so, He never turned away from me or left me alone.

"My grace is sufficient for you, for my power is made perfect in weakness."
2 Corinthians 12:9 (NIV)

This verse means so much more to me now as I look back on those months of pregnancy, for I was physically and emotionally weak. For me, I saw death as the only way out of what I was going through. I wanted everything to end – to escape and never have to deal with anything again. Death was my ticket out, and the One holding the key was God. But even then, I believed He had abandoned me, wasn't listening, and paid no interest in what I was experiencing… or so I thought.

I now realize that when we are at our lowest and think that God has left us because we can't hear Him, that simply isn't true. I've concluded that it could be one of two possibilities: He is fighting for you, or maybe, just maybe, we haven't shut up long enough to hear Him speaking to us.

We have so much to say and to tell God what to do and all He is doing is wrong. We forget to stop and just listen.

"Be still, and know that I am God." Psalm 46:10 (NIV)

We have an amazing and loving Father, who cares deeply, with an everlasting love for His children. He cares so much that He sent His One and Only Son to take our place on the cross to pay a debt that we could never repay, to bring us back to Himself, so that we may have a relationship with Him.

"For God so loved the world that He gave His one and only Son, that whoever believes in Him shall not perish but have eternal life." John 3:16 (NIV)

Who else can love like that? Answer: no one. Not even one – except JESUS CHRIST. We are told in 1 John 3:16, "This is how we know what love is: Jesus Christ laid down His life for us."

So, when you are going through tough situations, and you feel alone, or it looks like you are on your own, there is an army of people waiting to take their place – God's army. These people are the extension of God's hand working in your life. The only thing is, far too often, we miss it at first. Even now, whenever I have moments of doubt, I can look back at that season in my life to remind me of God's faithfulness, and each time, I take away something different – a new perspective, a deeper realization of Who God is.

He promised Joshua that He would never leave him nor forsake him:

"I will never leave you nor forsake you." Joshua 1:5 (NIV)

And that promise is true for us today.

During one of the darkest seasons of my life, God showed up in a big way. It was years before I recognized or realized His faithfulness. Looking back now, I can see His footprints where He was carrying me – because I wasn't able to walk on my own, much less stand.

Father God knows each one of us by name:

"Even the very hairs of your head are all numbered." Matthew 10:30 (NIV)

There are times when we will have to wait, but He knows what He is doing. We can trust His judgment.

Memorize these two verses and keep them close to your heart when questions or doubts arise about God's faithfulness:

"Cast all your anxiety on Him because He cares for you." 1 Peter 5:7 (NIV)

"Neither height nor depth, nor anything else in all creation, will be able to separate us from the love of God that is in Christ Jesus our Lord." Romans 8:39 (NIV)

I pray that as you walk through your Season of Faith, you allow God to steer you in the way He wants you to go.

Also, go ahead – I dare you – to ask the tough questions.

He's strong.

He can take it.

But please, remember to be quiet more often than you speak…

Two ears. One mouth.

Nasha T. Alexis - Co-Author

Safe in His Arms

The Goodness of God

Brain David Fuller

CHAPTER FOUR

A Testimony of Faith, Perseverance, and Purpose

I feel like a human pin cushion. That was the only way I could describe the sensations coursing through me after five different nurses, each in turn, attempted to locate a good vein deep within my arms to administer an IV (intravenous). Diabetes had made even the simplest blood draws a challenge: veins rolling, disappearing, or refusing to give way. On that day, preparing for cardiac surgery, finding a viable vessel felt near impossible.

Once the flurry of pokes and prods subsided, I was laid up on a gurney in the pre-surgical holding area waiting to go into the operating theatre, a heavy sense of dread gripped my mind. The silence pressed in the hum of hospital equipment, the muted footsteps, my own shallow breaths. But when I was finally wheeled into surgery, and the anesthesiologist began her countdown, I awoke to the news that my angioplasty was a success as though no time had passed. I was relieved beyond words, as the weight of my anxiety fell off like chains snapping from a prisoner's wrists. What began as an exploratory procedure unveiled more than anticipated: an arterial blockage in the left ventricle of my heart, with 75% occlusion, was cleared. The surgeon's words echoed in the recovery room and reverberated to the depths of my mind: "You were anywhere from two weeks to two years away from a major cardiac event." In that moment, I knew that God had intervened, sparing me from the brink of death. To borrow a phrase from Scripture: *"He spared my life."*

But grace would meet me again less than three months later, as I found myself once more in a pre-op holding room. This time, I was no longer anxiously anticipating pain. I had resigned myself to the pokes, pricks and pinches associated with the pre-surgical preparation process. I was determined not to allow the moment to shake me.

However, the weeks before my surgery were deeply distressing. Depression hovered at the edges of my mind, dark and relentless, seeking to devour me. But I refused to let the darkness overtake me. I had hope – tangible, planted deeply in the hearts of those who loved and prayed for me. My family, friends, and faith community surrounded me in prayer, forming a protective firewall against my spiraling thoughts.

On the morning of the surgery, as I laid in the pre-op area, something extraordinary broke through. A sense of peace – calm, resolute, holy – washed over me and would not recede. The Holy Spirit began softly echoing verses of scripture in my mind:

"Peace, I leave with you; my peace I give you. I do not give to you as the world gives. Do not let your hearts be troubled and do not be afraid." John 14:27 (NIV)

Instantly, the fear that once consumed my mind evaporated. My heart no longer pounded with dread; my tears of sadness dried up like rain drops under the heat of the sun; my breath steadied. I felt supernatural strength; a peace not of this world. I had no more fear. Just an abiding calm. The goodness of God kept my mind in perfect peace, even as my body was going through chaos.

Now that I've captured your attention, let me properly introduce myself. I am Brian David Fuller, and I live by the motto *"Faith it till you make it."* This is not just a clever play on words, it is a powerful mindset mastery hack grounded in scripture, and lived out through purposeful intention.

I have been a follower of Jesus for thirty years. My faith journey began one humid Saturday morning when I was eighteen. Two elderly women came to my apartment door and shared the gospel with me. That singular moment sparked a movement of the Holy Spirit within me, and began a journey of faith that has shaped my life.

Since that day, I have pursued faith with intentional passion. I've served in my local church in various capacities. I went to Bible college, and earned a Bachelor's Degree in Religious Studies. After graduation, I began the ministerial credentials process. However, life did not unfold as neatly as I planned. During that season, a diagnosis of Type 2 diabetes derailed my forward momentum. The next twenty years I battled with establishing good diabetic control. I've had stretches of good blood-sugar levels and seasons of struggle.

My father also suffered from Type 2 diabetes. He battled with the disease throughout his life. Unfortunately, he suffered two major heart attacks ten years apart. He did not survive the second one. The coroner's report revealed that he passed away from diabetic related heart disease. My father died six days before his 70th birthday. Although I inherited diabetes from my father, I have experienced far greater diabetic complications than he ever did.

In the summer of 2020, I began experiencing major health complications. Like a worn-out guitar string, my body, mind and soul were no longer in harmonious alignment. I was hospitalized for two weeks due to a life-altering infection in my right foot. During my time in the hospital, my faith was stretched as the pain from my infection had me in physical and emotional distress. Days before my release, I was given a troubling prognosis. I prayed aloud: "God, where do you want me to be?" That's when I heard Him say: "Be at peace." Instantly, fear loosened its grip over me. My heart filled with trust. A verse came to mind:

"And the peace of God, which transcends all understanding, will guard your hearts and your minds in Christ Jesus." Philippians 4:7 (NIV)

From then on, I understood that God doesn't promise us trouble-free lives. But He does promise His constant presence – peace that surpasses our understanding and anchors us to Himself, in the midst of the storm. In the years following my hospitalization, my diabetes became more severe.

Living with severe diabetic complications has been extremely challenging. With each crisis of health, my faith has been tested. I am no longer able to work, and my driver's license has been revoked. My eyes have become extremely light sensitive, which makes seeing contrast very difficult. I have lost my independence. I can no longer interact with a computer screen, fill out documents, read a book, or write this chapter you are reading without assistance from trusted friends.

As an individual living with visual limitations, I have learned that many people, in public spaces, do not have the compassion and capacity to show care for a person like me, who needs the help of a good Samaritan. Whenever I identify my impairment, it is often met with skepticism or reluctance. People tend to say, *"You don't look visually impaired,"* or *"Why aren't you wearing glasses?"* Most people are not aware that blindness exists on a spectrum. I often wonder if I wore dark glasses and carried a white cane, would people show more compassion towards me, whenever I need help.

In addition to my visual impairment challenges, I am suffering from the effects of heart disease. In order to save my foot from a deadly infection, I've had toes amputated. My kidneys are failing, and I require dialysis treatment three days a week. I struggle with chronic fatigue and bouts of insomnia. And due to the fragility of my feet, I require regular wound care management.

The greatest impact this disease has had on my daily life is how it restricts the relationship with my daughter. I pride myself on being a present and engaged father, but my impaired vision and limited mobility has stolen precious moments we once shared. The simple things like driving her to and from school, helping with her homework and partaking in our shared love of drawing is no longer possible for me to do.

My heart is broken by every loss, limitation and life-altering surgery that have marked my journey. Yet with every crisis of health I encounter, I have discovered fresh depths of grace. In my thirty years as a follower of Jesus, the last five years have truly refined my faith. During this season of suffering, I have learned that God truly walks with us, when life takes us through dark valleys. His Goodness can be found in the darkest of circumstances. God is Good – regardless of what we endure.

> *"And we know that in all things God works for the good of those who love him, who have been called according to his purpose."* Romans 8:28 (NIV)

Katherine Wolf, a podcaster that uses her experiences of suffering shared the following insights:

"God's goodness to us is not dependent on how good we are to Him…or based on how diligently we pray. God's goodness to us is based on His character and divine attributes. God is good even when life is not. God's Word is true. That truth resonates deeply. Outcomes don't define God's goodness – He does. Our suffering doesn't testify against His love – it refines it."

Philippians 3:10 (NKJV) reminds us that suffering brings us closer to God: *"That I may know Him and the power of His resurrection, and the fellowship of His sufferings, being conformed to His death."*

And James 1:2-4 (NIV) assures us: *"Consider it pure joy … whenever you face trials … because you know that the testing of your faith produces perseverance. Let perseverance finish its work so that you may be mature and complete, not lacking anything."*

Faith does not guarantee us a better outcome. Instead, it guarantees us a closer walk with Jesus. The trials we encounter in this life teach us perseverance that pushes us deeper into God's Heart, while shaping our character, and giving us hope to share. However, before we can effectively share our story of perseverance and hope, we must first allow ourselves the space and time to grieve the losses we have experienced. Grief is not a sign of weakness, but a natural response to the brokenness of life. It is the pathway to acceptance, and acceptance opens the door to true lasting peace. When we suppress or rush past grief, we risk carrying unhealed wounds that hinder our testimony and causes us to question the goodness of God. Jesus teaches us to manage grief, as He knelt in deep anguish at the Garden of Gethsemane (Matthew 26:38–39). In that moment, He did not deny His sorrow or push away His pain; instead, He acknowledged it fully before the Father. His Prayer, *"Not my Will, but Yours be done,"* models how grief can be transformed into purpose. As we surrender our grief into the Father's hands, He gives us strength and peace needed to persevere and hope to share with others.

In my journey of faith, I've learned five practical ways that have strengthened me during difficult times.

1. Read Scripture daily

- God speaks through His Word. His Promises, His Character, and His Comfort lie therein. Start with the Psalms. Psalm 46:1 declares, "God is our Refuge and Strength, a very present Help in trouble." Work through the Gospels or read through a Book of the Bible daily.

- Journal verses that speak to your soul and re-read them in your moments of doubt.

- Over time, your heart will be tethered to the unshakable truths of who God is—His Love, His Sovereignty, His Power to save and sustain.

- My commitment to reading the Bible regularly has transformed my life, while strengthening me through the momentary struggles of life.

2. Pray with honesty

- Bring your doubts, your anger, your desperation before the Lord. God isn't surprised by your struggle. He's already walking with you through it.

- Share your heart unfiltered.

- Ask for peace not because your pain is comfortable, but because you need strength to endure.

- Pray Scripture: *"Lord, fill me with your peace,"* (Philippians 4:6–7).

- Prayer isn't a magic wand. It's the pathway to communion with the Almighty. We often pray for God to change our circumstances. But I have found that prayer has an incredible way of changing our hearts first, while we are waiting for our circumstances to change.

3. Stay connected to Christian community

- Suffering is too heavy to shoulder alone. God designed community for our restoration and to uplift.

- Join a small group.

- Stay close to people who know your story and will pray for you.

- Let others carry your burdens and allow yourself to carry theirs.

- Ecclesiastes 4:9–10 reminds us, *"Two are better than one … if either of them falls down, one can help the other up."*

- My health challenges would be even more daunting, if I did not have the prayerful support, loving empathy and practical assistance of my church family. It is extremely important to have good people in your life, that can hold space with you, and do life alongside you.

4. Seek godly counsel

- Isolation breeds despair: wise counsel brings perspective.

- Talk with a trusted pastor, counselor, or mature believer.

- Lean on their spiritual insight and practical experience. Let them speak Scripture into your scars and remind you that you're not alone. God has given me a select group of individuals that I have been able to lean on. Over the years, I allowed them to challenge, correct and counsel me. Without their trusted wisdom and guidance, I wouldn't be the man I am today.

5. Cultivate an attitude of worship and thanksgiving

- Affirm God's character by giving Him praise – even in pain.

- Flood your mind with worship songs and scripture-filled prayers.

- Keep a gratitude list. Start with small things (*"I'm grateful for this morning's sunshine"*).

- Redirect your gaze from the storm to the shelter.

1 Thessalonians 5:18 instructs, *"Give thanks in all circumstances; for this is the will of God in Christ Jesus for you."* I have learned that gratitude and depression cannot exist in the same space. In order to win the war within our minds, we must choose to worship God in spite of our circumstances, and because He Is always Good.

Life will always press. We will encounter pain. The losses we experience will sting. But through it all, the covenant-keeping God remains – His character unshaken, His Presence unending. His goodness unfailing. Your current valley isn't the whole story; it's a chapter, and God is writing the ending.

Prayer

Eternal God and Ever-Wise Father,

Surround us with your Peace that passes understanding. Let Your Word be a lamp to our feet and a light to our path. Help us to trust You with the valleys and the peaks. Teach us to pray when we don't know what to say. Draw close to us and be our strength, our comfort, our ever-present help in trouble. May we walk in faith, not fear, knowing You're working all things out for our good and Your glory.

In Jesus' name, amen.

Through it all I have learned that, although my body may grow weak, and my vision is impaired, my spirit remains strong because I stand on the foundation of Jesus Christ, my Savior. I don't know what tomorrow may bring, but I do know this: God is good. His plan is purposeful. And His peace is powerful.

So, I encourage you to: faith it 'til you make it. Press on, lean in, and walk forward knowing Jesus walks with you, in every season, every struggle and every victory.

Brian David Fuller - Co-Author

Safe in His Arms
The Goodness of God

Chanroutie Superville

Chapter Five

Redeemed by Grace – My Journey from Darkness to Divine Freedom

My name is Evangelist Chanroutie Superville, Founder and *Visionary of Divine Freedom Church International*. When I look back over the many seasons of my life, I can say with absolute certainty that every chapter was written by the grace and mercy of God. What the enemy meant for destruction, God turned into redemption. I stand today as a living testimony of His goodness, His deliverance, and His unfailing love.

I was born on the beautiful island of Trinidad, into a devoted Hindu family. I was the third of nine children. Life was not easy for us. Poverty and hardship marked much of our early years. We lived day by day, never sure what tomorrow would bring. My father, whom I loved dearly, became very ill with cancer. His condition grew worse each day, and our household was filled with fear and sorrow.

One afternoon, my grandmother arrived at our home with hope shining in her eyes. *"I found a pastor who can help him,"* she said. At the time, I didn't understand what she meant – after all, we were Hindus – but I watched as that Christian pastor came into our small home, laid hands on my father, and prayed in the mighty name of Jesus. What happened next would change our family forever.

Through those prayers, God miraculously healed my father. The cancer disappeared completely. Doctors were astonished, but my grandmother simply said, *"It was Jesus."* I didn't know who Jesus was then, but a seed was planted in my heart that day; a seed that would one day grow into a mighty tree of faith.

I attended a Presbyterian school, and every morning and afternoon, we would recite The Lord's Prayer and Psalm 100. I repeated the words faithfully, not realizing that I was declaring God's truth into my own future. Those moments were divine appointments. They were daily seeds of faith being planted in a young girl who didn't yet know the Savior she was speaking to. I can still remember the sound of our voices echoing through the classroom, the teacher's calm tone as she led us, and the peace that always seemed to linger afterward.

Even at that tender age, God was weaving His promises into my spirit. The words I spoke became a quiet foundation, anchoring my heart for the storms I would later face. Jeremiah 29:11 (NKJV) says, *"For I know the thoughts that I think toward you, says the Lord, thoughts of peace and not of evil, to give you a future and a hope."* Even as a little girl, God's Word was taking root in my heart, preparing me for both the battles and blessings that would one day reveal His incredible grace.

As I entered my teenage years, life took a difficult turn. Our house burned to the ground, and with nowhere to go, my parents – out of love and fear – arranged for me to be married at the age of sixteen. They believed it was the safest choice to secure my future. But two years later, I found myself divorced and caring for a baby alone. I remember those nights vividly: sitting by the window, holding my child, wondering how life could change so suddenly. I was still a child myself yet already carrying the weight of adulthood on my shoulders.

In those early years, I felt trapped between two worlds. My father, though healed by a Christian pastor, remained Hindu, and our household continued to follow traditional practices with deep reverence. I attended temple rituals, lit incense, and recited chants, but my heart felt distant. There was a quiet longing in me for something more – a love that could fill the emptiness no ritual could reach. Yet, deep inside, something in me yearned for the God who had healed my father. I often wondered, *"Who was that Jesus? Why did His name carry such power and peace?"*

Not long after, our family experienced what we could only describe as a spiritual attack. Strange things began happening: illness, confusion, tension, and loss. We were exhausted in every way. Around that same time, a Christian crusade was being held near our village. Pastors and women of faith came to our home, offering prayer and sharing the love of Jesus. Their visits brought peace, and little by little, the heaviness lifted. One by one, members of my family gave their hearts to Christ. We had been known as one of the strongest Hindu families in our community, yet now we stood as living witnesses of God's transforming power.

I didn't know it then, but God was setting me apart for His purpose. My story of redemption had only just begun.

In my early twenties, I carried deep insecurities. I longed for education, success, and acceptance, but every effort failed. People whispered behind my back, *"No one will ever want you."* Their words pierced my soul. I began to believe them, speaking defeat over my life: *"I'm not smart enough. I'm not worthy. I'll never make it."* Fear and self-doubt became my constant companions. I hid behind a smile, pretending to be strong, but inside, I was breaking. I stopped dreaming. I stopped hoping. Yet somewhere deep inside, a small voice whispered that there was more to life than pain and rejection.

When I was twenty-five, I was given a chance to travel abroad. I believed this was my opportunity to rewrite my story; to earn money, support my family, and find a new beginning. I packed my few belongings and left with hope. But life in a foreign country was harsher than I could have imagined. I knew no one and had no place to stay. Some people offered help, but not all had good intentions. After weeks of uncertainty, a kind man offered me a small room to rent. I eventually found work through an agency and began renting my own apartment.

Still, fear haunted me. I would lie awake at night wondering, *"What if something happens to me here?"* Sadly, those fears were not unfounded. I was coerced into a relationship I did not want. At first, I convinced myself it might improve, but it soon turned abusive – emotionally, mentally, and physically. For five years, I lived under control and manipulation, raising two children in pain and silence.

During that season, I drifted far from God. I depended on my own strength, doing whatever I could to survive. I didn't pray. I didn't seek Him. I simply existed. But one day, something inside me began to stir. It was a holy discontent, a quiet voice that said, *"This is not the life I have for you."*

In desperation, I sought help from a Hindu priest, but he refused to see me. That rejection shattered me. I turned more intensely to rituals and fasting, but nothing changed. My body was weary; my spirit was broken. One night, in utter despair, I cried out, *"Who is the true God? Will anyone hear me? Please, if You are real, show me who You are!"*

With tears streaming down my face, I whispered, *"God, show me the way. Help me to know You. Deliver me safely. I don't know how to pray, but You know my heart."*

Then, in the stillness of that night, I heard a voice – gentle yet powerful – say, *"Go and kneel down and pray."*

Immediately, I remembered The Lord's Prayer and Psalm 100 from my childhood. The voice said again, "Join hands with the children." Trembling, I gathered my children, locked the door, and opened an old Bible. Together we read those verses, crying as we prayed. That night, I felt something shift. Peace entered our home.

In a dream that followed, I heard the Lord say: *"Give Me your brokenness, and I will make you whole."* When I awoke, I knew that God had heard me. Within a week, He made a way for me to escape that home and return safely to my parents. I was finally free.

Though I was grateful to be free, my heart ached for the children I had left behind. I prayed constantly for their safety. One morning, the Holy Spirit whispered, *"Go and take your child."* Obeying that voice, I traveled with my brother to bring my daughter home. Along the way, we saw her father, but by divine power, he did not recognize us. God blinded his eyes so we could pass safely.

A stranger appeared and said, *"I know why you are here. God sent me to help."* He led us straight to my daughter. Every step was divinely ordered. That Sunday, I took my daughter to church and gave public thanks to God. The pastor rejoiced with me, and for the first time in years, I felt peace flood my soul.

From that day on, I attended deliverance services faithfully. God broke every chain of fear, shame, anger, and doubt. I learned to walk with dignity, speak with grace, and see myself as God saw me. The woman who once cursed and feared was gone. I had become a new creation.

I often tell people: *"When no one else could help me, Jesus did."* The Holy Spirit became my teacher, showing me how to pray, forgive, and walk in faith. During prayer, I once saw a heavenly portal open above me. Another time, I saw myself dancing with Jesus – my feet resting on His, my head against His chest. I could feel His heartbeat. That was when I knew that I am truly safe in His arms.

The Lord began to instruct me to write down my prayers, and later, those prayers blessed others: Bible school students, friends, and believers hungry for more of God. He even revealed my future husband through dreams. In one dream, I saw four colored slippers. In another, our names written together on a page. Each vision came true, confirming that God still speaks today through dreams, visions, His Word, and His Spirit. We only need to listen.

Every storm in my life prepared me for the ministry I now lead. I discovered that God restores what the enemy tries to destroy. Psalm 23:1–3 (NKJV) declares:

"The Lord is my shepherd; I shall not want.
He makes me to lie down in green pastures;
He leads me beside the still waters.
He restores my soul."

The Lord truly restored my soul. He turned pain into purpose, sorrow into song, and captivity into calling. He gave me favor, provision, and the vision for *Divine Freedom Church International*, where I now preach to others still walking through darkness.

I've learned that each of us lives two lives – one physical and one spiritual. We must choose which one will lead us. I have chosen to walk by the Spirit, for Galatians 5:16 (NKJV) says, *"Walk in the Spirit, and you shall not fulfill the lust of the flesh."* When we walk in the Spirit, we soar like eagles. Life's storms no longer crush us. They lift us higher.

Today, I stand as a woman redeemed by grace. The same Jesus who healed my father's cancer and rescued me from abuse is still performing miracles today. I've witnessed blind eyes opened, hearts mended, and families restored through the power of prayer. I've seen the addicted set free, the broken made whole, and the hopeless filled with divine purpose. God's power is not a thing of the past. It is alive, active, and available to anyone who dares to believe. His Spirit still moves in homes, hospitals, prisons, and churches alike. He restores dignity to the forgotten, courage to the weary, and peace to those who thought it was lost forever.

If God could deliver me from despair, He can deliver you too. There is no bondage too strong for His mercy, and no sin too deep for His forgiveness. His love reaches into the darkest places and brings light where there was once pain. His grace doesn't just rescue. It transforms. John 3:16 (NKJV) reminds us, *"For God so loved the world that He gave His only begotten Son, that whoever believes in Him should not perish but have everlasting life."* That love rescued me, restored my purpose, and set me free. And it will rescue, redeem, and renew you too, if you simply open your heart and believe.

My dear friend, perhaps you are reading this and wondering if God could ever love or forgive you. I am here to tell you that He already does. You are His masterpiece, handcrafted with intention, shaped by love, and chosen for a divine purpose. No matter what you have done or what has been done to you, His mercy still reaches into the deepest parts of your heart. His arms are open wide, waiting to embrace you – not when you are perfect, but just as you are right now.

Psalm 139:14 (NKJV) declares, *"I will praise You, for I am fearfully and wonderfully made."* You were not created to live in fear, abuse, or shame. You were created to walk in freedom, joy, and divine destiny. James 1:17 (NKJV) says, *"Every good gift and every perfect gift is from above, and comes down from the Father of lights."* The same God who spoke creation into being still speaks life into your situation today.

The Lord is calling you to surrender; to release every burden, disappointment, and scar you've carried for too long. He's calling you to let go of the voices that told you you're not enough and listen instead to His voice of truth. Trust Him with every broken piece of your heart. When you do, He will restore your joy, renew your strength, and unveil the beauty of His perfect plan for your life. His grace is not limited by your past. It is powerful enough to rewrite your story, redeem your destiny, and turn your pain into a platform for His glory.

Prayer

Heavenly Father,

I lift up the precious soul reading this testimony. Reveal to them Your unconditional love and everlasting mercy. Let Your peace calm every storm in their heart. For those struggling with fear, abuse, or rejection, let them know You are near.

Lord, as they surrender their pain to You, wrap them in the safety of Your arms. Heal every wound – emotional, physical, and spiritual – that has kept them bound. Replace their sorrow with joy, their shame with confidence, and their fear with faith.

May they know, beyond all doubt, that they are never alone. You have redeemed them by grace, called them by name, and appointed them for divine freedom.

Thank You, Father, for hearing this prayer and for the victory that is already theirs.

In the mighty and matchless name of Jesus Christ, Amen.

Evangelist Chanroutie Superville - Co-Author

Safe in His Arms
The Goodness of God

Anita Sechesky

Chapter Six

Exploring the Attributes of God in Scripture

When we read through the Old Testament, we discover a portrait of God that is rich, layered, and overflowing with goodness. His nature is revealed through every covenant, every act of mercy, every moment of correction, and every expression of love. The Old Testament is not merely a historical account of events; it is a living testimony that invites us to see God as faithful, patient, and just, a Father who desires to dwell among His people and to bless them beyond measure.

From the very beginning, in the book of Genesis, we encounter a Creator who delights in His creation. After forming the heavens, the earth, the animals, and mankind, God looked at all that He had made and declared, *"It is very good."* His first recorded words over humanity were words of affirmation and blessing, establishing that goodness flows from His very being. His goodness is not something He occasionally shows. It is who He is. Even after sin entered the world, His mercy followed immediately, covering Adam and Eve's shame with garments of grace.

Throughout the generations, God's goodness remained steadfast. He called Abraham out of idolatry and made him a promise – to bless him, multiply his descendants, and make him a blessing to all nations. Abraham's story reveals that God's goodness is relational, not transactional. His blessings are not based on perfection but on promise. Even when Abraham doubted, God remained faithful.

Through Abraham's descendants, Isaac and Jacob, God continued to demonstrate patience and compassion. With Jacob, whose very name meant "deceiver," God saw not the trickster but the potential of transformation. Jacob's life reminds us that God's goodness meets us where we are, but it never leaves us there. When Jacob wrestled with the angel and refused to let go, he discovered a truth that still holds today: we may struggle with God, but His goodness always prevails.

The life of Joseph shines as one of the clearest examples of divine goodness amid suffering. Betrayed by his brothers, sold into slavery, and imprisoned unjustly, Joseph could have allowed bitterness to take root. Yet, when restoration finally came, he declared, *"You meant evil against me, but God meant it for good"* Genesis 50:20 (NKJV). His statement encapsulates the essence of divine goodness – that God has the power to turn pain into purpose. Through Joseph's obedience and endurance, an entire nation was preserved during famine. God's goodness, even when hidden behind human betrayal, still orchestrated redemption.

The story of the Exodus magnifies this same theme. The Israelites cried out under Egyptian bondage, and God heard their cries. He did not ignore their suffering. He responded with power and compassion. With a mighty hand, He parted the Red Sea and led His people to freedom. This act of deliverance is not only a historical event; it is a prophetic picture of the goodness of God that still liberates us today from fear, sin, and oppression. When Moses questioned God's presence and asked to see His glory, God replied, *"I will make all My goodness pass before you"* Exodus 33:19 (NKJV). Notice that God equated His glory with His goodness. To encounter God's goodness is to encounter His very essence. It was this revelation that shaped Israel's identity and still shapes ours as believers.

The Psalms are the heart songs of those who walked intimately with God. In their words, we find honesty, sorrow, repentance, and overwhelming gratitude. David, who experienced both victory and failure, proclaimed in Psalm 27:13 (NKJV), "I would have lost heart unless I had believed that I would see the goodness of the Lord in the land of the living." This verse is more than poetic. It is deeply prophetic. It reminds us that God's goodness is not reserved for eternity; it is available right here, in the middle of our chaos. Psalm 34:8 (NKJV) declares, "Taste and see that the Lord is good." Goodness must be experienced personally and must be tasted, savored, and remembered.

The psalmists continually point to gratitude as the response to goodness. Whether through praise, lament, or thanksgiving, they model the power of acknowledging God's hand in every circumstance. Gratitude is not only a form of worship; it is a weapon that guards our hearts from despair. God's goodness is not limited to blessings. It is also expressed through discipline. The prophets warned Israel of disobedience, not out of anger but out of love. His correction was an invitation to return. Even in exile, His voice of hope was clear. Through Jeremiah, He declared, "For I know the plans I have for you… plans to prosper you and not to harm you, plans to give you a hope and a future" Jeremiah 29:11 (NKJV). God's discipline refines, but it never destroys. It directs us back toward His purpose. Just as a parent corrects a child for their own good, God's loving discipline is evidence that we belong to Him.

The Old Testament closes with promises of restoration and renewal. They are reminders that the story of God's goodness is far from over. If the Old Testament shows us the promise of goodness, the New Testament shows us the Person of goodness: Jesus Christ. In Him, everything that was foreshadowed became flesh. He is the living expression of divine love, mercy, and compassion. From His humble birth in a manger to His resurrection glory, Jesus revealed the Father's heart. When He touched the untouchable, forgave sinners, healed the broken, and restored the rejected, He demonstrated that God's goodness is not distant. It dwells among us.

Every act of kindness, every word of truth, every miracle performed was an open window into heaven, revealing a God who cares deeply for His creation. Jesus' ministry was filled with divine interruptions of mercy. When He turned water into wine, it wasn't simply to save a wedding. It was to demonstrate that God delights in joy and celebration. When He fed thousands with a few loaves and fishes, He reminded us that God provides abundantly. When He healed the blind and raised the dead, He showed that God restores what seems beyond repair.

His parables, too, are love letters from a good God to a broken humanity. The Good Samaritan illustrates that compassion knows no boundaries. The Lost Sheep and the Prodigal Son reveal the relentless pursuit of divine love. The Father runs toward us, not away from us, embracing us with forgiveness before we can even explain ourselves. The cross is the pinnacle of divine goodness. It stands as a timeless reminder that God's love is stronger than sin, shame, and death.

At Calvary, Jesus bore the weight of our failures and extended His mercy to every generation. Romans 5:8 (NKJV) declares, *"But God demonstrates His own love toward us, in that while we were still sinners, Christ died for us."* The cross was not a tragedy. It was a triumph. God's goodness was revealed in full measure through sacrifice. It was not about judgment but redemption. Because of the cross, we are not just forgiven. We are restored, reconciled, and adopted into the family of God.

After the resurrection, the goodness of God continued through the early believers. In the book of Acts, we see a community transformed by grace. They shared possessions, cared for widows and orphans, and prayed with unity of heart. The same power that raised Jesus from the dead now flowed through them, bringing healing and deliverance. When Peter and John encountered a lame man at the temple gate, Peter said, *"Silver and gold I do not have, but what I do have I give you: In the name of Jesus Christ of Nazareth, walk"* Acts 3:6 (NKJV). That moment encapsulates the heart of Christian service – freely giving what we have received. God's goodness flows through us when we make ourselves available to be vessels of His love.

As a Registered Nurse, I have witnessed God's goodness in countless ways. In the Emergency Room, where life and death meet daily, I've seen His presence calm chaos. In coaching and mentoring sessions, I've watched hearts transform as people begin to understand that their pain has purpose. And in moments when individuals have requested personal ministering to strengthen their faith walk, I've stood beside them as God poured healing oil over their souls.

A dying patient once forgave a long-estranged son moments before passing into eternity. A grieving mother found the courage to lift her hands in worship through her tears. A young man bound by addiction finally surrendered and found freedom in Christ. These are not random occurrences. They are living parables of divine goodness still at work today.

The Apostle Paul, once a persecutor of the church, became one of the greatest proclaimers of God's grace. He wrote from prison with joy, declaring, *"Rejoice in the Lord always"* Philippians 4:4 (NKJV). His letters remind us that gratitude is not dependent on comfort. It is a choice to see goodness even in chains. Gratitude and faith work together like a heartbeat. When we thank God, we declare that His character is trustworthy. Gratitude shifts our focus from what we lack to what He provides. It transforms hardship into testimony.

Paul also reminds us that goodness is a fruit of the Spirit: *"But the fruit of the Spirit is love, joy, peace, longsuffering, kindness, goodness, faithfulness, gentleness, self-control"* Galatians 5:22-23 (NKJV). It is cultivated through closeness with God. The more we walk with Him, the more His nature becomes ours. Goodness is not something we perform. It is something we reflect.

The early church demonstrated that goodness thrives in community. They met in homes, broke bread together, and shared joy and suffering alike. Acts 2:46-47(NKJV) records, *"They ate together with glad and sincere hearts, praising God and enjoying the favor of all the people."* This kind of unity still carries the fragrance of God's goodness today. When believers gather, pray, and serve one another, the atmosphere shifts. Hope rises. Miracles manifest. As we embody His goodness, we become the hands and feet of Jesus in our neighborhoods, workplaces, and families. Whether through prayer, compassion, or mentorship, every act of kindness echoes heaven's heartbeat.

The miracles in Scripture are not relics of the past. They are previews of what God continues to do. Hebrews 13:8 (NKJV) declares, *"Jesus Christ is the same yesterday, today, and forever."* The same Savior who healed the woman with the issue of blood still heals today. The same Shepherd who sought the lost still restores lives in 2025. Every testimony we share adds another thread to the tapestry of His faithfulness. Each act of deliverance, healing, or reconciliation is proof that the God of Scripture is alive and active in our generation.

When we live from the awareness of His goodness, we become carriers of hope to those around us. The light of His love shines through our stories, our workplaces, and our ministries, reminding others that God is still near, still faithful, and still transforming lives.

Prayer

Heavenly Father,

Thank You for revealing Your goodness through every chapter of Scripture – from Genesis to Revelation, from creation to covenant, from the cross to resurrection life. Thank You that

Your nature is constant, Your mercy unending, and Your love unfailing. Open our eyes to see Your hand in every moment. Help us to recognize the quiet miracles that unfold around us each day. When we grow weary or discouraged, remind us that You have not forgotten us. Strengthen our faith and anchor our hearts in the assurance of Your goodness.

Lord, may our lives be living testimonies of Your compassion and grace. Let our words and actions reflect the beauty of Your Spirit in the world around us. We thank You for Jesus – the ultimate expression of goodness and love.

In the precious and powerful name of Jesus Christ, Amen.

Anita Sechesky - Visionary Compiler & Publisher

Safe in His Arms

The Goodness of God

Cheryl Gardner

Chapter Seven

Redeemed by His Goodness

I woke up in the dark of my grandmother's room to the sound of dogs howling and the low chatter of voices coming from outside the house. As I followed the voices, I could see a small crowd of neighbors along with family members gathered on the stairs and in the yard outside our home. I would soon learn that my grandfather had passed sometime that day. I was six years old.

That is one of the earliest clear memories I have, and it took place during my time spent in the Caribbean. I had not been there long, and as a result, I never really had a relationship with my grandfather. I was, however, blessed to have my aunt, my cousin, and of course, my grandmother Grace. They showered me with love throughout the four years that I would go on to stay in that family home.

I was the only child of my divorced parents when I left my mother's home, and upon my return to Canada years later, as you can imagine, everything had changed. Both of my parents had remarried. At the age of 10, I was now faced with juggling a number of new situations.

I had to adjust to being back in the country, going to a new school, and making new friends. At home, assimilation involved living with two complete strangers: my stepmother, whom I knew nothing about, and my father, whom I had not seen in four years. This was not during the computer age of facetime and cell phones, so I literally had not laid eyes on my father in four years.

At my mother's house, in addition to getting to know her again, there was a stepfather and two younger siblings. Everything and everyone felt unfamiliar – everyone except my cousin, whom I had lived with during the time I was away from my parents. She, too, had traveled to Canada.

Life with my father and stepmother came with many challenges. My father was very quiet and took a back seat to my stepmother, who was the disciplinarian. She was a drill sergeant and left little room for error. My cousin, being older than me, soon became engaged, married, and moved out.

I was now the main focus of the sergeant, and the heat was intense. There was no peace.

Being a teenager can be a challenge on its own. It's an awkward time for most. Feelings of discomfort in my own skin were heightened by a move north of the city just in time for my first year of high school. The area lacked diversity, and my experience was less than desirable. There was no peace.

This, coupled with the ongoing battle between myself and my stepmom, came to a climax, and by the time I turned 16, I ran away from home. I left without permission from my dad and went to live with my mother and her family back in Toronto.

I've discovered that life can easily pass you by. While you're busy trying to live it, you can actually miss it. We make plans, but God is the Author and the Finisher not only of our faith but of our lives.

There are a number of definitions of peace in the Bible. One of my favorites is: *"Peace is an individual virtue or state, that is, tranquility or serenity."*

Living without restrictions in my late teen years led me to make some decisions that I lived to regret. I had no relationship with God.

In my early 20s, I fell in love and got married. We were blessed with my firstborn, a boy. I now realize I suffered from undiagnosed postpartum depression. This contributed to our separation and, eventually, our divorce.

The Word of God says, *"Seek, and ye shall find."* Looking for peace in all the wrong places led me into a relationship that lacked restrictions. Void of standards, I entered a relationship with a married man. He indicated that although he and his wife were living in the same home, they were no longer in a relationship (but a married man is a married man).

Had I known who I was as a child of God, those restrictions would have kept me away from that. Living in darkness, I was led to make immoral decisions I would not have made if I had been living in the light of Christ.

I was thrown into a life of chaos, confusion, heartbreak, isolation, shame, and pain. Broken became my new normal. There were many lows, but there were also highs – unbelievably, the same person had a part in both! He seemed to be able to pull the strings responsible for either.

How could someone who made me feel so loved also cause me so much shame and pain? Why did I constantly find myself having to make excuses or find ways to explain why the man I loved was missing – especially on major occasions, like the christening of our daughter? How could the same mouth that once spoke words that lifted my spirit and made me smile also so easily say the most awful things anyone has ever said to me?

In the midst of that season of my life, God still blessed me – this time with a baby girl.

We purchased a home (definitely a high), but there was so much financial stress, especially due to the double life my partner was leading. The home meant we were physically closer to my family; however, I couldn't have foreseen the problems that would arise as a result.

If the walls of that home could speak, they would tell so many stories. Funny enough, when I first saw that house, I hated it. I was very pregnant with my daughter, and as is known, pregnant women can have extreme reactions to smell. The home had been locked up for some time, as it had been foreclosed. It was not in great condition, but my partner saw potential. I did not. I could not get past the smell! But the price ultimately won me over.

We eventually moved in a couple of months before I gave birth in December of that year. Many years later, I realized one major thing we did not do was have that home blessed – a significant oversight.

It wasn't long before the noise began. It's amazing how much turmoil was packed into just a few years. Unfortunately, those were also the first few years of my daughter's life. Those years were so heavy.

A few months into my pregnancy, I discovered that my partner (amidst his divorce) was expecting another child with his wife. The child was born a few months later, and my partner began to spend many weekends with his "son." By default, those weekends were also spent with his "wife." This continued throughout our relationship – including the days after our daughter was born.

She came into the world on a Tuesday, the day after his birthday. We returned home on Thursday, and he was gone by Friday. He openly lived a double life, which I facilitated. He spent his weeks with us and his weekends in another home he purchased with his wife, who eventually had another child. Yes – also his child. This was the second of four outside children he would father during our time together.

I did my very best to hold down the home front mostly on my own. In the midst of verbal abuse that turned physical, arrests, and even a friend's bold-faced betrayal, I pushed through. There was no peace, but I was determined to make the relationship work. I couldn't imagine another failed relationship.

Soon, those hidden glances, actions, and even words began to seep out from behind the closed doors. Initially, I did my best to cover bruises, glue broken glasses, make excuses for red eyes, or explain missing family functions – but I was unable to cover the evidence of my bruised ribs, the outside children, or the police cars and Children's Aid visiting our home.

If one is not intentional about making change, history has a way of repeating itself. As life and circumstances had resulted in me being separated from my parents on and off in my early years, I had always told myself I would never send my children away. However, in this very season, I not only had to be apart from my teenage son but also my baby girl.

It broke me. But it also woke me up! Every weekend for an entire summer, I drove three and a half hours each way to spend the weekend with my 2-year-old daughter. That summer was possibly my most difficult – it was traumatic not only for my children but also for me.

On my way there, I would drive with anticipation and excitement to see my child. This high was swiftly followed by the realization that I would be leaving her again in a matter of hours. I would often leave while she was asleep to avoid her crying, and then I would cry as I drove all the way back home.

Keep in mind that because I was away every weekend with my daughter, this also meant I couldn't see my son, who was now staying with his dad. And so, the generational cycle of abandonment repeated itself before my very eyes.

I was in a deep state of depression, but somehow still managed to push through. There were many days when I just didn't want to get out of bed. I was battered and bruised – not only on the outside but on the inside as well.

I was putting on a mask at work. I was avoiding friends and family. I missed my children terribly. I felt distraught and betrayed. This was not the life I had envisioned for myself and my children. I felt helpless.

Recently, I saw a picture of myself that had been taken that summer, and I didn't recognize myself. I was a hot mess and barely surviving the chaotic storm that was my life.

A friend from work had given me a couple of worship CDs, and I began to listen to worship music as I drove back and forth. I would lose myself in worship as I sang and began to communicate with God. I acquired messages on CDs, and as I drove and listened to those messages, the dark space I was operating within began to clear. The broken pieces began to stack themselves. The fog began to lift, and when my vacation pay arrived – in a much-needed, very timely fashion – I saved it and began to make plans to leave.

In my soul, I knew that if I didn't somehow get out of this situation, my children would no longer have a mother. So, I began to create a game plan. I found a place and paid the first month's deposit. This gave me a new reason to live and push through that summer.

"I promise not to leave this house with your daughter without your permission."

SIGNED: _____

As the summer came to an end, I had not only paid the deposit but also my first month's rent, collected the key, and secretly started moving items into our new place. My ex discovered my plan, and after many hours of being threatened and locked in a room in the basement of our house, I was released after signing and agreeing to the statement above.

All hope was lost. I struggled to figure out how I would ever get myself out of this situation. I knew I couldn't do it on my own.

Needless to say, I lost my deposit and first month's rent – but that was the least of it. I felt lost and beaten down. I had not only failed at my game plan, but I had also broken my promise to my son. My fresh start affected him coming home – it was supposed to be our fresh start. I was heartbroken, but now my son was also heartbroken.

As we made arrangements for him to continue his stay with his dad, I lost a part of myself that I thought would never return. Having to make this decision, I knew it was best for my son, but I was angry, and I promised myself this would not be the end of our story.

In complete desperation, I reached for God. (Like the woman with the issue of blood… I reached for the hem of His garment.)

I had to admit I was an abused woman. This realization – and the revelation of being at my lowest point – had me look to Christ. This was something I had never done before. No man or woman could help dig me out of this deep hole. I had to get up and get out of that toxic relationship.

I didn't know how – only by the grace of God! I had turned my back on Him, but He surely did not turn His back on me. In my weakness, He gave me strength!

I began to make prayer a part of my lifestyle and visited a church in the area from time to time. Approximately six months later, as my ex planned a trip to his country of birth, I saw the opportunity to turn things around.

Running away had become my go-to response whenever things got difficult. Having been left quite young, I unknowingly developed abandonment issues that caused me to react by leaving – or abandoning – situations. But this time was different. I knew I had to leave. Leaving would mean living.

I gained the strength to start over with my dignity intact. It was difficult, but we left. Of course, upon his return, he hunted us down until he found us. Thank goodness my employer allowed me to take some time off, and my daughter and I stayed at a women's shelter. This gave me the opportunity to look for an apartment.

"The axe forgets, but the tree remembers."

Trauma experienced traps itself in our fibers. It can affect how we think, what we see and say, and how we breathe. It affects what and who we become.

Growing up in a time and environment where it was understood that "children are seen and not heard" taught me that I didn't have a voice. As a child, I learned to be observant, and I was great at keeping secrets. In my tween years, I was taught that my opinions and feelings didn't matter – that I should just do as I was told.

I remember one day when my ex and I had company over, and the topic of politics arose. I voiced my opinion, only to be asked, *"Since when do you have one?"* My inner voice cried.

Life had taught me to run. If it's not working… leave. I got married at a young age and, unfortunately, wasn't mature enough to understand that I had to work to make it successful. So, I ran.

LIFE is work.

HEALING is work.

RELATIONSHIPS are work.

PEACE is work.

I lost a lot in the past, but I've had to face the mistakes head-on. As I let go of the regrets from many decisions made in the dark, I forgive, I heal, I reclaim, and I recover. I experience the wholeness that comes with being FREE.

I've discovered I am made in HIS likeness. I've discovered God on the inside of me. I've discovered LOVE on the inside of me. As I seek HIM, slowly but surely, I've begun to find my PEACE – knowing that there is nothing I could have done in my own strength.

As the old poem *Footprints* indicates: when I look back and see one set of prints in the sand, I know HE carried me.

As I mentioned, my grandmother's name was Grace. My daughter's middle name is Grace. Throughout my life, I see that the grace of the Lord has always surrounded me – and continues to do so.

"For it is by grace you have been saved, through faith – and this is not from yourselves, it is the gift of God." Ephesians 2:8 (NIV)

Cheryl Gardner - Co-Author

Safe in His Arms
The Goodness of God

Cindy Dawkins

Chapter Eight

Strength, Joy, and Peace

"Have I not commanded you? Be strong and courageous. Do not be afraid; do not be discouraged, for the Lord your God will be with you wherever you go." Joshua 1:9 (NIV)

My name is Cindy. I am a mother of two incredible young adult children whom I love with all my heart. I am a Christian and have been serving the Lord since I was about six years old, as far as I can remember. I currently work as an instructor therapist for children on the autism spectrum, with a background in business. I was born in Jamaica to Jamaican parents, but I've lived in Canada for most of my life.

I have always been very aware of God's presence through prayer, Bible reading, and church attendance. I grew up surrounded by family members who loved the Lord and who introduced me to His goodness by sharing their testimonies. Listening to their stories of healing and divine encounters as a young girl brought me peace and assurance, knowing that God was always with me throughout my life's journey.

Even now, as I approach my senior years, I continue to experience God's presence firsthand through powerful testimonies of healing. Some examples include overcoming congestive heart failure and surviving a stroke. The fact that I can breathe, walk, and talk without pain today is a miracle I do not take for granted.

I am passionate about encouraging others to hope and believe in the reality of God's presence. I've experienced His power for myself, and my prayer is that others will come to know Him in a personal and transformative way as well.

When I was about three or four years old, I had a terrifying experience by the riverbank in Jamaica. We were on our way to Sunday school, with my older cousins responsible for walking the younger ones. I remember wearing a lovely yellow dress. Along the way, the older cousins decided to stop for a swim and left me sitting on the riverbank, watching from a distance since I was too young to join them.

Swimming looked easy to me, so without understanding the danger, I jumped into the water fully clothed. Immediately, I was gasping for air. My head went under, and water filled my lungs. As I flailed, none of my cousins seemed to notice. I remember silently repeating the name of Jesus in my mind because I couldn't cry out loud. Suddenly, one of my older cousins swooped in and pulled me from the water, saving my life.

I knew in that moment, it was God who saved me.

When I was a vibrant teenager, probably around seventeen years old, I had a lovely Mustang with a soft top. It was an incredible gift from my parents in recognition of my successful grades. That car quickly became the center of my social world. I was one of the first young women in my friend group to get a driver's license, so every opportunity to drive was a chance I never passed up. I proudly drove my friends all over town in that Mustang.

One day, while the car was parked in our driveway, I remembered I had left something inside the house. My little brother, who was around eighteen months old at the time, was in the car. As I turned to grab the forgotten item, I realized – to my horror – that the car had somehow been shifted into reverse. It began rolling back on its own. Speeding around the corner was a large white van, moving far too fast for our quiet Burlington street. The Mustang, with my baby brother inside, was heading straight into its path.

All I can remember is instinctively prying open the car window with my hand, reaching in, and slamming the gearshift into park. There was barely six inches between the Mustang and the van when everything came to a screeching halt. God's hand of protection was undeniable that day. His presence was real, and I know He spared my brother's life…and mine.

Another unforgettable moment of divine intervention came one Saturday morning. I had a dentist appointment scheduled, but I absolutely did not want to go. I had plans for the day and fully intended to skip it. I decided instead to spend the day with my children, enjoying regular Saturday routines like chores and errands. That appointment was the last thing on my mind.

Yet at the very last moment, something shifted in me. Without understanding why, I scrambled to get the kids ready and rushed out the door to make it to the dental office. I now thank God for that sudden prompting because it truly saved our lives.

While we were at the appointment, an electrical short occurred in the toaster oven back at home, which began sparking and igniting the nearby plastic on our refrigerator. When we returned home, we were met by a street filled with concerned neighbors and firefighters. We were informed that the house had caught fire and was engulfed in flames within just forty-five minutes of us leaving.

I remember my little girl, only five years old at the time, looking up at me and saying, *"We seem to have lost everything, but Mama, we have everything because we have each other."* In that moment, she was able to grasp what truly mattered. It wasn't the furniture, the toys, or the electronics we lost. It was our lives, our togetherness, that was the real treasure.

Once again, God's protection and His goodness covered what could have been a devastating situation. We lost tangible, earthly possessions. But my family – my loved ones – were spared. I was able to hold them, kiss them, and thank God for their lives.

In 2019, I was dealing with my mom's cancer treatments and the terrifying possibility that we could lose her. She was battling both kidney failure and breast cancer, and the treatments were taking a heavy toll on her. Not long after her diagnosis, I began experiencing my own symptoms: difficulty breathing, a weakening voice, and an inability to sleep at night.

One night, before trying to sleep, I cried out to God, saying, *"What's happening? I need sleep, and I can't breathe."* Walking even short distances – like from the house to the car – left me gasping for air. Deep down, I sensed in my spirit that God was showing me I had congestive heart failure. I had gone to the doctor, who prescribed puffers, assuming it was asthma. But I kept hearing congestive heart failure echo in my spirit, and that alarmed me because it was the very condition my father had died from.

I made a decision that I would not die from congestive heart failure. I believed the Lord was showing me what He planned to heal. So, I returned to the doctor and insisted they test me specifically for congestive heart failure, and they confirmed the diagnosis. From that point on, I underwent tests, heart monitoring, and the full protocol for treatment.

After about six months of dealing with the illness, my stomach was distended, my legs were swollen, and I was physically worn down. One day, I cried out to God again, *"I do not have congestive heart failure. I thank You that I do not have it."* Day after day, I stood in front of the mirror, looking at the puffiness in my body, and I kept declaring in faith, *"I do not have congestive heart failure. I don't want it. I don't accept it. Thank You, Lord, that I don't have it."*

One day, I looked in the mirror and noticed that the swelling was gone. I took a deep breath and my breathing was completely clear. Filled with excitement, I rushed back to the doctor. They were astonished and simply told me to keep doing whatever I was doing. They even began to reduce my medication.

Then, in 2021, I suffered a stroke. In that moment, I recall being unable to speak, but in my spirit, I kept calling on the name of Jesus. I could hear people around me saying, *"Stroke,"* but I couldn't respond. Still, I held on to God in my heart.

While I was in the hospital, they pulled up my medical records. They saw the 2019 diagnosis of congestive heart failure, but the doctors confirmed there was no current evidence of it. I now have documented medical proof of my miraculous healing.

The stroke affected the left side of my body and impacted my ability to drive. But I am here today to testify to God's grace and His goodness. My speech has returned, and I've recently been able to drive on the highway again. I'm so grateful for the mercy of God because many people do not survive one of these diagnoses, let alone both.

As I've walked this faith journey, knowing that God is always with me, it has become my natural default to expect things to work out despite challenges, difficulties, or what the circumstances may look like. There's something deep within me that knows it will be okay. My trust in God has grown stronger and more sustained over time. Every time He shows up, His faithfulness renews my faith.

God's constant presence and unwavering love have helped me embrace the unknown without needing to have everything figured out or see the full picture. I've learned to live day by day, by faith, and I now find myself confidently encouraging others because I know that God has always come through for me. When I journal and reflect, I see a pattern: God coming alongside me, pulling me through, answering prayers in ways I never expected. I realize I don't need all the answers. I can boldly walk this walk of faith, not knowing what's next, simply because I know that God has me.

I walk in His favor and peace. And when circumstances are intense and challenging, I rise above them and experience joy that doesn't match the chaos around me because the peace of God sustains me. I keep going with strength and confidence. I can truly say I have joy unspeakable.

I've come to realize that my relationship with God is deeply personal, specific, and intimate. And I want to encourage you to pursue that kind of closeness. God knows every single one of us so well that He even knows the number of hairs on our heads. He took the time to design you uniquely and intentionally. His love is unconditional, bountiful, and so rich that it surpasses anything we could ever comprehend.

So, no matter what you're facing, hold fast to your faith. Do not waver. Never give up. The same God who created you also aligned the sun and the moon, gave us light by night, warmth during the day that does not scorch us, and breath in our lungs. He meticulously created you for His glory. He protects you, wakes you up, surrounds you with His shield, and assigns angels to guard you, even from dangers you may never see.

His Word tells us:

"For I know the plans I have for you," declares the Lord, "plans to prosper you and not to harm you, plans to give you hope and a future." Jeremiah 29:11 (NIV)

Because it's God's plan, it is a good plan – and you can count on that.

Whenever your mind is filled with racing thoughts, telling you to give up or question what's possible, remember: life's greatest victories are born from the challenges and battles we face. You are never alone. You can face life with courage and fierce resilience.

My prayer for you is this: that you would sense God's presence in every moment, bringing comfort and peace in all circumstances. May His unconditional, relentless love surround you, and may His healing power drive out anxiety, suffering, and every form of pain or grief. May His grace lift you up, and His love envelop you.

One of my favorite songwriters, Crystal Lewis, put these thoughts beautifully in her song *"Beauty for Ashes"*:

God replaces fear with strength, brings joy in times of sorrow, and offers calm in the midst of deep distress.

Cindy Dawkins - Co-Author

Safe in His Arms
The Goodness of God

Nasha T. Alexis

Chapter Nine

To Be Known by God

"But now that you know God—or rather are known by God—how is it that you are turning back to those weak and miserable forces? Do you wish to be enslaved by them all over again?" Galatian 4:9 (NIV)

Does anyone fully understand what it means to be known by God? If you do, or know someone who does, please let me know. And thank you in advance. This is a concept that I have had difficulty fully understanding – or should I say, accepting. The truth is, we know ourselves how we think and what makes us tick, for the most part. So then, to believe that I am known by God – the Ruler and Creator of the universe – is baffling to take in, because He knows us so much better.

In my mind, I know and understand that He *"knitted me together in my mother's womb"* (Psalm 139:13, NIV) and *"the very hairs on [my] head are numbered"* (Matthew 10:30, NIV). Still, I wonder – who am I that He would have the time to know me? There are so many more important people doing amazing things. So, who am I that He would want to know me? That is so overwhelming to think about – or accept, to say the least.

But the truth is, we are known by a loving and faithful God, who loves us endlessly. There was a time when I didn't believe that, but the Holy Spirit reminded me through an experience I had some time back. In essence, He was showing me that if a human being can take the time to get to know me, how much more should I believe that

God Himself knows me?

I believe it was a timely experience – something I could relate to – to help me on my journey back to the Father; to believe what He says in His Word.

It was the time when I first started attending my current home church. I am not – and was never – a person who announced their presence. I would go in and come out quietly, with my daughter in tow. I participated in Bible studies and training, while my daughter attended programs geared toward her age group.

Not long after, I became pregnant with my second child and was very ill from the beginning. I remember being sick in people's vans – church members who would give my daughter and me a lift to and from church services or events. Sometimes they would have to take me back home as soon as we arrived at the building – or even before we got there. Most people carry their wallets, tissue, and makeup in their bags when going out. On the other hand, I had to make sure my bag had throw-away plastic bags – the kind we paid for at some grocery stores. I couldn't and wouldn't leave without first ensuring I had an ample supply of those bags with me at all times, all neatly folded.

Eventually, I became too sick to attend church services or any other programs in person. I was either in the hospital or on bed rest at home. That's when I started receiving phone calls from church members I didn't know. I had no idea how they got my phone number or how they even knew who I was or what was happening with me. These women would pray for me over the phone – something entirely new to me.

Then a couple of those ladies visited me, bringing food, flowers, and even cash. I was so taken aback that I didn't know how to respond. I am forever thankful to my church family for bringing my name before the throne of God – those who went out of their way to pick up me and my daughters and bring us home safely again. I am forever grateful to each one, even those who have gone home ahead of us. May they rest in peace.

Among all these acts of kindness, one of my most treasured memories was the day one of the visiting ladies told me the pastor of the church had sent his greetings and a card. My first question to them was, *"How does the pastor know who I am?"* Their simple response was, *"He knows,"* as they laughed quietly.

I must confess, I wrestled with that for a very long time. I know it's nothing grand, but it affected me deeply, even without fully understanding why. I found it hard to believe that the pastor of a good-sized church – especially when I wasn't even a member yet – would actually know me, recognize me, or be interested in my health. There were people much closer to me who didn't care about any of that.

Just thinking about it now, as I write, is overwhelming. I'm not putting this person on a pedestal by any means (besides, he would knock it down if I tried), but I still ask: why bother? I'm sure he had more pressing matters and issues to deal with. Yet that was – and still is – his nature. He made every effort to welcome people and get to know something about those he is leading, which I found truly commendable.

God uses every experience we go through to help us make sense of the world we live in and to bring us back to Him. No experience, no matter how insignificant we may think it is, is too small or useless. It all works for our good and His glory.

I write all this to say that a mere man took the opportunity to know who I am, without him or even me realizing it would play a significant role in my relationship with the Father. How much more do you think God will go for you? After all, He is the One who made you and me. We are made in His image. Only the craftsman knows his vessel better – inside and out – than anyone else. God, in all His infinite power, wants to have a relationship with His creation and His children.

As mentioned before, He already knows us, so the other end of building that relationship rests with us. Psalm 139:14 (NIV) says, *"I praise you because I am fearfully and wonderfully made; your works are wonderful, I know that full well."* Have you noticed how many times certain words in this verse are emphasized? That is how important you are to God. That is how much He cares for you and me – so much so that He says repeatedly we are *"fearfully and wonderfully made."*

Tell me, what else should we need to know to fully understand how well God knows each one of His children (and we are His children) individually? He meets each one of us where we are, even when we can't see or feel Him. There have been plenty of times when I felt unheard and unseen by God. It didn't matter whether anyone else saw me. All I needed to know was that my Heavenly Father saw me and was with me. Still, there are days when I have to remind myself of that truth – that I am seen and known by God.

Just like the woman at the well, He already knows all that we have done, are doing, and will do in the future. There is nothing about us that will ever surprise God. He knows us better than we know ourselves. I have also realized that relying on people can only lead to disappointment, when it's God who can truly meet all our needs.

We sometimes get to a place where we depend on others to fulfill us instead of God, or we seek recognition from others. We must learn to turn our focus to God – the One who knows us best. For me, reminding myself of God's truths may look different from time to time, depending on the situation I find myself in, or even where I am physically, mentally, emotionally, and spiritually.

At times, it is through dance movements – with or without flags. Sometimes, it's through singing, *"Shout for joy to the Lord, all the earth, burst into jubilant song with music!"* Psalm 98:4 (NIV).

And again, in Psalm 100:3–5 (NIV), we are reminded:

"Know that the Lord is God. It is He who made us, and we are His; we are His people, the sheep of His pasture. Enter His gates with thanksgiving and His courts with praise; give thanks to Him and praise His name. For the Lord is good and His love endures forever; His faithfulness continues through all generations."

So now, let's do just that. Let us exalt the Lord our God.

Prayer

Father, thank You for being who You are. I honor and magnify Your holy name. I worship You now and always. May praise be on my lips continually as I cry out, *"Holy, holy is the Lord God Almighty, who was and is and is to come"* Revelation 4:8b (NIV).

King and righteous Judge, You are forever sovereign. A mighty warrior in battle, a conqueror of nations, who fights for His people. It is written in 1 Samuel 17:47 (NIV), *"All those gathered here will know that it is not by sword or spear that the Lord saves; for the battle is the Lord's."*

Battles may come, trials may raise their heads, even the fiery darts from the enemy may come our way, but we stand firm – knowing and trusting that You, God, will defend us, for the battle belongs to You.

Thank You, Mighty Warrior, for You know that I cannot fight any battle on my own and win; I need You always and forever. I stand on Your promises, which are yes and amen, as it says in Your Word in 2 Corinthians 1:20 (NIV):

"For no matter how many promises God has made, they are 'Yes' in Christ. And so through Him the 'Amen' is spoken by us to the glory of God."

Gracious and awesome Abba, there is no one like You. You are from everlasting to everlasting, oh Sovereign King. Holy and righteous Father, I give thanks and praise. I adore You and lift You higher above all things and everyone in my life, for You are God alone.

You knew me even before I was born. You saw my beginning, and You alone know my end – and everything in between. I thank You, Lord, for breath in my lungs, blood in my veins, and a brain to think. I praise You, for I am fearfully and wonderfully made in Your image.

Thank You, Sovereign King.

May we also remember that no one and nothing compares to You. You, who created the heavens and the earth, which You have made Your footstool. You reign supreme as *"the King of glory, the Lord strong and mighty, the Lord mighty in battle"* Psalm 24:8 (NIV). Who or what can ever be compared to You or even come close to matching Your greatness? There is none – not even one.

You command the waters of the seas on how far they can go. You displayed that miracle for Moses and Your people when You led them out of Egypt by Your mighty hands. You split the seas and made a way for them to walk on dry land. Oh, my Father, You are wonderful and an ever-present help. You know all I need, even before I think about it or even know it myself. There is no place that Your arms cannot reach. And so, I say, thank You, Lord.

Nothing is out of Your sight or knowing, for You hold the world in the palm of Your hand. Spirit of the Living and One True God, I reverence and bow low before You, for You are too magnificent for my eyes to behold. Your loving-kindness is overwhelming, but I long to be in Your presence. Your grace and mercy are too difficult to comprehend, but I am grateful that they are new every day. Your presence is too powerful, but I desire to be wherever You are.

Psalm 23:6 (NIV) says, *"Surely your goodness and love will follow me all the days of my life, and I will dwell in the house of the Lord forever."* Holy Spirit, help me to walk and live my life on this side of eternity with a grateful heart that is pleasing to You. May I be obedient to Your Word and Your ways.

Today, I echo the words of King David in Psalm 8:4 (NIV), *"What is mankind that you are mindful of them, human beings that you care for them?"* In essence, who am I, that You are mindful of me, a human being that You care for me? I may never fully understand the depths of Your love for me, so I ask, Holy Spirit, please remind my soul of that truth – that I may live in that truth with understanding.

You demonstrated that love for Your people by sending Yeshua to take our place on that old wooden cross, to die for all the sins of the world, to bring us back to You. As John 3:16 (NIV) declares, *"For God so loved the world that he gave his one and only Son, that whoever believes in him shall not perish but have eternal life."* And again, in 1 John 4:10 (NIV), *"This is love: not that we loved God, but that he loved us and sent his Son as an atoning sacrifice for our sins."*

Father, Ancient of Days, we thank You for the life, death, and resurrection of Yeshua, our Savior and hope. We praise You with a grateful heart, singing praises unto You for Your sacrifice. May we live our lives worthy of Your sacrifice, Lord.

Father, we thank You for the presence and counsel of the Holy Spirit, through whom we can commune with You daily, and for making our bodies a living sacrifice, holy and pleasing to You.

Thank You, God, for knowing and receiving us despite our faults. We are forever grateful that we are known by You, God, our Heavenly Father. Amen.

Remember, there is nothing wrong with being known or recognized by our fellow brothers and sisters, whether at our workplace or in our community. However, when God is not present, it is useless. Our eternal and ultimate hope is found in Christ alone. And when He knows us, everything else will fall into place.

It is better to be known by God than by the whole world, which neither loves us nor can save us.

Nasha T. Alexis - Co-Author

Safe in His Arms
The Goodness of God

Dhanmatie Persaud

Chapter Ten

From Palmyra to Purpose – The Goodness of God in My Life

"Oh, give thanks to the Lord, for He is good! For His mercy endures forever."
Psalm 136:1 (NKJV)

As a young girl growing up in Palmyra Village, Berbice, Guyana, I never could have imagined how God would transform my life. Looking back now, I can see His fingerprints everywhere: in my childhood, my struggles, my family, and even in the pain I didn't understand at the time. I realize now that every moment, every hardship, and every unanswered question was preparing me for a life anchored in faith and purpose.

Our family background was Hindu. My parents believed in God, but we did not actively practice Hinduism. In our home, there was no temple, no idols, and no daily rituals. Yet, deep inside, I always sensed there was one true and living God who saw me, who heard me, and who cared. I used to look at the sky at night, wondering who created all the stars and how He could know someone as small as me.

When I went to school, Christian missionaries often visited our classrooms. They prayed before lessons began and spoke about Jesus with such warmth and peace that it stirred something in my heart. Even as a little girl, I felt drawn to the name of Jesus. There was a gentleness in His story, a love that felt personal. I didn't understand everything they said, but I knew I wanted to know Him more.

As a teenager, I began to pray quietly on my own. When things were difficult at home or when my parents argued, I would whisper, *"Father, help me."* I didn't know how to pray properly, but somehow, I knew He was listening. Many nights, I fell asleep talking to God like a friend. It wasn't religion – it was relationship.

When I was sixteen or seventeen, my father became very sick. I was frightened, and I didn't know what to do. A friend from school noticed my sadness and said, *"Jesus can help you."* She invited me to church, and that one invitation changed my life forever.

A Heart Touched by the Savior

The day I walked into that little church, I felt something I had never felt before. The people were clapping, singing, and lifting their hands in worship. Their faces were glowing with joy, and the atmosphere felt holy and peaceful, yet powerful. It was as if Heaven itself had descended into that humble place. The air felt different; it was filled with love, acceptance, and a presence I could not describe. As I stood there, a warmth spread through my heart, and tears filled my eyes. I didn't understand it then, but I now know that it was the presence of the Holy Spirit surrounding me, calling me home to the Father's love.

When the pastor began to preach about the goodness of God, it felt as if he was speaking directly to me. Every word pierced my heart, as though God Himself was revealing that He had seen my pain and heard my prayers. He said, *"God can turn any situation around, no matter how hopeless it looks."* That message broke something open inside of me. I went home that day full of faith and hope, determined to believe that this Jesus could help my family and change our story.

That night, I walked around our small home, praying out loud for the first time. I didn't know the right words, so I simply said, *"Jesus, protect my family."* I pleaded the blood of Jesus over every room, every wall, and every person under our roof. From that day forward, something shifted. Peace entered our home like a gentle breeze. My father began to get stronger, my siblings started attending church with me, and our hearts became united in faith and love.

That was the day I knew Jesus was real. That was the day He came into my heart and into my family's life. He didn't just change my circumstances, He changed me from the inside out. From that moment on, I made a decision that no matter where life took me, I would live for Him and testify of His goodness for the rest of my days.

Growing up in Guyana wasn't easy. Many families in our community lived in poverty, and ours was no exception. I can still remember the smell of wood fires burning in the mornings as mothers prepared simple meals for their children before school. Sometimes, my siblings and I had to share what little we had. There were days when dinner consisted of rice and a small piece of fish, yet we never went to bed hungry. God's unseen hand always made a way.

Psalm 40:2 became one of my favorite verses: *"He also brought me up out of a horrible pit, out of the miry clay, and set my feet upon a rock, and established my steps."* That verse described exactly what God did for me. He didn't just lift me out of poverty, He gave me a vision for something greater.

As I served Him and trusted Him, He began to open doors I never thought possible. Slowly, our lives began to change. My father's health improved, and new opportunities came our way. Neighbors who once pitied us began to ask, *"What happened to your family?"* and I would smile and say, *"It's Jesus. He made a way where there was no way."*

Then came one of the greatest blessings of my life. God made it possible for me to come to Canada. I had never even imagined living in another country, but God had a bigger plan for me. Moving to Canada was like stepping into a new chapter of destiny. It wasn't easy at first. I had to adjust to a new culture, weather, and way of life, but God's grace carried me. What I learned in that season was that when God calls you out, He always provides the strength and favor you need to succeed.

I went from being a poor village girl in Palmyra to a woman blessed to bless others. Every step of the way, I saw His hand of provision. Truly, Jehovah Jireh has never failed me.

God's Hand of Protection

There have been many moments in my life where I've seen God's protection firsthand, but one moment stands out vividly. It was in 2008. I was living in Canada and heading to work one cold morning. I remember feeling exhausted but determined to push through my day.

As I approached a major intersection, I prepared to make a left turn. I checked both directions, and everything appeared clear. But as I began to turn, out of nowhere, a car came speeding toward me and slammed into my vehicle. The impact was so violent that my car spun several times across the road.

I could hear the sound of tires screeching, metal bending, and people gasping. It was an industrial area filled with large trucks, and for a moment, I thought my life was over. But God! In that instant, I felt His hand shielding me. Though the car was destroyed, I walked away alive. The doctors later said it was a miracle that I survived with only minor injuries.

Psalm 91:11 became my lifeline: *"For He shall give His angels charge over you, to keep you in all your ways."* That day, I knew those angels were real. God's goodness wasn't just something I read about. It was something I lived through. That accident could have taken my life, but instead, it became a testimony of His mercy and protection.

Another season that tested my faith was when my mother became sick. I had brought her from Guyana to Canada so she could have a better life and spend her later years in comfort and peace. For a while, she was strong, joyful, and adjusting well to her new surroundings. She loved attending church, singing hymns, and joining me in prayer each morning. Her laughter filled our home, and her presence brought warmth to everyone she met. But then the diagnosis came – cervical cancer – and our world felt as though it had stopped.

The news hit me like a storm. My mother was my confidante, my encourager, my prayer partner, and my closest friend. Watching her grow weak and lose her strength broke something inside of me. I remember kneeling beside her bed, holding her hand, crying, *"Lord, please don't take her yet."* Those nights were filled with tears, but also with desperate prayers that drew me closer to God's heart.

Matthew 11:28 brought me comfort during those sleepless nights: *"Come to Me, all you who labor and are heavy laden, and I will give you rest."* I clung to that promise with everything I had. She went through painful rounds of radiation and treatments that left her frail, yet through it all, she never stopped praising God. Her faith became my strength. Slowly, she began to improve. God gave us two more precious years together – two years of laughter, love, stories, and moments that will forever live in my heart.

When she eventually went home to be with the Lord, I didn't grieve like those who have no hope. I knew she had given her heart to Jesus before she passed, and that assurance gave me peace beyond words. Even in her final days, she radiated serenity and whispered prayers for her children. It reminded me once again that the goodness of God endures even in the valley of sorrow. Psalm 34:19 became my strength: *"Many are the afflictions of the righteous, but the Lord delivers him out of them all."* Her journey became a testimony of His mercy, and her legacy of faith continues to inspire me every single day.

Called to Serve

Today, as an ordained minister and a pastor's wife, I can say without hesitation that serving the Lord is the greatest honor of my life. But ministry has not been without challenges. It requires faith, humility, endurance, and a constant dependence on the Holy Spirit. There are moments when the spiritual battles feel heavy, when the needs of others seem endless. Yet every trial pushes me to lean harder on God's strength and less on my own. It's in those moments that I feel His grace carrying me, reminding me that the calling is greater than the cost.

Through every season, I've seen how God uses brokenness to birth compassion. Every hardship I faced, whether poverty, accidents, grief, and illness, prepared me to minister to others with understanding and empathy. What once wounded me has now become the very tool God uses to heal others. I've stood beside women weeping over sick loved ones, and I've been able to say, *"I know how that feels, and I've seen what God can do."* My pain became my platform, and my tears became my testimony of His unfailing love.

My husband and I now serve together, leading others to Christ with one heart and one vision. Our ministry focuses on healing, restoration, and community outreach. We've witnessed God's power move through prayer meetings, altar calls, and even casual conversations in grocery stores or hospital rooms. We've seen hardened hearts softened by His love, prodigal sons return home, and weary souls find rest in His presence. Each soul that comes to Jesus reminds me why I said yes to the call: because every life transformed is evidence of His faithfulness.

No matter how dark things seem, I've learned that there's always light when you call upon the name of Jesus. Hebrews 13:8 says, *"Jesus Christ is the same yesterday, today, and forever."* That truth gives me courage to keep pressing forward, knowing that His faithfulness never wavers. He is still healing, still saving, and still using ordinary people like me to accomplish extraordinary things for His glory.

If you're reading my story today, I want you to know that Jesus loves you deeply. You are not forgotten. You are not too far gone. No matter where you are or what you've done, God's mercy is greater than your mistakes. His love reaches into the darkest places and brings light, healing, and hope. Even when you feel unseen, He knows your name, your tears, and your silent prayers. He has a plan for you – one that is far better than anything you could imagine.

Maybe you've prayed and nothing seems to change. I've been there too, in those moments when you wonder if God still hears you. But I'm here to tell you to hold on. God is still writing your story. Sometimes, the waiting is where He builds your strength and prepares you for the blessing ahead.

Matthew 19:26 says, *"With men this is impossible, but with God all things are possible."* What looks hopeless to you is only a setup for His glory. You might be crying today, but joy is coming in the morning. Don't give up before the breakthrough. Your pain has a purpose. God specializes in turning ashes into beauty and tears into testimonies.

Call on Jesus. He still heals, He still restores, and He still answers prayer. If you give Him your heart, He will give you a future filled with peace, purpose, and divine favor. Surrender everything to Him, and you will see His goodness unfold in ways that will leave you in awe.

A Mother's Blessing and Prayer

My dear sister or brother-in-Christ, if I could sit with you right now, I would hold your hand and tell you that everything is going to be alright. You may not see the way forward, but God already has a plan written for your life – one filled with hope, restoration, and purpose. You are not forgotten, and every tear you've cried has been seen by Him.

Heavenly Father,

I thank You for this precious sister or brother reading my story. You know their pain, their tears, their dreams, and their fears. I ask You to meet them right where they are today. Wrap Your loving arms around them and remind them that they are never alone. Strengthen their heart and renew their mind with Your promises.

If they're battling sickness, I speak healing over their body in Jesus' name. If they're worrying about their children, remind them that You are their keeper, their protector, and their guide. If they're burdened by financial need, open doors that no man can shut. Replace their anxiety with Your perfect peace, and give them the confidence to trust You even when they cannot see the outcome.

Lord, turn their mourning into dancing. Let their testimony be one of victory, overflowing with joy and faith. Surround their home with Your presence and fill their heart with hope. Restore their strength, renew their courage, and let them know that better days are coming. May Your goodness overflow into their generations to come, leaving a legacy of faith that will never fade.

In the mighty and matchless name of Jesus Christ, Amen and Amen.

Pastor Dhanmatie Persaud - Co-Author

Safe in His Arms
The Goodness of God

Anita Sechesky

CHAPTER ELEVEN

The Goodness of God in Times of Suffering

There are seasons in life when the world feels unbearably heavy, when the air itself seems thick with sorrow, and the sound of hope fades into a distant echo. These are the moments that test the very core of who we are and what we believe. In such times, our hearts ache for answers, for reasons, and for rescue. Yet even in the deepest shadows, there remains a gentle radiance that cannot be extinguished – the steadfast light of God's goodness. It does not flicker or fade with our circumstances. His light remains constant, unbroken, and true, even when our world feels like it's falling apart. And though our minds may struggle to understand what our spirits already know, His presence becomes the quiet anchor holding us steady when life feels like shifting sand beneath our feet.

Pain has a way of magnifying everything around us. It amplifies our fears, exposes our doubts, and often isolates us from others. It makes ordinary days feel overwhelming and simple decisions feel impossible. Yet if we are still long enough, if we quiet the noise of our racing thoughts, we can sense something sacred in the silence. Deep within that quiet space, the whisper of God calls out, reminding us that He has not left us. He is Emmanuel, God with us, in the joy and in the sorrow, in the peace and in the storm. Even when our tears blur the path ahead, His compassion steadies us one breath at a time. And it is often in the depths of suffering that we become most aware of His nearness.

He is the same yesterday, today, and forever (Hebrews 13:8, NKJV). His character does not waver when we stumble, nor does His love diminish when the storms of life rage against us. In fact, His goodness often shines brightest against the backdrop of our brokenness. When everything familiar falls apart, when we can no longer see the way forward, He is still there, gently weaving the tangled threads of our pain into a greater story of redemption. Nothing in our lives is wasted in His hands. What feels like the end to us often becomes the beginning of a new chapter written by a God who specializes in restoring, rebuilding, and renewing His people. Even when suffering feels senseless, His goodness refuses to let our pain have the final word.

Our tears may blur the picture, and our hearts may question His timing, but while we only see fragments, God beholds the full masterpiece. What looks like chaos in our hands is order in His. What feels like delay to us is preparation in His plan. When we feel as though life is unraveling, He is quietly aligning every thread with divine precision. Nothing escapes His notice – not a sigh, not a struggle, not a single sleepless night. He is the Master Artist who works in layers, and though we may not understand the strokes He is making, we can trust that His hands never create anything without purpose.

"Even though I walk through the darkest valley, I will fear no evil, for You are with me." Psalm 23:4 (NIV)

This verse is a divine promise. The same God who rejoices with us on the mountaintop also walks beside us in the valley. His presence doesn't vanish when the road grows painful; it becomes our very strength. He steadies us when the ground beneath our feet trembles. He becomes the quiet assurance in the middle of the unknown.

Every believer eventually faces a valley where God's goodness seems hidden, where prayers echo back with silence and faith feels fragile. Yet those valleys are sacred places where His presence often becomes the most tangible. When all we have left is trust, we discover that trust truly is enough. God's goodness does not always remove us from pain, but it will always redeem it. In His hands, even suffering becomes a seed that will one day bloom into testimony.

Suffering is not a punishment. It is often a process. It is the refiner's fire through which faith is purified and purpose revealed. Gold cannot shine without heat, and faith cannot mature without testing. Though it rarely feels this way in the moment, our pain often carries a purpose greater than our understanding. What feels unbearable today may become the very testimony that strengthens someone else tomorrow. God is not careless with our wounds. He uses them intentionally, shaping us into vessels who carry resilience, compassion, and authority. Sometimes the very places where we break become the places where His glory is most clearly seen.

Throughout Scripture, we see countless examples of people who encountered God's goodness not after their suffering, but within it. Joseph was betrayed, sold into slavery, and imprisoned, yet he later stood before his brothers and declared, *"You meant evil against me; but God meant it for good"* (Genesis 50:20, NKJV). Job lost everything – his family, wealth, and health – yet still proclaimed, *"Though He slay me, yet will I trust Him"* (Job 13:15, NKJV). David hid in caves, running for his life, yet still wrote psalms of praise and refuge. Esther risked her life before the king. Paul worshiped in the darkness of a prison cell. Each story testifies that God's goodness is not the absence of suffering but His presence within it. Their breakthroughs came not because they avoided hardship, but because God met them in the middle of it.

In my years of serving as a Registered Nurse across the Greater Toronto Area and Southern Ontario, I have seen this truth unfold time and time again. I have held trembling hands in emergency rooms, whispered prayers over those fighting for life, and stood with families waiting for news that could alter their world forever. In those sacred moments between life and death, I have seen miracles take place – not always in the way people expected, but in ways that revealed God's heart. A silent room suddenly filled with the sound of a heartbeat. A breath returning after being still. A family finding peace in the middle of loss. A hardened heart softening as forgiveness was extended. A dying patient experiencing an unexplainable calm as they slipped into eternity.

Those moments have taught me that God's goodness often steps in when human strength runs out. Sometimes His miracle is not in changing the situation, but in changing us through it. He doesn't always calm the storm, but He gives us the courage to stand firm until it passes. His grace holds us upright when our knees buckle under the weight of grief. His love becomes the lifeline we cling to when everything else falls away.

There were nights in the hospital when exhaustion and sadness pressed down heavily, but the presence of God would fill the room like a gentle light. I have watched patients smile through pain, whispering, *"God is good,"* even when their bodies were failing. That kind of faith can only come from walking through fire and realizing that the flames cannot consume what God has already redeemed. I have seen families gather around a bedside, holding hands and praying through tears, not because the situation made sense, but because God was still worthy. In those moments, heaven felt close. The atmosphere would shift, and the peace of God would settle over the room in a way no medication or machine ever could. Those sacred encounters taught me that suffering does not diminish God's presence; it often magnifies our awareness of it.

At first glance, gratitude and suffering seem like opposites. One is born of abundance, the other of lack. But gratitude is not about what we have; it is about recognizing Who is with us. Gratitude in times of pain is an act of defiance against despair. It says, *"Even here, even now, I will see the goodness of God."* It is choosing to open our eyes to the subtle fingerprints of His grace woven throughout our day: the unexpected text message, the strength to get out of bed, the quiet reassurance that we are not alone.

Giving thanks in the middle of hardship doesn't mean denying our pain or pretending everything is fine. It means acknowledging that God is still working behind the scenes, even when we can't trace His hand. Gratitude shifts our perspective. Instead of fixating on what we have lost, we begin to notice what remains: the air in our lungs, the people who care, the promises that still stand firm. It becomes the lens that helps us see light in places once covered by darkness. Gratitude is a candle that refuses to be extinguished, even in the fiercest wind. It invites hope back into the room.

"Though the fig tree may not blossom, nor fruit be on the vines... yet I will rejoice in the Lord, I will joy in the God of my salvation." Habakkuk 3:17–18 (NKJV)

This verse captures the essence of spiritual maturity. The prophet's praise was not rooted in circumstance but in confidence, knowing that God's goodness is unchanging. Gratitude is not conditional; it is intentional. It becomes the melody that drowns out fear, the rhythm that keeps our faith steady, and the anchor that tethers our hearts to truth when emotions threaten to overwhelm us.

When we thank God in the middle of the storm, we are not ignoring the pain. We are surrendering it. We hand over the broken pieces of our hearts to the One who specializes in restoration. Gratitude doesn't erase grief, but it redeems it. It becomes a bridge between despair and hope. It shifts the atmosphere within us, reminding our souls that darkness does not have the final say. Every "thank You" becomes a declaration that God is still on the throne, still faithful, still working even when our natural eyes see no progress. Gratitude is a spiritual weapon, gently yet powerfully pulling us out of the heaviness that tries to suffocate our faith.

In my own journey, I have learned that thanksgiving in hardship can open the door to healing. There were moments when tears fell freely, yet even then, I whispered, *"Thank You, Lord."* Not because everything made sense, but because He was still with me. That small act of praise became a lifeline, a thread connecting me to His unshakeable goodness. Over time, I realized that gratitude doesn't change God. It changes us. It softens our hearts, quiets our fears, and makes room for His peace to settle where despair once tried to reign.

When we think of miracles, we often picture dramatic scenes such as the blind receiving sight, the seas parting, and the dead rising. But miracles are not always loud or visible. Some arrive quietly, like a peace that surpasses understanding (Philippians 4:7, NKJV), or the strength to forgive when bitterness seems justified. Others appear through simple acts of grace like a timely phone call, an unexpected provision, or a heart transformed through suffering. Sometimes the miracle is simply having the strength to take the next step when everything in you wants to give up. Other times, it is the sudden awareness that God has been carrying you all along, even when you felt abandoned. Miracles in suffering remind us that God's goodness is not restrained by our circumstances. It flows through them.

I have seen these miracles unfold in hospital corridors, in living rooms filled with prayer, and in the silent surrender of weary souls. I once met a mother who survived a life-threatening condition. As she recovered, she told me, *"I didn't understand why God allowed it, but it changed how I live, love, and trust. I cherish life differently."* Her words have stayed with me as a reminder that God can take even our deepest pain and use it to cultivate new life. Her testimony wasn't wrapped in neat answers, but it carried the unmistakable fragrance of transformation – proof that suffering, when surrendered to God, can birth a new way of seeing, living, and loving. I have watched others experience similar moments: a hardened heart softened through illness, a fractured family reunited around a hospital bed, or a person who once lived in fear suddenly walking in bold, unshakeable faith. These are miracles too – quiet ones, hidden in the folds of ordinary days, but miraculous nonetheless.

Miracles often bloom from broken ground. Sometimes the miracle is that we endure at all. Other times, it's that we emerge softer, wiser, and more compassionate than before. Psalm 30:5 (NKJV) says, *"Weeping may endure for a night, but joy comes in the morning."* This verse is not merely about time passing; it's about transformation. It speaks to the divine exchange that takes place in the heart of a believer who refuses to give up, even when everything around them feels dark. "Morning" is not a specific hour on the clock. It is a spiritual awakening.

"Morning" does not always mean sunrise. Sometimes it's the moment peace replaces panic, or when your heart dares to hope again. It's the quiet assurance that though sorrow visited, it will not stay forever. Morning can be the phone call that brings clarity, the strength to forgive, or the unexpected courage to face another day. The goodness of God guarantees that joy will return. His promises are not delayed; they are developing. What feels like waiting may actually be preparation for breakthrough. God is never idle. He is always shaping, healing, and redeeming, even in the hours when we feel most abandoned.

Prayer

Heavenly Father,

I lift before You every heart that is weary, wounded, or waiting for breakthrough. You see each story in its entirety – every sleepless night, every silent cry, every question whispered in the dark. Lord, remind Your children that You are near, even in the valley of sorrow. Wrap them in Your peace like a comforting blanket and let Your presence be their resting place.

For those struggling to believe, breathe fresh faith into their spirits. For those grieving, comfort them with the assurance that You hold their loved ones in perfect peace. For those facing sickness or fear, release Your healing power into their bodies and minds. Where confusion reigns, bring clarity. Where hopelessness resides, release divine hope.

Teach us, O God, to trust Your process even when we do not understand it. Help us to give thanks even when the miracle is still forming. Remind us that Your goodness has not abandoned us. It is carrying us. Turn our pain into purpose. Turn our tears into testimonies. Let every wound become a well of wisdom for others who walk the same path.

And finally, Lord, may every person reading these words feel the warmth of Your love wrapping around them right now, reminding them that they are seen, known, and cherished by You. You are our healer, our sustainer, and our everlasting hope.

In the precious and powerful name of Jesus Christ, Amen.

Anita Sechesky - Visionary Compiler & Publisher

Safe in His Arms

The Goodness of God

Harrichand Persaud

Chapter Twelve

Raised Up by Grace – The Testimony of Pastor Harry

"Surely goodness and mercy shall follow me all the days of my life; and I will dwell in the house of the Lord forever." Psalm 23:6 (NKJV)

Today, I just want to share the goodness of God in my life. When I look back over the years, from the time I gave my heart to Jesus until now, I can see the hand of God working in ways that still amaze me. I have learned that it was not my own strength or my own plans that brought me this far. It was His grace.

I was born in Betsy Ground, Berbice, in the beautiful country of Guyana. I came from humble beginnings, and I often say, *"If it had not been for the Lord on my side, where would I be?"* That statement has become more than a phrase to me. It's the story of my life. I have seen God take what was small and make it great, take what was broken and make it whole, take what was impossible and make it possible.

As the youngest of nine children, I watched my parents work tirelessly to provide for us. We didn't have much, but we had love. And I believe that love was God's way of showing me that He was with us even then. My mother was a praying woman. She might not have had riches, but she had faith, and that faith shaped who I would become.

When I look at my life today, I see blessings far beyond what I ever imagined. God has given me a beautiful wife, two wonderful sons, and three precious grandchildren. I work full-time while pastoring full-time, and somehow, by His strength alone, He allows me to balance it all. It is not always easy, but every day I am reminded of the truth that *"My grace is sufficient for you, for My strength is made perfect in weakness"* 2 Corinthians 12:9 (NKJV).

In ministry, my days are filled with serving others: weddings, funerals, counseling sessions, visiting the sick, and organizing programs for seniors and children. We have a thriving Sunday school and an active outreach team that ministers to our community. When I think of how far God has brought me – from a young man with no clear direction to a pastor leading a registered church in Canada – I am humbled. Starting a ministry was never part of my plan. It was part of God's plan. And His plan has always proven better than mine.

For more than twenty years, I have served faithfully in this nation, helping people, sharing the gospel, and praying for those in need. Every time I felt weary or discouraged, God reminded me of His promise in Philippians 1:6: *"He who has begun a good work in you will complete it until the day of Jesus Christ."* That scripture became my anchor when I felt overwhelmed, unsure, or under attack.

Growing Up with Little but Learning to Trust Much

I came from a poor family. My parents raised nine children, and we often had very little. My mother worked tirelessly to make ends meet, sometimes taking odd jobs just to put food on the table. I remember nights when dinner was simple – just rice and a small piece of fish – but we never went to bed hungry. Somehow, God always provided, even when it seemed impossible. Looking back now, I realize that what we lacked in material things, we gained in faith, love, and resilience. Those humble beginnings shaped my heart and taught me to see blessings in the smallest things.

Those early days taught me the value of gratitude and faith. I learned that you can be content even when you don't have everything you want because God supplies what you need at the right time. I watched my mother pray over empty cupboards and then see unexpected provision come through a neighbor's kindness or a friend's visit. When I gave my life to Christ, something shifted within me. My eyes were opened to see that the same God who sustained us in lack was calling me into a deeper walk of trust.

I began reading the Word of God, and one particular verse changed everything.

> *"Bring all the tithes into the storehouse, that there may be food in My house, and try Me now in this," says the Lord of hosts, "if I will not open for you the windows of heaven and pour out for you such blessing that there will not be room enough to receive it."* Malachi 3:10

That scripture challenged me to trust God completely. Even when I didn't have much, I decided I would honor Him with my tithes. I remember times when I had only a few dollars left, and my mind told me to hold onto it, but my spirit said, "Give it to God." Every time I obeyed, He provided more than I expected.

When I first came to Canada, I couldn't find work for seven long months. I was new to the country, unfamiliar with the systems, and unsure of my next step. Yet I held on to faith. I spent that time praying, reading, and seeking God's direction, trusting that He was preparing me for something greater. Then, finally, the breakthrough came – I found a job. When I received my very first paycheck, I made a vow to give it all to God as my first fruits.

I went to church that Sunday, and when the pastor called for an offering, I walked forward and placed the entire check in the basket. Tears filled my eyes as he took my hand and prayed for me. He asked God to open doors and provide supernatural favor. That moment marked the beginning of a new chapter in my life. From that day forward, I never stopped tithing.

God has honored His Word in my life. I have seen Him provide in miraculous ways. Bills were paid when there was no money, jobs opened up when others were being laid off, and my family lacked nothing. Proverbs 3:9–10 (NKJV) says, *"Honor the Lord with your possessions, and with the first fruits of all your increase; so your barns will be filled with plenty, and your vats will overflow with new wine."* That truth became my testimony. I learned firsthand that obedience unlocks provision, and faith activates the miraculous. God truly blesses those who trust Him without reservation.

From Conversion to Calling

From the time I was converted to Christianity, I have seen the greatness of God revealed in my life and in my family. Through prayer and faith, God transformed not only my heart but also the hearts of my loved ones. My parents, sisters, nieces, nephews, uncles, and aunts all came to know His saving grace. Each life changed is a testimony of His mercy and power, proving that God's love reaches deeper than our failures and stretches wider than our understanding.

God's greatness is shown in His ability to heal, restore, and unite families in love and truth. What seemed impossible became possible through Him. Truly, there is no limit to the greatness of our God. When one person in a family says yes to Jesus, it can open the door for generations to be blessed. I've seen entire family lines changed because one person decided to pray instead of complaining, to believe instead of doubt, to worship instead of worry. Every prayer offered in faith became a seed of transformation that eventually bore fruit in the lives of those around me.

Twenty years ago, I founded a church with a vision to share God's love and power with the world. What began as a small gathering of faithful believers in a living room has grown into a thriving ministry where countless lives have been transformed. Through prayer, faith, and the presence of the Holy Spirit, we have witnessed miraculous healings, restored families, and renewed hope in the hearts of many. God's glory fills the sanctuary each time we gather, and I often stand in awe of how far He has brought us.

Each miracle is a reminder that the God we serve is still the same yesterday, today, and forever. I have seen people delivered from addictions, marriages restored after years of separation, and hearts healed from trauma. I have seen young people rise up to serve God boldly, unashamed of the gospel. Some of our members have gone on to start their own ministries, missions, and community programs that continue to spread the light of Christ beyond our walls. When I see these things, I am reminded that this work is not about me. It's about Him.

As I look back over the years, I am humbled and grateful for the journey. The same God who called me from humble beginnings in Guyana continues to lead me here in Canada. He has proven Himself faithful in every season – through triumphs and trials alike. I continue to trust Him for greater works ahead, because Ephesians 3:20 reminds me: "Now to Him who is able to do exceedingly abundantly above all that we ask or think, according to the power that works in us." Every day, I hold that promise close, knowing that the story God is writing through my life and ministry is still unfolding, for His glory alone.

Faith Through the Storms

There were times in my life when everything seemed to fall apart: finances were tight, when sickness struck, and when people I loved walked away. Those moments tested my faith, but they also refined it and drew me closer to the heart of God. I learned that even when God seems silent, He is still working behind the scenes, orchestrating every detail for my good. What I once saw as loss, He later revealed as preparation for something greater. Every trial became a teacher, showing me that His delays are never denials, but divine redirections meant to strengthen my trust in Him.

I remember once when our church faced financial hardship. The bills were piling up, and it seemed like we wouldn't make it. But instead of panicking, we prayed. Our members gathered one evening, and we cried out to God together, trusting Him to make a way. Within a week, unexpected donations came in, and every need was met in full. That experience taught me that God never fails those who trust in Him. He simply waits for us to place our confidence in His timing rather than our own.

I have also seen Him heal. One Sunday, a woman came to the altar, barely able to walk. The church gathered around her in prayer, and by the next service, she testified that the pain had left her body completely. Another time, a man who had lost all hope came forward in tears, asking for prayer for his family. Today, that same man and his family are active members, serving in ministry with joy. I've seen marriages restored, hearts mended, and broken dreams revived through prayer and faith.

Through every trial, I've discovered that faith is not about avoiding problems. It's about trusting God through them. When we fix our eyes on Jesus, the storms may rage, but we remain standing. His grace sustains us, His presence strengthens us, and His promises remind us that no storm lasts forever. And when the clouds finally clear, we realize that even in the storm, God was there guiding, teaching, and shaping us for His glory.

Looking back, I realize that obedience was the key to my growth. Every time I said, "Yes," to God – whether it was in giving, forgiving, or serving – He opened new doors that I never even knew existed. Each act of obedience became a stepping stone to a deeper level of faith and maturity. Gratitude became my lifestyle. No matter how small the blessing, I learned to give thanks, because I discovered that thankfulness attracts the presence of God and ushers in even greater favor. Obedience taught me patience, and patience taught me trust. Every test became an opportunity to see God's promises fulfilled in ways I never could have imagined.

"I have been young, and now am old; yet I have not seen the righteous forsaken, nor his descendants begging bread." Psalm 37:25 (NKJV)

I have lived this verse every single day. God has taken care of me, my family, and our ministry in ways that still amaze me. He has been Jehovah Jireh, my Provider, Jehovah Rapha, my Healer, and Jehovah Shalom, my Peace. Even in seasons of lack or uncertainty, His hand never left me. There were days when I didn't know how things would work out, yet God would send help at just the right moment; sometimes through a stranger, a friend, or a member of the congregation. Each divine intervention strengthened my confidence that obedience never goes unrewarded.

When I see my grandchildren worshipping in church, I am reminded that God is faithful through generations. The seeds of faith planted long ago continue to bear fruit in their lives. I often watch them lifting their hands in worship, and tears fill my eyes knowing that what I started in obedience has now become their inheritance. That is the beauty of walking with God. His blessings never end with us; they continue through us, multiplying into the hearts and destinies of those who come after us. We are living proof that God keeps covenant to a thousand generations of those who love Him. This legacy of faith, hope, and love is the greatest reward of all—a testimony that time cannot erase and a reminder that every "yes" to God echoes into eternity.

A Pastor's Blessing and Prayer

Heavenly Father,

I thank You for every reader who has taken the time to hear my story. May they see through my journey that You are a faithful God who raises us up by grace.

Lord, for the one who feels lost today, remind them that they are never too far gone for You to reach. For the one struggling to provide for their family, show them that You are still Jehovah Jireh—the God who provides. For the one battling sickness, let them feel Your healing power right now.

I pray that Your peace will guard their hearts and minds in Christ Jesus. Let every person reading these words experience Your presence in a personal way. Give them courage to trust You, faith to stand strong, and grace to finish their race well.

And Father, help us all to remember that Your goodness and mercy follow us all the days of our lives. Thank You for protecting, healing, and providing for me. Thank You for every miracle, every open door, and every testimony born out of trials.

I declare that the same grace that raised me up will raise up every person who calls upon Your name.

In Jesus' mighty and precious name, Amen.

Pastor Harrichand Persaud - Co-Author

Safe in His Arms
The Goodness of God

Jasmine E. Clarke

CHAPTER THIRTEEN

The Steps of The Righteous – Getting into Alignment

"For I know the plans I have for you," declares the Lord, "plans to prosper you and not to harm you, plans to give you hope and a future." Jeremiah 29:11 (NIV)

Growing up as children, we can remember going to school, hanging out with our friends, playing games, doing things that we liked, and just enjoying ourselves at those moments – not thinking much about our futures. *"Why am I here?"*

How many of you have reached that place?

We finished elementary school and then high school. We may have decided to become nurses, doctors, dentists, architects, teachers, or even singers. Some of us may not have even known what we really wanted before we went to college or university.

Unfortunately, some of us may have lost our way and ended up going in the wrong direction, not serving the Lord. Our parents, teachers, or friends may have told us to become doctors, teachers, or whatever, and we know deep in our hearts that it doesn't sit well with us. Right down in the core of our hearts, we know something is missing. We don't feel right. We feel like a fish out of water. We feel so out of place. Many of us have been there – maybe you are there right now – because we didn't know any better. We stay in that position or whatever we are doing just to make ends meet and provide for our families.

"Lord, I know that people's lives are not their own; it is not for them to direct their steps." Jeremiah 10:23 (NIV)

I strongly believe that the well-seasoned believers should be the ones to encourage us, as the new sheep within the flock, to seek the Lord for direction and to observe the gifts that they carry for that particular time and season, so that we are walking in His purpose. Some may notice the gifts and encourage you to pursue them, but there are many believers who have not yet reached the point of using their gifts.

For this reason, some may have been placed in a position within the church where they're not called to be, nor has God placed that calling upon them. This causes the individual to feel out of place and prevents them from using their God-given gifts. Within the body of Christ, we all have different functions. If you look at the whole body, every single part has its own responsibility. So it is with us. We're all here to fulfill His purpose in our lives with our gifts. We must remember that His ways are not our ways. We need to submit to His call and ask for direction.

God sent us into this world because He has a purpose for each of us to fulfill. Everyone has a part to play in His Kingdom. We are placed here to serve the Lord and to build up His Kingdom. Many of us have gifts that would help us financially and could even make us destiny helpers for someone else needing help to get their calling started. Many of us are in financial difficulty these days and do not realize that the very gifts God has given us are the ones that are going to set us up and build His Kingdom.

I'm sure many of you have experienced joy, peace, happiness, and contentment using the gifts God has given you. When you're using those gifts, time doesn't even matter to you - you just enjoy that space and time. I believe each of the gifts God has given us is to be used because they will leave an impact on others. Their lives will be blessed and changed just by your presence and by using the gifts that have been given to you. God can work within you so that He can minister to those individuals.

I'm sure we all have a passion or desire to do something, and you just can't shake it off. You have been chosen. You have been separated. The Lord has planted it within your heart.

When I look back over my life, I realize that I have many gifts, but I didn't know which one I was supposed to focus on at that particular time. I thought I would be using just one gift, but I understand now that each gift can be used in various seasons of my life. Everybody will experience something different in their lives according to the season that they're in. God has a way of making you use your talents so that He receives all the glory through them all.

I love to bake Jamaican fruit cake, which is usually baked during Christmas time. I know people who don't bake and would love a fruit cake made a certain way. Because of the method I use to make the cakes, people enjoy them and put in their orders. So, I am blessing individuals with one of the gifts God has given me. You see, our talents are not meant for us to keep to ourselves. We are to share them with others so that they can be blessed by them.

A young lady whom I saw interviewed had painted a picture, but she painted it as the Holy Spirit had led her. I can't recall what the picture was about, but it was three-dimensional. She had it on display in a studio, and the viewers were just so drawn to it. The artist herself was amazed at how the people would just stand there, gazing at the picture with tears streaming down their faces. It was because the picture itself ministered to them. This is just an example of how God can use a person's gifts in ways they could never imagine.

Maybe you're a seamstress who sews a variety of different items, like clothes for children. There could be a mother with young children, and she's having a hard time finding clothes that fit them, and here you are – a seamstress who's able to make outfits for the children that would look most suitable for them. Could you imagine the smile on those children's faces and on the mother's face because you used your God-given talent to make their outfits?

When I baked, that was for a different season. I chose to work in the dental field because that was where I was needed at the time. I did it for quite a few years, but then I began to feel out of place. That was my cue to leave because that season of my life was over. I started having the desire to be around God's people, reading His Word, spending more time in His presence, blessing His people, and giving Him the glory. It was time for me to start participating in a praise and worship team. I enjoyed singing. I love worshipping God. I loved ushering His people into praise and worship, so I pursued it. And yes, I loved it. It made me feel as if I was at the foot of His throne, giving Him my all in worship. This was it! I loved being in the presence of God dearly. On any given day, I would be singing and playing my music. You would think that I was having church while I was doing my house chores.

Many of us have gifts that we can use without any effort. They're just natural to us. Some people may have to go to school and receive training, and that's all right. I can remember playing the piano after church at the tender age of five, and no one taught me. Music will always play a great role in my life.

"Thou wilt shew me the path of life: In thy presence is fullness of joy; At thy right hand there are pleasures for evermore." Psalm 16:11 (KJV)

Yet, there are other seasons in your life where God will have you take a detour to do something else. This has taught me to be obedient, patient, and humble in this particular season. As I sit here sharing what I have walked through, I truly understand now why I had to take this turn. When this season is over, I will pursue the next thing He'll have me do. I thank the Lord for what He's brought me through because I wouldn't be who I am today without Him. I have learned so much. It wasn't easy, but I have grown so much in the Lord. There are many other paths and seasons that we will experience.

Of course, everyone's path is different, but you have to be in alignment with God so that you won't lose your way. Another thing that I've realized is that whatever season you're in, He will provide and sustain you while using whatever gift you'll be using at that particular point in time.

Let's take a look at David. He was a young shepherd boy who took care of his father's sheep. God had plans for him even though he was young. David was anointed to be the new king after Saul. During his time of waiting, God still used him. God used the little shepherd boy to stand up against Goliath and kill him. That was the earlier season of David's life. God used him in different ways, even though David committed many sins against God. David still went back to God, asked for forgiveness, and repented of his sins. When all that was done, God still said David was a man after His own heart.

There are things that can hinder your walk with God: sin, disobedience, self-centeredness, generational curses, trauma, and so on. You will need to put all these things before the Lord and take care of them before you can go any further. Your Heavenly Father loves you so much that He doesn't want you to lose your way.

"Let all things be done decently and in order." 1 Corinthians 14:40 (KJV)

You need to take some time in prayer. Repent of your sins daily because you can sin without even realizing it. Fast, meditate on the Word, and build a relationship with the Lord. This will give God the opportunity to speak to you. Listen to His voice. When you do, that's when you'll be able to hear and know what He wants you to do. Meditating on His Word builds you up and strengthens you because it's God Himself speaking to you.

When you fast, it gives you power and strength to prepare for your tasks. When you spend time in prayer, you're communing with

Him and building a personal relationship with your Heavenly Father. Sometimes, while taking your walks or drives, talk to Him and get to know Him as your Father. It also gives Him a chance to share things with you. Communing with God gives Him great joy when you take time to be in His presence. It gives you power and strength. It gives you the assurance that you will make it because God's got your back. You can walk with boldness, authority, and confidence, knowing that He is right there with you.

God is going to pave the way for you. When there is disorder and confusion, remember that Satan is the author of confusion. We do not want to give any foothold to the enemy because he's only there to steal, kill, and destroy.

"The steps of a good man are ordered by the LORD: And he delighteth in his way. Though he fall, he shall not be utterly cast down: For the LORD upholdeth him with his hand." Psalm 37:23-24 (KJV)

In fact, when your purpose is bigger than you, God will make provisions for you, such as connections to your destiny helpers. But you will still have to take care of your part, like educating yourself. You are assured that no matter what trials and hardships you may face, He will never leave you nor forsake you. All you need to do is put your complete trust in Him. What you cannot do, God will provide a way. Make time to give Him praise and worship. This is your weapon to fight back against the enemy when times get rough.

"Finally, my brethren, be strong in the Lord, and in the power of his might. Put on the whole armour of God, that ye may be able to stand against the wiles of the devil." Ephesians 6:10-11 (KJV)

Lastly, you will always need to walk by faith and not by sight. Live with integrity, gratitude, and humility, and be committed to the call on your life. In everything that you do, give thanks and praise to the Lord. He must get the glory.

Prayer

Father God, I repent for all the sins that I have committed, both known and unknown. I ask that You forgive me for my sins. Dear Heavenly Father, I come to You at this time, knowing that Your plan is to prosper me and not harm me. Lord, help me to follow in Your footsteps, to walk in the order that You have placed me, and to be attentive to Your call. Please help me to fulfill Your purpose in my life.

Father God, You have given me so many gifts, and I want to use them for Your glory. I know that, according to Your Word, You used many other servants. You blessed them with talents that they used for Your glory. Father God, I just want to use all that You've given me for Your glory. I come to You with a willing heart so that I can be used for Your purpose. Teach me Your ways, O Lord, so that I will be able to walk uprightly in Your sight. I thank You for being there for me along this journey. I thank You for guiding and directing me, even though at times I may have lost my way. So, Lord, I come to You humbly and with gratitude for what You've done and what You're about to do in my life. I would like to serve You and to be used for Your glory.

In Jesus' name, I pray. Amen!

Jasmine E. Clarke - Co-Author

Safe in His Arms

The Goodness of God

Jean Lawrence-Scotland

Chapter Fourteen

Through Loss, Still Good

On October 20, 2023, my life shifted forever.

My younger brother, Jr., passed away. As I write those words, the tears are streaming down my face. It still feels so unreal. We weren't twins, but our bond felt like we were. From childhood to adulthood, we moved through life side by side – laughing, dreaming, growing. He was my brother, my mirror, my friend.

How do I see the goodness of God in his passing?

The memory of that day is still vivid in my mind. I was at work, in the middle of a five-day training session. It was a Friday afternoon. I noticed my phone had rung a few times – one call from my mother. I didn't answer right away, figuring I'd get back to her during the afternoon break.

At 2:45 p.m., we were finally on break. I checked my messages. A text from my sister-in-law read: *"Jr. collapsed. They are working on him."*

I froze.

As I reached the door to exit the room, my knees gave way. I fell right there at the threshold. I remember my co-workers picking me up gently and taking me into a quiet room. One co-worker immediately began to pray, her words filling the silence with hope. The other one volunteered to drive me straight to the hospital. The entire car ride, I cried and begged God, *"Please let Jr. be okay."*

But it wasn't God's plan for him to be okay. One hour into the ride, my sister-in-law called again. Her voice trembling, she said the words I dreaded: *"He's gone."*

There are moments in life that define us – not by what we achieve or gain, but by what we survive. That day became one of those moments. I entered a season of profound pain, confusion, and heartbreak.

So where is the goodness of God in that?

It's a question that doesn't always get a quick answer. It's one that sometimes echoes in silence, in tears, in the ache of empty arms and unanswered prayers. Faith, in these moments, isn't about easy answers. It's about holding on when everything in you wants to let go.

And yet, even in the valley of grief, something deeper whispered, *"I am still with you."*

When we speak about the goodness of God, it's easy to associate it with blessings, breakthroughs, and beautiful moments. And yes, God is good in those times. He's good when we get the promotion, when we're healed, when our loved ones are safe. But is He still good when everything falls apart?

Yes.

That's the deep, enduring, almost scandalous truth of God's nature: His goodness isn't circumstantial. It's eternal. It doesn't disappear in our pain; it holds us through it.

Psalm 34:18 (NIV) says, *"The Lord is close to the brokenhearted and saves those who are crushed in spirit."*

I have lived that verse. I've felt His closeness when I could barely breathe from the pain. I've experienced His saving grace – not in the form of preventing my loss, but in the way He carried me through it.

In the days and weeks following Jr.'s passing, I began to see glimpses of God's goodness. Not through dramatic miracles, but in the presence of others. In the way people simply showed up. My husband was a steady source of comfort. And my sister-friends dropped everything to sit with me, pray with me, and cry with me. My sisterhood of nine women was incredibly active and present, as they still are today. Interestingly enough, each of them has experienced and is managing their own grief journey.

Family members, especially our cousin wrapped our parents in love and unwavering support when we didn't know what to do next. My older brother demonstrated incredible strength and resilience, even while navigating the deep pain of losing his only brother. My one co-worker drove me without hesitation while the other prayed with such authority and tenderness.

Two of my choir members were just amazing humans! And to our church family: words will never be enough to express our family's gratitude.

Grief is overwhelming. There are times I cried so hard I couldn't breathe. But God's love can show up in the most unexpected ways: in a friend's embrace, a stranger's kindness, or even in the stillness of the early morning when you realize you've made it through one more sleepless night. That is the goodness of God. His goodness comes running after us, just like the song by CeCe Winans says. Sometimes we don't have the strength to run toward Him, but His love pursues us anyway.

I prayed hard that day. I pleaded with God to let Jr. live. I bargained. I begged. And He still said no. It's hard to accept that. We think of God's goodness as giving us what we ask for. But in His higher wisdom, God sometimes answers in ways we cannot understand.

Isaiah 55:8–9 (NIV) reminds us: *"For my thoughts are not your thoughts, neither are your ways my ways," declares the Lord. "As the heavens are higher than the earth, so are my ways higher than your ways and my thoughts than your thoughts."*

That verse has been a lifeline for me. He knows the very second of our birth and the very second of our death. It doesn't erase the pain, but it gives me peace in knowing that God sees the full picture, even when I can't. Sometimes the greatest act of faith is trusting in God's goodness when life feels anything but good.

Remembering Jr. Through the Lens of God's Grace

Jr. was full of life – his laugh, his spirit, his kindness. He made people feel seen. He has left a positive legacy and impact on many lives. His wife, three children, and his bonus daughter are left with loving and wonderful memories of their dad. Losing him left a hole in our family that no one else can fill.

And yet, when I remember him, I also remember the grace that surrounded his life. I thank God for the years we had together. I thank God that he knew he was loved. I thank God that even in his final moments, he was not alone. Sometimes God's goodness isn't about preventing the storm, it's about calming us in the middle of it.

I now see Jr.'s life as a gift. Short, yes, but filled with moments of beauty. I choose to celebrate the goodness of God in the way Jr. lived, the love he gave, and the legacy he left behind.

Since Jr.'s passing, I've met others walking through grief. We share stories, tears, and sometimes even laughter. And in these shared experiences, I see how God uses even our deepest wounds to help others heal.

It reminds me of 2 Corinthians 1:3–4 (NIV): *"Praise be to the God and Father of our Lord Jesus Christ, the Father of compassion and the God of all comfort, who comforts us in all our troubles, so that we can comfort those in any trouble with the comfort we ourselves receive from God."* That verse is no longer just words to me. It's real.

When we allow our pain to become a testimony, God uses it to minister to others. Our scars become sacred when we offer them to Him.

Surrendering to the Goodness of God

There's a line in an award-winning song by a well-known female Gospel artist that encourages me that surrender is not weakness. It's worship. It's saying, God, I trust You – even when I don't understand.

That has been my daily prayer: "Lord, I give You everything – even my questions, even my grief." And every time I do, He meets me with peace. Not all at once. Not in a magical, pain-erasing moment. But in steady, gentle waves that remind me He's still God. Still good. Still with me.

The image in the same song of God's goodness running after us is powerful. It's not passive. It's active. It's intentional.

Even in our wandering.

Even in our anger or numbness.

His goodness is in pursuit.

In my brokenness, He came running.

In your brokenness, He will too.

Choosing to Sing Again

One of the hardest things for me was going back to worship – singing again, praising again. But I learned something important: worship is not just for the mountaintop; it's for the valley too. There is power in singing about God's goodness when your heart is still aching. That kind of worship is raw. Real. Costly. But it is also incredibly beautiful. It says to the world – and to the enemy – I still believe. I still trust. I still declare the goodness of God.

As I reflect on the months since October 20, 2023, I still grieve. I still cry. But I also stand in awe of the God who has sustained me.

Here's what I've learned:

- God's goodness is not dependent on my circumstances.
- He can be good, and I can be grieving at the same time.
- His love never stops pursuing us, even in our pain.
- He is present in the silence, in the sorrow, and in the support of others.
- He gives us strength to face what we never thought we could.

So, how do I see the goodness of God in Jr.'s passing?

I see it in the love that surrounded him.
I see it in the people who held me up.
I see it in the strength God gave me to keep going.
I see it in every moment I choose to live and love fully because Jr. would want that.

I still sing of the goodness of God, not because life is easy, but because God is faithful.

Even in loss.
Even in the valley.
Even when the tears fall again.

God's kindness keeps pursuing me, even when I least expect it.
And with every breath I have, I will testify to His unfailing goodness.

Jean Lawrence-Scotland - Co-Author

Safe in His Arms
The Goodness of God

Joan M. Steward

Chapter Fifteen

All Things Are Possible with God

"Jesus responded, 'What appears humanly impossible is more than possible with God. For God can do what man cannot.'" Luke 18:27(TPT)

My life is a testament to the transformative power of God's love. As I sit down to write this chapter, I am fully consumed by a sense of awe and reverence for the God who has transformed my life. The life of a little black girl whose memory of her childhood days reflects fear, pain, and sorrow. Today, I see myself as a remarkable woman of faith. I, Joan Margaret Steward, can testify to the power of God's love and redemption, a reminder that with Him, *"all things are indeed possible"* (Matthew 19:26).

Growing up in my parents' home was a constant nightmare for me. A house filled with domestic violence, a childhood plagued by fear, anxiety, and a deep sense of unworthiness.

My father, who was supposed to be my protector and provider, was instead the source of my pain and suffering. This led to a long period of struggling to form healthy relationships with others. It has been, and still is, very challenging to trust people, fearing that they would ultimately hurt and cause me pain.

My self-esteem was severely damaged not only by my dad but also by other family members and my environment, and I often felt like I was walking on eggshells, never knowing when the next explosion would occur.

Despite the chaos and unpredictability of my home life, there was a wee bit of light from my aunt, who tried her best to provide a sense of stability and normalcy for me. She was a teacher, a very strong woman of faith and courage. I remember her praying with me and teaching me about adulthood and the love and goodness of God. Those were the only shining lights in my life – the times that I felt safe and loved, even though they were short-lived.

However, the emotional scars of living with domestic violence ran deep, and I struggled to reconcile the love and affection I craved with the harsh reality of my father's behavior.

The absence of love and affection from my father left an emotional void in my life. I struggled to understand why my dad couldn't love me the way he loved my other siblings or the way I deserved to be treated. As I grew older, I began to internalize the negativity, unheard, thinking that I was somehow to be blamed for my father's behavior. I remember asking my mom on various occasions if he was truly my dad, her response being, *"What kind of question is this?"*

Despite the chaos and dysfunction in my home, my mom worked tirelessly to provide for the family. She was a pillar of strength, a constant source of comfort and reassurance. However, the strain of living with an abusive husband eventually took its toll on my mom. After my dad tried to poison the family, my mom secretly left the house and country. This was a great move for my mom but not for me. My shield was gone, and I was open to all forms of emotional abuse.

Feeling lost and alone, I turned to God as a young teenager. I had always believed in Him, but it wasn't until I hit rock bottom that I began to seek Him out in a much more meaningful way. I started attending church regularly, reading my Bible, and praying as I poured out my heart to God, asking Him to get me out of that home.

I was clinging to the hope that God would somehow intervene and rescue me from the darkness that had consumed my life. I would often pray, asking God to send a wonderful, God-fearing man to say that he was my real father. But there was no change.

I began to feel like I was living in a war zone. My dad would enter the house via the front door, and I would jump out via the back door. Eventually, my dad got word of where my mom was, and he too left the country to find and kill her.

At this point, the tension and stress of living with domestic violence had taken its toll on my mental and emotional health. I was struggling through school but continued anyway because, deep inside, I felt there was going to be a change somewhere along the line.

I felt lost, alone, and unloved, like I was just a tiny boat adrift in a stormy sea. But even during such darkness and despair, I began to sense that there was something more, something greater than the pain and suffering I was experiencing. I started to feel a spark of hope, a glimmer of light in the darkness.

That spark of hope was fanned into a flame when I encountered God's love for the first time.

I was invited to a church crusade service by a friend, and it was there that I heard the gospel message of God's love and redemption. The pastor was speaking about the Father-heart of God, and something within me was ignited. For the first time in my life, I felt like I was seen, heard, and loved. I felt a sense of connection with a Father who loves me unconditionally. I realized that God was not like my earthly father but a loving and merciful God who really wanted to have a relationship with me and had been waiting for this for a long time. This was the beginning of a new journey for me, one marked by healing and restoration.

As I began to learn more about God's love, I also encountered people who truly loved and supported me. I realized that I was not alone, not unloved, and that I was not worthless. I began to understand that God's love was not based on my performance or behavior, but on His character and nature. He loved me because He chose to, not because I deserved it.

I came to realize that God had been working in my life all along. He had been providing for and protecting me, even when I didn't realize it, and He had ultimately delivered my family and me from the abusive relationship that had caused us all so much pain.

This revelation was like a balm to my soul. It healed my wounds, restored my dignity, and gave me a sense of purpose and belonging. For the first time in my life, I felt like I was home, like I had found a place where I truly belonged.

With this newfound Father, I began to experience a sense of peace and joy that I had never known before. I was no longer alone; God was with me every step of the way, and He loved me.

As I continued to grow in my faith, I began to experience the transformative power of God's love in my life. I started to see myself as God saw me as a beloved child, worthy of love and respect. I began to understand that my identity was not defined by my past or my circumstances, but by my relationship with God. I also learned that I wasn't alone. Many had gone through, and many are still going through, the same and even worse experiences.

This newfound understanding gave me the courage to confront the pain and trauma of my past. I began to work through my emotions, process my experiences, and find healing and closure. It was a difficult and painful journey, but with God's love and support, I was able to find freedom and release.

Years later, I was able to look back on my journey and marvel at the incredible transformation that had taken place in my life. I had gone from being a broken, wounded, and lost soul to being a confident, courageous, and compassionate woman of faith.

My life is a powerful reminder that with God, all things are possible. He took the broken pieces of my life and turned them into something beautiful. He healed my wounds, restored my dignity, and gave me a sense of purpose and belonging.

As I often say, *"God took the ashes of my life and turned them into something beautiful. 'And provide for those who grieve in Zion – to bestow on them a crown of beauty instead of ashes, the oil of joy instead of mourning, and a garment of praise instead of a spirit of despair. They will be called oaks of righteousness, a planting of the Lord for the display of his splendor.'"* Isaiah 61:3 (NIV).

He took the pain and trauma of my past and turned it into a message of hope and redemption. I am living proof that with God, all things are possible.

No matter what we may have gone through or are going through in life, God is able to redeem and restore us. He is a God who heals the brokenhearted and binds up their wounds. As Psalm 147:3 says, *"He heals the brokenhearted and binds up their wounds."*

He is a God who loves unconditionally and wants a personal relationship with us.

I pray that from my story, you can learn several valuable lessons about redemption and the transformative power of God's love.

Firstly, know that no matter what you've been through, no matter how broken or wounded you may be, God can take the pieces of your life and turn them into something beautiful.

Know that you are not alone. No matter what you're going through, know that God is real and that He cares deeply about your many struggles. If God can hear me and restore peace in my life, He can do the same for you or anyone else.

We live in a world filled with darkness and despair, but with God, we can overcome even the most daunting challenges.

As you reflect on my story, may you be inspired to trust in God's goodness and know that He is always working to bring light and life into this broken world.

Secondly, I would like you to see the importance of confronting the pain and trauma of one's past. It is only by facing our fears, working through our emotions, and finding healing and closure that we can truly experience the transformative power of God's love.

Finally, be reminded that our identity is not defined by our past or our circumstances, but by our relationship with God. We are not who we were, but who we are becoming in Christ.

I would like to challenge your faith. As you reflect on my story, I hope you will be challenged to examine your own faith. Do you believe that God can take the broken pieces of your life and turn them into something beautiful? Do you trust that He can heal your wounds, restore your dignity, and give you a sense of purpose and belonging?

Do you believe that with God, all things are possible?

I encourage you to hold onto hope, to trust in God's goodness, and to believe that He can do exceedingly, abundantly above all that we ask or think, because with Him, all things are possible.

May my story be a source of inspiration and encouragement to you. May you be reminded that no matter what you are facing, you are not alone. God is with you always, and with Him, all things are possible.

"And we know that in all things God works for the good of those who love him, who have been called according to his purpose." Romans 8:28 (NIV)

"Jesus looked at them and said, 'With man this is impossible, but with God all things are possible.'" Matthew 19:26 (NIV)

"He heals the wounds of every shattered heart." Psalm 147:3 (TPT)

"Jesus looked at them and replied, 'With people it is impossible, but not with God – God makes all things possible!'" Mark 10:27 (TPT)

"Not one promise from God is empty of power. Nothing is impossible with God!" Luke 1:37 (TPT)

Prayer

Heavenly Father,

Today, I bring to You my dear brother or sister who is suffering in a domestically violent and abusive relationship. Father, You know what they're going through. You know the depth of their pain and the weight of their fear. My God, You see the ways in which they are being hurt and manipulated. Lord, I ask that You be their rock and their solace. Father, be their shield and protection during their storm. Surround them with Your loving presence and give them the courage to stand strong as You lead them through it all. Father, protect them from harm and keep them safe from their abuser. Give them wisdom and discernment to know when and how to seek help and how to get out of the situation.

Precious Father, heal their emotional and physical wounds. Lord, restore their sense of self-worth and dignity. Help them to see themselves through Your eyes as beloved, valuable, and precious. Provide them with a support system of loving friends, family, and professionals who can help them through this difficult time.

Gracious Father, give them the financial resources they need to walk out of the old and start anew. Lord, I pray for the abuser. I pray that You would intervene in his or her life and bring them to a place of repentance and healing. Help them to see the harm they are causing and to seek help to change their behavior. Open their eyes to recognize the pain they are inflicting, and lead them to seek help so that they may come to know You and Your love. Transform their heart, Lord.

Thank You, Lord, that You are a God of justice and mercy. Thank You that You are always with us, even in the darkest of times. Thank You, God, that You are the only One who can take every impossible situation and transform it into something possible.

In Jesus Christ's Name, I pray, Amen.

Joan M. Steward - Co-Author

Safe in His Arms
The Goodness of God

Anita Sechesky

Chapter Sixteen

The Role of Gratitude in Recognizing God's Goodness

Gratitude is more than polite acknowledgment; it is the heartbeat of faith. It is a living force that changes how we see, how we think, and how we experience God's presence in everyday life. A grateful heart has the power to pierce through even the thickest darkness, illuminating the path toward peace and perspective. Gratitude anchors us in the truth that God's goodness does not fluctuate with our circumstances. It flows from His unchanging nature. When we thank Him, we are not simply responding to blessings; we are recognizing His hand at work, even when the outcome is still unseen. Gratitude becomes the lens through which we witness God's fingerprints on every detail, whether through a small kindness, a moment of clarity, or a quiet reassurance whispered into our spirit.

What I've learned over the years is that gratitude is not only expressed when life feels gentle or predictable; it's expressed when faith chooses to speak louder than fear. Gratitude steadies us when life trembles. It is our reminder that even when life shifts, God remains. A grateful heart becomes a sanctuary where God's peace can rest. When our minds feel overwhelmed, thanksgiving reorders our thoughts. When discouragement whispers lies, gratitude declares truth. When life feels unsettled, gratitude restores balance. It teaches us to pause, inhale deeply, and remember that even in uncertainty, God has never lost control. Gratitude is the spiritual discipline that opens our eyes to what is right, even in the midst of what is wrong.

As a Registered Nurse, I have witnessed gratitude unfold in life's most fragile moments. I have seen humanity laid bare – raw, vulnerable, and often afraid. Yet even in those places, gratitude has the power to soften what feels hard and breathe hope into what feels hopeless. A grateful heart opens a window for God to enter, even when doors seem closed. And sometimes that one moment of gratitude becomes the turning point in a person's healing – physically, emotionally, or spiritually. I have watched patients who felt defeated suddenly find strength when they whispered, *"Thank You, God, for another breath."* I have seen families shift from panic to peace as they gave thanks simply for the gift of being together. Gratitude does not erase suffering, but it invites God into it, transforming the atmosphere, renewing the mind, and awakening the soul to His goodness.

To thank God in times of suffering is not denial; it is holy defiance. It's standing face to face with pain and saying, *"You will not define me. My God is still good."* Gratitude in hardship is an act of spiritual resistance against the enemy's attempts to discourage or defeat us. It declares that our hope is not tied to circumstances but rooted in the character of God. It is choosing to lift our eyes above the storm long enough to remember who holds the winds and waves in His hands. In that sense, gratitude becomes warfare. Every "Thank You" is an arrow aimed at fear. Every expression of praise dismantles the lies that try to take root in our hearts.

During my years in the emergency department, I learned that gratitude is often born in places where fear tries to dominate. There were nights when exhaustion pressed heavily upon my shoulders, when the emotional weight of caring for others felt overwhelming. But when I stepped aside for a moment and whispered, *"Thank You, Lord, for allowing me to be Your hands today,"* something shifted inside me. Gratitude didn't erase the chaos, but it repositioned my heart within it. It restored my purpose. It awakened resilience. It breathed life into weary bones. Gratitude reminded me that I was not alone in that room. God was working through every touch, every word, every decision.

Pain has a way of stripping life down to essentials. It removes distractions and exposes what truly matters. And in those raw places, gratitude becomes a lifeline that tethers us to hope. I have witnessed families receiving devastating news, yet instead of withdrawing from God, they held onto one another and prayed with thanksgiving, not for the outcome, but for God's nearness in the storm. That kind of gratitude is not fragile; it is fierce. It is the kind of faith that refuses to let darkness have the final word.

Gratitude reminds us that even though we walk through valleys, we never walk alone. It keeps us grounded in the assurance that God not only sees our suffering, but He walks through it with us. His presence becomes our comfort, His promises our compass, and His goodness our reason to keep moving forward, one step at a time.

Modern science now echoes what Scripture has declared for generations: gratitude heals. It calms anxiety, strengthens the heart, and restores mental clarity. But more than that, gratitude is medicine for the soul. It softens hearts hardened by disappointment and clears the fog left behind by grief.

I often think of a beloved woman I visited in a nursing home. Her body weakened by illness, yet her spirit unshakably vibrant. Each morning, she greeted the day with the same words: "I'm still here. Thank You, Lord." Her gratitude didn't come from the absence of suffering. It came from the abundance of God's presence. Even confined to her bed, she ministered through her thankfulness. Gratitude became her strength, her testimony, her identity.

In another moment, I witnessed a reconciliation so profound that only gratitude could have opened that door. A father and son, separated by decades of pain, found healing in one simple phrase: *"Thank you for forgiving me."* That moment changed the atmosphere of the room. Gratitude dismantled years of bitterness in seconds.

Paul reminds us that thanksgiving is not an addition to prayer; it is foundational to it. When we thank God before answers arrive, we declare that He is trustworthy. Gratitude prepares our hearts to receive peace even before resolution comes. It positions us to recognize the hand of God long before breakthrough manifests.

True worship is born out of gratitude. It is not limited to music or moments in church. It is a posture of the heart. Gratitude says, *"God, You are worthy,"* with or without an audience. It transforms ordinary routines into sacred rhythms. It turns chores into worship, conversations into ministry, and quiet moments into encounters with God. Gratitude shifts worship from something we do to something we live. It awakens an awareness of God's presence in places we once overlooked: morning commutes, kitchen tables, waiting rooms, hospital hallways. When gratitude fills the heart, worship becomes a natural overflow.

As a Professional Life Coach and mentor, I often encourage individuals to begin each day with intentional gratitude. This simple exercise, writing down three things they're thankful for, shifts mental patterns and spiritual posture. Gratitude trains the heart to seek God's fingerprints, even in small things. It becomes a daily act of spiritual alignment. Over time, this simple practice rewires how we see challenges. Instead of asking, *"Why is this happening?"* we begin to ask, *"Where is God in this moment?"* Gratitude helps us recognize that He is always near, always active, always speaking.

Jesus Himself modeled this. Before multiplying food, He gave thanks. Before resurrecting Lazarus, He gave thanks. Even before the cross, He gave thanks. Gratitude was the doorway to every miracle He performed. This shows us that thanksgiving is not mere politeness; it is a supernatural catalyst. It primes our hearts for God to move and positions us to recognize His intervention. Gratitude invites miracles because it aligns our spirit with heaven's perspective.

Gratitude is also a weapon in spiritual warfare. The enemy thrives on complaint, fear, and distraction. But when we say, "Thank You, Lord," chains begin to break. Darkness begins to flee. Peace begins to rise. Paul and Silas sang hymns in the darkest prison cell, and their gratitude shook the foundations of the earth. When we choose thanksgiving in adversity, we wage war with praise. Gratitude is not passive. It is powerful. It is prophetic. It is victorious. It declares that even in the valley, God is still worthy and the victory is still assured.

Gratitude was never meant to be kept quiet. It grows when shared. When we testify about God's goodness, we give others permission to see blessings in their own stories. Gratitude spreads like fire, with one spark igniting another. A single testimony can breathe hope into someone who has forgotten how to hope. A simple *"God has been good to me"* can soften a heart that has been hardened by disappointment. Gratitude has a way of breaking through walls that words alone cannot penetrate. It speaks to the soul. It reminds people that light still exists, even when they have only seen darkness.

In ministry and publishing, I have watched gratitude knit hearts together. Many authors come to me carrying wounds that feel too deep to speak aloud. Yet when they begin to express gratitude – thanking God for strength, for survival, for lessons learned – healing begins. Their story becomes someone else's breakthrough. Their gratitude becomes someone else's courage. Testimonies have a prophetic echo; they declare, *"If God did it for me, He can do it for you."* Gratitude transforms personal victories into communal encouragement.

Communities flourish where thanksgiving is spoken. Families heal. Churches revive. Burdens lift. Gratitude dissolves isolation because it reminds us that God has been faithful to all of us in different ways. It shifts conversations from complaints to praise, from what's missing to what God has already provided. A grateful community becomes a strong community – rooted, unified, and expectant of God's continued goodness.

Psalm 107:1 reminds us that God's mercy endures forever. Gratitude anchors us in that truth. It keeps our hearts soft and our spirits expectant. It opens our eyes to blessings that would otherwise go unnoticed. When we are grateful, we become aware of God's goodness everywhere: in laughter, in tears, in silence, in seasons of waiting, and in seasons of joy. Gratitude becomes the lens through which we interpret life, and through that lens, we begin to see that God has been with us every step of the way.

When gratitude governs the heart, everything shifts. It changes the tone of our conversations, the direction of our thoughts, and the posture of our spirit. Gratitude makes us more patient, more present, and more aware of God woven into the details of our everyday lives. It softens places within us that stress once hardened. It cultivates humility, reminding us that every breath is a gift and every moment carries purpose. Gratitude draws our attention away from what is broken and toward the God who restores. It transforms ordinary days into holy ground, where even the smallest joys become reminders of His unfailing love.

A grateful life is intentional. It is cultivated through daily choices to see blessing instead of burden, to look for God instead of focusing on what is missing. Gratitude is not blind optimism; it is spiritual clarity. It teaches us that even when storms arise, God's goodness has not disappeared. It simply becomes easier to see through eyes trained by thanksgiving. Gratitude slows us down long enough to notice the fingerprints of God on moments we once rushed past: sunrises, conversations, answered prayers, and unexpected kindnesses. It turns moments into miracles.

Gratitude must be practiced until it becomes reflexive. It becomes the song of a mature heart that has wrestled with sorrow, walked through uncertainty, and still chooses praise. Gratitude doesn't deny pain, but it reframes it. It reminds us that God can redeem every chapter, every loss, every disappointment. Gratitude gives us language for worship, even in the dark. It whispers, *"God is here,"* when everything else feels silent.

A life shaped by gratitude becomes a life that shapes others. It becomes a testimony others can follow, a fragrance that lingers, and a light that shines. Grateful people carry an atmosphere of peace that influences every room they enter. Their presence brings reassurance, comfort, and hope. Gratitude becomes a ministry all on its own that points people back to the goodness of God.

Prayer

Heavenly Father,

Thank You for the priceless gift of life and for Your unending mercy that renews each morning. Teach us to cultivate hearts that overflow with gratitude; hearts that recognize Your goodness in every breath and blessing. When fear or sorrow clouds our vision, lift our eyes to see Your hand at work behind the scenes.

Bless every reader walking through difficulty today. Let gratitude be their anchor and peace their portion. May families across cities, nursing homes, hospitals, and homes throughout the GTA and Southern Ontario feel Your presence even now. Turn pain into praise, and uncertainty into unshakable trust.

Lord, may gratitude become our daily worship and our love offering back to You. As we thank You for all You have done, may our lives shine as living reflections of Your everlasting goodness.

In the precious and powerful name of Jesus Christ, Amen.

Anita Sechesky - Visionary Compiler & Publisher

Safe in His Arms

The Goodness of God

Joshua Otabor

CHAPTER SEVENTEEN

The Last Bus to Mercy

If you've ever questioned whether God is still good, I understand you.

In fact, the story you're about to read is my own testimony. I'm not sharing theory – I'm sharing life. Real life. Na real wahala I enter, but God showed up like the fourth man in the fire. You'll see.

This is the story of how I almost missed the bus – literally and spiritually. But God, in His tender mercy, made a way where there was no way. It is my prayer that as you read, the same mercy will meet you, overtake you, and settle your matter once and for all, in Jesus' name.

When Life Felt Like It Was Closing In

It all began on a very hot afternoon in Lagos – one of those days when even the sun seems to have a personal vendetta. I had just received another rejection email from a job I had applied for. That made it the 21st rejection in two months. And that's not even counting the ones that just ghosted me.

I had been serving as a full-time pastor with Living Faith Church, a.k.a. Winners Chapel International, for years. Now, I felt the Lord leading me into something new – a transition, a new chapter. But everything seemed dry after this move in 2018. Doors were not just closed; they were padlocked with multiple chains. I prayed, fasted, even sowed seeds. Yet, nothing.

At this point, I had exhausted my savings. My rent was due. My daughters needed school fees. My wife was doing all she could, but it wasn't enough. The devil started whispering lies. "*So, this is what obedience to God looks like? You left everything to follow Him, and now look at you – stranded.*"

But in my spirit, I still held on. I would kneel beside my bed and whisper, "Lord, I know You're good. I don't understand what You're doing, but I trust You."

The Day of Divine Setup

It was a Thursday morning. I had an interview scheduled at a company in Victoria Island. I didn't even have enough money to put gas in my car, so I had to take public transportation because I felt a push in my spirit. *"Go. Your help is on the way."*

I got dressed, ironed one of my good shirts, and headed to the bus stop in Yaba. When I got there, the queue was insanely long. People were sweating, complaining, and pushing. I stood there and prayed under my breath, *"Lord, I need You today. Please, don't let me miss this bus... and don't let me miss my moment."*

That was when I saw him – a young man I had once prayed for years ago when I was serving as an assistant pastor in LFC Jikwoyi-Abuja. He was now a manager at one of the big banks. He spotted me and said, *"Pastor! Ah, it's been ages!"* Before I could respond properly, he dragged me out of the line and into his car.

"Where are you going?" he asked. *"VI,"* I told him. *"Perfect. I'll drop you off. I'm headed to Lekki."*

Just like that, God sent a ride. But that wasn't all.

On our way, he began to share how his life had changed since I prayed for him. He said, *"Sir, I've been looking for a way to give back. Please, I want to be a blessing to you and your family."*

Right there in the car, he transferred enough money to cover my rent, school fees, and more. I almost shouted in that car! I held back tears, just whispering, *"Jesus, You did this?"*

He then said, *"By the way, the company I work with is looking for someone with your exact experience. Send me your CV this evening."*

That very week, I got the job. Not just any job – it was the kind of job that was beyond my qualifications. Grace opened the door. Mercy gave me the seat.

The Prophetic Word Came Alive

Many years before this moment, a prophet had spoken over my life, saying, *"You will get to a junction in your life where only God can help you, and that is where His mercy will locate you."*

That word came back to me as I sat in my new office weeks later. I wept, because I had truly reached the junction of no return. But God showed up.

"Thou shalt arise, and have mercy upon Zion: for the time to favour her, yea, the set time, is come." Psalm 102:13 (KJV)

That was my Kairos – my set time.

Looking back now, I realize that God sometimes lets us reach the edge so that we will learn to fly by His Spirit, not by our plans. That delay was not denial – it was a divine setup. That rejection was redirection.

I also learned that God's mercy doesn't follow protocol. He bypasses systems, breaks norms, and rewrites rules. And here's the most powerful part: when God decides to be good to you, nothing and no one can stop Him – not the economy, not your past, not your background, not even your own doubts.

I don't know where you are in your journey, but I sense strongly that someone reading this is at their own "bus stop" moment. You've tried everything. You've been faithful. Yet, you feel stuck.

I declare over you: You will not miss your bus of mercy.

In the name of Jesus, the same God who located me at the eleventh hour will locate you.

This is your turn. This is your time.

The God who turned my story around will turn yours around.

In the courts of heaven, your name is on the mercy list.

Your destiny is being remembered.

Your help is on the way!

The Goodness of God Is Not a Theory – It's a Testimony

As I write this, I'm living proof that the goodness of God is real.

I'm not where I used to be.

I now combine my calling to ministry with a growing career in data analytics, and God is opening doors in ways I never imagined.

And I know this:

God is not done with me yet.

And neither is He done with you.

So, if you're still waiting for your own "last bus," don't give up.

Sometimes, the last bus is not the least – it's just the one God reserved for you.

To Him who sits on the throne, and unto the Lamb, be all glory, honor, and praise. Amen.

Joshua Otabor - Co-Author

Safe in His Arms
The Goodness of God

Nasha T. Alexis

Chapter Eighteen

My New Name

"Sticks and stones may break my bones, but words shall never hurt me." This is said to be an old English-language children's rhyme, with the earliest publication in 1844 by Alexander William Kinglake in his book *Eothen, or Traces of Travel, Brought Home from the East*. This rhyme is usually used to stand up against bullies after they call another person a mean name. It's often used in retaliation to demonstrate resilience after name-calling.

I remember myself as a child, with hands on my hips, defiance on my face, and an attitude to match, saying those words. No one would make me – or even see me – cry over something so silly as name-calling. Yet, at night, as I lay down to sleep, those words would play over and over in my mind, and a little bit of me would die.

Over the years, I started saying things like, *"I'm a duck, and whatever you say just runs off my back,"* to deflect the negative things said either directly to me or about me. Even recently, in my forties, I remember thinking and repeating that same rhyme when someone called me a negative name. But something different happened. I remember thinking those words did hurt, and they are still hurting.

Then I started recalling some names from long ago and things said about the way I looked or the way I behaved. That realization hit me very hard: I have been carrying all this weight from name-calling, from when I was a child up to the present.

The question that came to my mind then was, *"How much longer am I going to carry that weight?"* Not one of those names is who I am. I am so much more than that.

Our loving and gracious Father has planted in each of us a Seed of Hope, but the enemy, who is always on the prowl, comes in and kills those seeds. This happens in so many ways, one of which is name-calling. It may seem so harmless, but name-calling goes deep down, and it cuts even deeper than an actual knife or sword. It reaches the soul. We then carry that wound in our soul with us, usually without realizing it.

As I think back now, I can see where God was reaching out to me. He planted many Seeds of Hope along the way to help me find my way back to Him. I was so wrapped up in bitterness and resentment that it took me a long time before I found the path He had set out for me.

Some of us spend so much time missing out on many opportunities and never understand why. We are fearful to try new things, to take any type of risk, to venture out on our own because we believe that we can't do it. Some of us pass up wonderful opportunities because we think we are not good enough or smart enough to succeed. We also self-sabotage out of fear.

There are still some of us who wouldn't even consider a particular career or life path because we think that we don't have what it takes to succeed. How can something as simple as words hold so much power over us as to stifle – or even kill – our dreams and aspirations before we even have the chance to fully think about them?

I have experienced, if not all, then most of the situations mentioned above. We are told in Proverbs 15:4 (NIV), *"The soothing tongue is a tree of life, but a perverse tongue crushes the spirit."* When your spirit is crushed, you have no zeal or passion for most things. Trust me, we can go about our lives acting like we have it all together and everything about us is fine, but our spirit is in turmoil.

Like an old television or a slide show, when you least expect it, those words come back to taunt you, playing again and again in your mind…reminding you, *"That's why you'll never move forward,"* or *"Nothing will ever work out well for you."* You can insert your own mind show here.

But we know, as stated in Proverbs 18:21 (NIV), *"The tongue has the power of life and death…"* This is where the narrative changed for me – and it can change for you too. Our words have power, but more importantly, the Word of God is more powerful than anything. We can start by believing in Jesus and all that He has done. When we change our focus to Jesus as our firm foundation, then we can think about and trust in His faithfulness.

With our strong and firm foundation in Jesus, we can then believe in what He says about us. As the only One with the authority to change our names, Jesus' words are the only ones of importance we must claim. He has the final say in how our lives should go, and when we give that power to others, we are sinning against Him. When we believe in the lies of the enemy, we are essentially saying that God is a liar, and He is not in control.

One truth I recently learned is that even Satan must give an account to God. Even Satan must present himself before God, as in the story found in Job 1:6 (NIV): *"One day the angels came to present themselves before the LORD, and Satan also came with them."* When questioned by God about his whereabouts, Satan replied that he was roaming the earth, going back and forth. That's what he is still doing today – roaming the earth, looking for souls to devour.

And just like he did in the Garden of Eden when he entered the serpent and deceived Eve, he continues to use people by entering their minds to wound and kill other people's souls. Satan continues to use what worked for him then, even today. He continues to cast shadows and doubts on all that God says is "Good," and the boundaries that He sets out to keep us safe and protected.

When you're young and don't know much better, you may be led to believe all the lies. But I implore you, as you get older, allow the Holy Spirit to dismantle and tear down all those lies. I'm by no means an overnight success story, for I am still a work in progress. But I can honestly say that I am not where I used to be.

With counseling from a Christian counselor and the miraculous work of the Holy Spirit, I eventually started to believe in not only who God says I am, but in WHOSE I am.

This is how God stepped in and changed the way that I saw myself, and the names that I believed about myself for so long. He showed me that I am who He says I am, not who others say I am. Frankly, it's none of my business – or your business, for that matter – what other people think. Their perspective is their perspective only.

With that in mind, let us walk through some of the names that God calls me. I hope that you too can hear and accept most, if not all, of these names, for you are precious to Him also.

He calls me blessed.

"But blessed is the one who trusts in the LORD, whose confidence is in Him." Jeremiah 17:7 (NIV)

You see, our confidence is not in ourselves but in the One who is with us – the One who knows all things and does all things for our good and His glory. Each one of us is blessed in our comings and goings to do the will of the Father. We are not blessed to keep it to ourselves. He provides all that we need; He fills us to overflowing so we can be a blessing to others. We must see and think big picture here – the Kingdom-building picture. We are blessed to be a blessing.

I am also called fearfully and wonderfully made.

Psalm 139:14 (NIV) declares, *"I praise You because I am fearfully and wonderfully made; Your works are wonderful, I know that full well."*

As we begin to understand the depth of God's love for us, we will then see that all His works are wonderful, including us. There will come a time when we'll know that without a doubt. We are not copies of each other, even though we are created in the image of God. He made each one of us unique and special. I cannot do what you were created to do and touch the lives you are meant to touch, any more than you can fill the place and space that was meant for me. God is creative and sovereign; there's nothing He cannot do. He makes no mistakes.

I am called anointed.

Psalm 28:8 (NIV) says, *"The LORD is the strength of His people, a fortress of salvation for His anointed one."*

We have the LORD on our side. We live and walk not on our own, but in His strength. He has also called Himself our fortress of salvation, which means we are lacking nothing; we have strength and protection. We are not left on our own to fend for ourselves. God has also anointed each one of us to accomplish all that we are here to do. He equips us with the right skills, knowledge, mindset, gifts, and the right people to help us.

When God anoints you to do His will, nothing can stop what He has spoken. As it is written in Isaiah 55:11 (NIV), *"So is my word that goes out from my mouth: It will not return to me empty, but will accomplish what I desire and achieve the purpose for which I sent it."*

His Word will not return void. It will do exactly what it was sent to do.

God calls me successful. When we commit our plans to Him, He will bring us success according to His will. As stated in Psalm 37:5 (NIV), *"Commit your way to the LORD; trust in Him and He will do this."* We are to do these two things only – commit and trust – whatever we have into the strong hands of God. God, in His sovereignty and might, will do the rest.

We don't have to go about seeking success on our own. Success will come when, *"Whatever you do, work at it with all your heart, as working for the Lord, not for human masters"* (Colossians 3:23, NIV). In everything that we do, we are to put God first and foremost. Whatever the job or task that you are doing, do it with pride, excellence, and joy.

He calls me righteous. 2 Corinthians 5:21 (NIV) tells us, *"God made Him who had no sin to be sin for us so that in Him we might become the righteousness of God."* Again, this righteousness is not in us, but it is found in Jesus Christ. So, when God looks at us, He sees the cleansing blood of Jesus all over us. When we become the righteousness of God, He no longer sees our sins, shame, filth, or guilt. He only sees the blood of Jesus Christ.

The Apostle Paul says it best in Galatians 2:20 (NIV), *"I have been crucified with Christ and I no longer live, but Christ lives in me. The life I now live in the body, I live by faith in the Son of God, who loved me and gave Himself for me."* Jesus already paid my debt and your debt. We are only to believe in Him and receive that gift, so we can live in His righteousness.

God says that I am, and you are, forgiven. Knowing that you are a sinner and doing nothing about it is also a sin. We are invited to come before the Father to confess our sins, and as we're told in 1 John 1:9 (NIV), *"If we confess our sins, He is faithful and just and will forgive us our sins and purify us from all unrighteousness."*

It's not that God can't forgive without us confessing, but confession allows us to experience the depth of our relationship with

Him. He wants to hear from us – to humble ourselves before Him, to acknowledge our weakness to sinning – so He can make things right. Remember, the work was already done by Jesus on the cross.

I am loved by God.

If no one else loves me, God's love for me is enough. This was one I wrestled with for a long time. I was not able to comprehend – much less accept – God's love for me. I felt unloved by the people I saw every day, so how could God love me? I didn't even love myself, so how could He love me?

Then one day, I had an epiphany. It wasn't that God didn't love me. It was me who didn't love Him. I had blamed Him for neglecting me and allowing me to go through so much turmoil. I had blamed God for every negative experience I had gone through, so much so that I stopped acknowledging Him. I don't know how long it was that way, but I knew I couldn't continue down that path. I had to fully surrender all that bitterness and anger to God. I had to give it all away, which meant giving up control too. And that was not easy to do. Let's be honest, who doesn't like to be in control?

When all those thick walls came crashing down, I fell to my knees in surrender and asked for forgiveness. When you know what you know – when you truly know it – nothing can change your mind. At that moment of surrender, I felt the love of God all over me. It cannot be explained, only felt. And I knew it then. I still know it today.

Last, but not least, and the best of all, I am called a Child of God.

John 1:12–13 (NIV) says, *"Yet to all who did receive Him, to those who believed in His name, He gave the right to become children of God – children born not of natural descent, nor of human decision or a husband's will, but born of God."* When we receive and believe in Jesus, we are adopted as children of God. We are then grafted into the family of the Most High. We are no longer orphans, but are called children of God.

This is so exciting to me for so many reasons that whenever I think about it, my soul rejoices.

These are just a few of the names that we're called by our Heavenly Father. The Bible is full of other wonderful names and thoughts God has for us and toward us. When we start calling ourselves and seeing ourselves in the light that Jesus sees us, our spirit changes. We become more alive – revived, joyful, and happy people. We become more confident in ourselves and our abilities.

Brothers and sisters, I pray that you were able to find a seed of hope in my story.

Seek God first, and He will change your life.

Nasha T. Alexis - Co-Author

Safe in His Arms
The Goodness of God

Judy Brown

CHAPTER NINETEEN
Planted by Grace, Growing by Faith

"I remain confident of this: I will see the goodness of the LORD in the land of the living." Psalm 27:13 (NIV)

The following reflection incorporates the verse above and encourages us, as quoted in Psalm 27:14 (NIV), *"Wait for the Lord; be strong and take heart and wait for the Lord."* Philippians 1:6 (NIV) also reminds us, *"He who began a good work in you will carry it on to completion."* He is faithful to complete what He has started.

First, let us create the scene. I tend to enjoy using imagery as I process my thoughts and what I learn. So, picture yourself standing outside early in the morning. As the sun rises, the landscape becomes more visible. You are in a field with rows and rows of planted crops. As you look from left to right, you see vegetation at various stages of growth – strong, deeply rooted cedar-like trees to the left with vibrant, richly colored fruit. You just know they are sweet and full of nutrients.

Then, as your gaze shifts from right to left, you notice vegetation still maturing. To the extreme right, you imagine there are planted seeds just beneath the surface. This imagery reflects how I see the passage of my life. It reminds me of scriptures like Isaiah 61:3 (NIV), *"…They will be called oaks of righteousness, a planting of the Lord for the display of his splendor."* Another favorite of mine is, *"They will be like a tree planted by the water… its leaves are always green."* And finally, Proverbs 13:22 (NIV), *"A good person leaves an inheritance for their children's children…"*

As I look through my life, I reflect on what I've experienced. I think about what I've overcome and what I've made it through. I remember those who have gone before me: my parents, aunts and uncles, grandparents, and perhaps even great-grandparents. I think about all they endured so that I could be here in this moment and in this place.

I reflect on the challenges they faced and overcame. I know that if I could ask each one of them what they attribute their success to, they would point to the hand of God on their lives – to the goodness of God. Psalm 145:4 (NIV) says, *"One generation commends your works to another; they tell of your mighty acts."* That is exactly what they did. I am grateful for the stories passed down through generations – how the Lord made a way when there seemed to be no way. Stories that testify of the Lord being in control of every detail, guiding every step of the journey through life.

I am especially thankful that I can now pass these stories on to the generations that come after me. These are the stories that help me get through each day – and sometimes even each moment. So often, I feel like I am in the middle of my story. But I know that one day, I'll look back, just as I've done before, and I'll clearly see the goodness of God in my life. His goodness has always been there. He is always present. And with every step forward I take, I am being strengthened and matured for the journey to come.

Sometimes, when we look at our lives, we only see the challenges and difficulties. We focus on how far we still have to go instead of recognizing how far we've already come. We worry about the challenges we'll face tomorrow instead of remembering all the things we've already overcome – again and again. We forget that there were times we thought we'd never make it, but God helped us through. And the truth is, He is still helping us and will continue to help us.

"They triumphed…by the blood of the Lamb and the word of their testimony." Revelation 12:11 (NIV)

This highlights the importance of hearing the stories of others and sharing our own. Testimony matters.

We don't always recognize that we already carry the proof of success. That proof is woven into our story. Yet we spend so much time meditating on the challenges of life that we sometimes forget we are already successful. We are overcomers living a victorious life. Instead of taking those stories and applying them to our current situation, we often stand in defeat before we've even reached the outcome. We fail to see that the victories of our past are actually the seeds of encouragement we need for the future.

When we read the Bible, we see what others have overcome – the trials they faced, the hardships they survived, and the breakthroughs they experienced. Instead of letting their testimonies encourage us, we sometimes minimize them or write them off. We forget the value of those stories and the lessons they carry. We also forget that facing and overcoming challenges allows us to plant lasting seeds of faith and endurance in our lives.

With each success, we gain new skills, new wisdom, and a stronger foundation for the next challenge. We are not the same as we were five, ten, or twenty years ago. We are stronger. We are wiser. We are changing.

"We are being transformed into His image with ever-increasing glory…" 2 Corinthians 3:18 (NIV)

The most important knowledge we carry is the knowledge of who God is and how He works in our lives. We study His Word to understand how He moved in the lives of those who came before us. We listen to the stories of our parents, elders, mentors, and even younger believers to learn how He has shown up in their lives. And we remember: What He does for one, He can do for all. That means I can expect His hand to work just as powerfully in my life. I can expect to know Him more deeply just as others have grown to know Him more in their journeys.

So, as I move forward, I will reflect on all that God has done in my life. I will look at what He has brought me through. I will remember the lessons He has taught me. I will recognize the strength I now carry because of Him. I will see Him for who He is in my life – and see who I am in Him, who He has created me to be.

I will meditate on these things so that my hope will be renewed. So here we go.

First Lesson

My mom loved her sons and prayed that God would also bless her with a daughter. He granted her that miracle. God answered her prayer. A seed of faith was planted in her heart as He provided for her in that way, giving her the desire of her heart. Not only did she have two sons, but she also had a daughter she could call her own. As she shares that story with me, a seed of faith is also planted in my heart.

But He didn't stop there.

As a single parent, my mom experienced God's provision time and time again. He not only met her needs in the present but had already set things in motion from the past that would support her through the journey of raising her three children. He gave her godly parents who encouraged her and taught her the value of giving. These parents gave from what they had to help her succeed.

Because of the way they raised her – with faith and wisdom – she was able to step out boldly. She left a place of safety, her home country, to pursue a dream. With the trust she had in God, she moved to another country to study and establish a career that would sustain her for years. She trusted God to care for her when she left home to attend school. She trusted God when she chose the man she would marry. She trusted God again when she moved from one new country to yet another unfamiliar place.

She believed that God would give her opportunities to help her siblings and bring them to a better life. She trusted God to provide for her financially. She believed that He would meet her every need. And when her circumstances changed and she had to raise her three children on her own, she continued to trust God as her faithful Provider.

Each challenge she faced revealed more of who God was, who He is, and who He will always be. Seeds of faith were planted in her heart – nourished continually by God – enabling her to take one step forward each day of her life. Each step became a testimony of progressive success, not just for her own benefit, but for the generations after her.

As she moved forward, she planted seeds of faith in her children too, teaching us by example to trust God more and more.

So how does this translate to my life?

I faced the challenge of growing up in a single-parent home. My mom had to work, and perhaps she couldn't put as much into my upbringing as she would have under different circumstances. Yet, the goodness of God upon her life allowed her to overcome each challenge and provide for her children. There has never been a time when I was without a roof over my head, clothes on my back, or food to eat. I've never had to fear losing any of those basic necessities.

Now, I must say, my mom probably protected me from those fears when I was little. Years later, she would tell me about the challenges she faced – times when there was uncertainty about her job, or when she had to work more than one job just to make enough to care for us. Still, at the end of it all, she would say, *"It is by the goodness of God that we had all we needed."* She told me how she had to pray and trust God to provide for every need. She often spoke of the friends God brought into her life in times of need, and she would reflect on how God had also provided for her parents as they were growing up.

So, I think of all that God has provided for me. Opportunities to learn through French immersion. The privilege of attending a high school that helped develop my gifts and talents. Opportunities to travel for sports and be mentored by leaders who excelled in those areas. Opportunities in university to build a deeper relationship with Him. The chance to grow in leadership and influence the lives of others for His glory.

He gave me the ability to maintain a job for many years and experience exponential growth – not just in position, but in character and skill. He even transitioned me from the academic world to ministry, further developing my leadership through leading a group at church. And when it was time to grow in a new direction and know Him differently, He introduced me to new people and new environments. He opened new doors to grow and learn.

If I were honest, I would say that I don't feel like I'm growing as fast as I would like. At times, it even feels like I'm doing less. But even though I may feel that way, I cannot deny that God has been good to me. He has been faithful, and continues to be faithful. He continues to teach me and reveal Himself to me.

Yet at times, I still struggle to see His goodness in my life.

This brings us back to that field. Although I may not always see all that He is doing, I know He is doing.

Let's look at that imagery again. I am standing in the field, observing the vegetation progressing from huge, fruitful trees on the left to perhaps grass – or even bare dirt – on the far right. But what if this timeline of growth and development is not only my own? What if the strong, fruitful trees to the left are the result of seeds planted by those who came before me?

They shared their stories of God's faithfulness in their lives. When I look at them, I see giants in the faith. The fruit I see in their lives is the result of seeds others had sown and the nourishment they received to flourish. The deep roots they have are due to everything God provided for their growth – combined with their active pursuit of Him through spiritual disciplines like studying the Bible, praying, and serving faithfully.

As I examine each section of the field, I realize it can represent a generational timeline of spiritual growth; of deepening one's relationship with God and understanding how He works in our lives. I recognize that, one day, someone who comes after me will stand in this same field and see the thriving, fruitful trees to the left as the result of my own faithful acts that were enabled, guided, and sustained by the hand of God.

They will be able to identify parts of their life along the journey, and they will be encouraged to practice the same disciplines and share their stories for generations to come. As Joel 1:3 (NIV) says, *"Tell it to your children, and let your children tell it to their children, and their children to the next generation."* Psalm 78:4–7 (NIV) echoes this, *"We will tell the next generation... so they would put their trust in God."*

When we act in obedience to this Word, just as those before us have, we leave behind a legacy of faith. Those who follow will also proclaim the goodness of God in what they say, do, and share with all who see, participate, and listen.

Our lives will reflect seeds once planted in faith, watered by stories, prayer, and perseverance. As those seeds grow, the goodness of God will be revealed again and again – bearing fruit for generations to come, in ways only He can orchestrate.

Judy Brown - Co-Author

Safe in His Arms
The Goodness of God

Karen Jiron

Chapter Twenty

A Daughter of God

In this season of my life, I have been invited to speak about the goodness of God and what it means to me personally. I have witnessed many miracles throughout my life, and I would love for others to hear about them. My hope is that these stories will encourage those who may be facing difficult times – moments when it feels like there's no light at the end of the tunnel. I want others to see, through my own testimony, that the goodness of God is not only real but also life-changing in the most fulfilling and transformative way. God can illuminate a path for us, even in a world filled with darkness.

The scripture in Isaiah 40:31 (NRSV) declares, *"But those who wait for the Lord shall renew their strength; they shall mount up with wings like eagles, they shall run and not be weary, they shall walk and not faint."* This verse has spoken deeply to both my spirit and heart. In times when circumstances felt insurmountable, God stepped in, took the lead, and transformed things that were meant to break me into moments that built me up for His good purpose.

In my past, there were times when I did not have a close relationship with God and strayed far from Him. In one particular season, I found myself lost, seeking love and affection from the wrong people. I entered into a very toxic and unhealthy relationship. During this time, I stopped going to church and even began to doubt whether God was real. I thought that if there truly was a God, He certainly wasn't there for me.

That relationship, instead of fulfilling my longing, only brought heartache, loneliness, and deeper resentment toward the God I was already questioning. Yet, in His mercy, God used even that painful season as a catalyst to draw me closer to Him. Despite my hardened heart and doubts, He was still pursuing me.

Around the same time I was in that unhealthy relationship, I was also working as a registered nurse in trauma and ICU, clocking in long hours and leading an incredibly stressful life. As time went on, I began to feel unwell, and over time, the symptoms I was experiencing became increasingly debilitating. Despite feeling terrible, I kept trying to maintain a normal routine, continuing to work and function as usual. But as the illness progressed, it became harder and harder. Emotionally, I was falling apart, especially because none of the doctors had answers yet.

After more than a year of tests and uncertainty, I was finally diagnosed with a rare condition called Postural Orthostatic Tachycardia Syndrome (POTS). Anyone who has been diagnosed with this understands just how life-altering it can be. I became bedridden. I could no longer take part in regular activities. I had to stop working, couldn't drive, and even cooking for myself became impossible. It was then that I began to realize how many things I had taken for granted. Watching my independence slip away was deeply painful.

With no income, I fell into financial hardship, compounded by feelings of loss, despair, and hopelessness. After seeing several specialists, I was told I would never be the same again. This was an illness I would have to live with for the rest of my life. There was no cure. I remember wondering what my life would look like from that point forward. I grieved my old life with a heavy heart. I cried out to God, asking, *"Why me? What did I do?"* But even in the midst of grief, I held on to hope. I became determined to beat the odds.

One particular moment stands out in my memory. Lying in bed, broken and crying, I poured out my heart to God and asked Him for a miracle. I pleaded with Him to provide me with a nursing job I could do from home. I had worked so hard to build a career in nursing, and I didn't want to let it go. I asked Him to open a door that would allow me to keep serving in the field I loved, even if it meant doing so in a completely new way.

I kept praying. I kept believing. That season of illness and loss drew me closer to God. Because when you've lost everything – your health, your finances, your independence – and even the doctors can't help you, you begin to realize that God is the only one who can.

By His grace and mercy, nearly two years later, I found exactly what I had prayed for: a remote nursing position that allowed me to work from home. For that, I will always be grateful. It was a miracle – one that only God could have orchestrated. He made a way where there seemed to be no way.

During that time, I often felt disconnected from God. The isolation was heavy, and turning to friends or family didn't always bring the comfort I needed. I searched everywhere for guidance. Therapy helped to a certain extent, but it wasn't until I truly immersed myself in worship, prayer, and the Word that I experienced a dramatic shift in both my mind and spirit.

I remember listening to a sermon by Pastor Steven Furtick, and something he said struck a deep chord within me: *"If you're close to Dad, He won't let it go bad."* It resonated powerfully. In that moment, I realized God wasn't just "God." He was my Father – a true Father who filled every void I had ever carried. Through this growing intimacy with Him, I finally discovered my identity: a daughter of God.

As I saw my life changing and my health slipping away, I often wondered how I was going to pay my bills or even survive. I remember being overwhelmed by thoughts of whether I would live much longer. The physical symptoms I was experiencing often made me feel like I was dying, which only intensified the anxiety and fear already consuming me. I was also nearing the end of an unhealthy relationship and found myself wondering, "Who will be there for me? Who will help me? Who will be my support system now?"

These terrible circumstances revealed who my true friends were, as my circle grew smaller. Those I thought would show up simply didn't. There was a deep sense of isolation and sadness as my world seemed to crumble. My partner at the time abandoned me when I needed him most. That was the moment I realized that yes, my family would do their best to support me, but ultimately, it was just me and God. There was no one else on earth who could take me through the storm I was in.

Many times, I reached breaking points and cried out to God, unable to see a way out. There were moments when I couldn't even find the words to pray – only tears. But somehow, I knew God didn't need me to say anything; He already understood everything I was feeling and thinking. At times, I felt like He wasn't listening, but looking back, I see that some of those prayers were answered years later.

I often felt desperate for God to pull me out of the situation immediately, but He didn't. Sometimes, I felt angry with Him, wondering why things were taking so long and whether this new life, marked by loss and limitation, was something I had to accept. I had gone from working full-time as a registered nurse to becoming the patient, on disability. This reality pushed me deeper into Scripture, where I found hope and light in the darkness.

One verse that carried me through was Isaiah 43:2 (NIV): *"When you pass through the waters, I will be with you; and when you pass through the rivers, they will not sweep over you. When you walk through the fire, you will not be burned; the flames will not set you ablaze."*

I began to see that God was showing up for me in unexpected ways, even when I couldn't recognize it at first. When that toxic relationship finally ended, I sank into a place of deep sadness and uncertainty. I didn't know how I would heal or what the future would hold. But as I drew closer to God, He began to reveal His mercy in tangible ways.

I felt led to return to church for the first time in years. Even if I had to go alone and find a new church, I was determined to show up. And as I did, something started to shift in me. I began to believe that I was valuable, worthy of love – the kind of love God gives. Volunteering at church and giving back to the community helped me feel purposeful again.

God's mercy showed up in that season through the rebuilding of my self-esteem. I started to love myself in a deeper way and began to see myself as God, my family, and true friends saw me. I realized I was valuable, both inside and out. I began to walk with greater confidence in myself, my abilities, and the unique things I have to offer this world.

There was a lot of fear and anxiety surrounding the diagnosis of a disease that is considered incurable. Through the pain and the constant pleading with God for help and healing, my faith began to grow mainly because I had no choice but to believe and wait patiently. Although I didn't receive an overnight miracle, I experienced gradual healing over time.

The slow manifestation of God's goodness became evident when I visited my specialist and was told that my condition had improved dramatically. I could see it for myself. I was slowly able to be more active, return to work, and begin to see my life normalize again over the course of several years. I had no doubt that this was the result of answered prayers and God's grace and mercy at work in my life. I am eternally grateful, especially knowing that many people with the same diagnosis never experience any improvement at all.

Although the journey was painful and traumatic, God was with me through it all. That season of suffering created a deeper bond between me and the Lord. After walking through it, I have zero doubt that He is real and able to do miraculous things.

Even in moments when I felt deeply disconnected from God, He always found a way to make His presence known. There were times when I didn't feel like worshiping, but I would push myself to try. And in those moments of worship and seeking the Holy Spirit, I could feel a shift in my spirit. That divine connection gave me the strength and courage to keep going – to fight, to press forward, and to keep my eyes on Him for guidance.

My friends and family began to notice the transformation within me. They saw an increase in my faith, a calmness in how I approached life, and a greater acceptance of the things I could no longer control. I became more positive, more loving, and more joyful. It was as if a new light had begun to grow within me.

After going through so many obstacles, struggles, and dark seasons, God has placed within me a deep confidence, knowing that He is always with me and that I am never alone. This is one of the greatest changes I've seen in myself. When I wasn't as connected to the Lord, I felt the weight of the world on my shoulders. I believed I had to fix everything and control every outcome. Now, I've learned to accept that in life, we will face ups and downs, trials, and tribulations – but we are never alone. We have a Lord and Savior who eases our pain and gives us supernatural strength to keep moving forward, even when we think we can't.

I now truly identify as a child of God and can feel His presence with me every day. He is my Father and my Provider, and I know that I can cast all my burdens on Him because I no longer have to carry them alone. I've become hungrier to seek His Word and gain deeper understanding. Through all the pruning, refining, and molding, I've begun to see that I have a purpose in this life – a heart that longs to serve in God's Kingdom. Though we will never reach perfection or live without challenges, I've come to understand that God's mercy is greater than we could ever comprehend, and His love is endless. He calls us to love one another, to help each other through difficult seasons, and to be the salt of the earth He created us to be.

God's goodness is not something we are entitled to. It's something He gives simply because He loves us. We are all His children, and His love is deeper and more profound than the ocean. My prayer for you is that you find comfort in these words, that you draw closer to the Lord, and that you discover your identity in Him.

Prayer

I pray blessings upon you and your family. May you find your purpose and your joy in this lifetime, and even when your smile fades, may you know that God is always with you – and that you will smile again. Don't give up on God, and He won't give up on you. Amen.

"Taste and see that the Lord is good; blessed is the one who takes refuge in Him." Psalm 34:8 (NIV)

Karen Jiron - Co-Author

Safe in His Arms
The Goodness of God

Anita Sechesky

CHAPTER TWENTY-ONE

Stories of Miracles Reflecting God's Goodness

In a world where anxiety and uncertainty often cloud the hearts of many, the stories of miracles continue to remind us that the God of yesterday is still the God of today. His goodness has never ceased to operate. It flows steadily, reaching into hospitals, homes, and hearts – transforming impossibility into reality. Every miracle, whether it unfolds quietly or dramatically, reflects the same truth: God is still good, and He still moves among His people.

I have witnessed the fragility of human life and the overwhelming beauty of divine intervention during my career as an RN. There were moments where medicine could explain only part of the story, but faith completed it. I've seen patients recover when doctors had exhausted all options. I've seen families who were moments away from despair suddenly lifted by peace that surpassed all understanding. These are not coincidences; they are divine fingerprints.

Miracles come in many forms. Some are dramatic, others subtle. Some heal the body, while others heal the heart. I have seen marriages restored after years of separation, families reunited through forgiveness, and individuals freed from addictions that once controlled their lives. Each of these moments reflects God's relentless pursuit of wholeness for His children. One woman I coached was battling deep grief after losing her husband. She felt abandoned and angry at God. Through prayer and faith mentoring, she began to sense God's presence again. Months later, she said with tears streaming down her face, *"I thought my story ended with loss, but now I see that it began with His grace."* That was her miracle: not the return of her husband, but the restoration of her heart.

God's miracles aren't confined to the dramatic; they're often hidden in everyday life. A timely phone call, an unexpected opportunity, a bill paid just in time. These, too, are miracles of provision. When we look closely, we realize that divine goodness surrounds us daily. It may not always be loud or visible, but it is always real.

"Every good gift and every perfect gift is from above, coming down from the Father of lights, with whom there is no variation or shadow due to change" James 1:17 (ESV).

Some of the most powerful miracles I've witnessed were not of healing, but of hearts. I once prayed with a mother and daughter who hadn't spoken in years. Bitterness had built walls between them so high that neither thought reconciliation was possible. But during prayer, something shifted. The mother suddenly began to cry uncontrollably, whispering, *"Lord, forgive me for holding onto pain."* Within minutes, both were in each other's arms. That room, once filled with tension, became a sanctuary of peace. That's the beauty of God's goodness. He restores what was broken and breathes life into what seemed dead. The miracle of forgiveness is one of the greatest demonstrations of divine power. It softens hearts that years of anger could not touch.

Gratitude is the key that unlocks our awareness of God's miracles. Many people experience divine intervention without recognizing it because their hearts are burdened by worry or doubt. Gratitude refocuses our vision from what we lack to what God has done. I remember sitting beside a woman in a nursing home who was unable to walk. Every day, she would say, *"I thank God I can still see the sunlight and hear the birds."* Her gratitude radiated joy. She once told me, *"I may not have legs that walk, but I have a voice that gives thanks."* That statement pierced my heart. She taught me that miracles aren't always about what changes, but about how God changes us. Gratitude magnifies God's goodness. It invites us to see Him in everything – the simple, the silent, the subtle.

"Give thanks in all circumstances; for this is God's will for you in Christ Jesus." 1 Thessalonians 5:18 (NIV)

I have watched gratitude turn hospital corridors into places of worship. I have seen families, still in gowns and slippers, form a circle around a bed and sing softly through tears. The diagnosis had not shifted, but the atmosphere had. Peace entered, anxiety lifted, and courage rose. Sometimes, the miracle is the peace that guards the heart while the process unfolds. Other times, it is the sudden turnaround that leaves even the most seasoned physician speechless. Either way, miracles often bloom from surrendered hearts.

From the pages of Scripture to the testimonies of modern believers, divine intervention has always been God's language of love across generations. In the Old Testament, the Israelites witnessed God's miraculous hand repeatedly. When He parted the Red Sea, when manna rained from heaven, and when the walls of Jericho fell with a shout, each event declared His goodness and faithfulness. These weren't random displays of power; they were intimate expressions of His covenant love. God delivered His people not only to prove His might but to show His mercy.

Similarly, in the New Testament, the ministry of Jesus was defined by miracles, with each one revealing a different facet of His divine compassion. He opened blind eyes, raised the dead, cleansed lepers, and calmed storms with a word. But His greatest miracle was redemption itself through the cross and resurrection that secured eternal life for all who believe. The miracles of Scripture remind us that the God who acted then is still acting now. His nature hasn't changed; His goodness hasn't diminished. *"Jesus Christ is the same yesterday, today, and forever,"* Hebrews 13:8 (NKJV).

Today, we often look for God in spectacular displays, yet He often reveals Himself in whispers. A quiet prompting that prevents an accident. A dream that warns or comforts. A child's laughter that reminds us of joy still exists. These are not small things. They are sacred moments where Heaven touches Earth. As I reflect on my own life, I can count countless miracles – some I noticed immediately, others I recognized only in hindsight. There were seasons when everything seemed uncertain, but looking back, I see how every detour was part of God's divine plan. Each closed door protected me from something that would have harmed me. Each delay developed patience and trust.

"He has made everything beautiful in its time." Ecclesiastes 3:11 (NKJV)

I recall a young mother pacing a waiting room, clutching a small pair of shoes. Her child was in surgery, and fear pressed heavily on her chest. We prayed together with simple words and steady faith. Hours later, the surgeon emerged with a smile. The complication they feared was not present; the child would fully recover. We stood there in the hallway, not with loud celebration, but with holy reverence. Sometimes, gratitude is the only language that makes sense after God moves.

God rarely performs miracles in isolation. He often uses people – ordinary vessels – to bring His goodness to others. In churches, workplaces, hospitals, and neighborhoods, we see His love expressed through the compassion of His children. In my years of ministry and publishing, I've seen this repeatedly. When someone shares their testimony of healing or provision, it ignites faith in another. When one believer prays for another, Heaven responds. Miracles multiply in environments of unity and gratitude.

There is also a miracle in direction. I have watched people on the brink of destructive choices pause because of a Scripture that came to mind at just the right moment, or a phone call that interrupted the spiral. Guidance is not glamorous, but it is God's gracious miracle of protection. Doors close as often as they open, and both are mercy. Sometimes, the "no" saves our lives.

Every miracle is an invitation – an open door calling us deeper into trust. Miracles don't just happen to us; they happen for us, to remind us that we are not alone and that God's promises are alive and active. And while we celebrate the moments when a body is healed or a need is met, we also acknowledge the mystery: sometimes, we don't receive the miracle we hoped for. A healing doesn't come, a door remains closed, or a prayer seems unanswered. But even in those moments, God's goodness remains. Sometimes the miracle isn't in what changes but in how He sustains us through it. The peace that guards your heart, the comfort that surrounds your grief, the strength to keep believing – that, too, is miraculous.

Trusting God through uncertainty is itself an act of faith that births miracles of perseverance, hope, and transformation. I have seen widows become pillars of encouragement to others. I have seen people who lost everything become generous beyond measure. I have seen those who walked through fire emerge with compassion that could only have been forged in flames. Suffering refined their vision; gratitude refilled their hearts; God's goodness redirected their story.

Miracles are meant to be shared. They're not private trophies but public testimonies that point back to the heart of God. When we speak of His goodness, we become conduits of faith to others who may be struggling to believe. Every story, whether it's a dramatic rescue or a quiet answer to prayer, is a reminder that God sees, hears, and loves us. The world needs these reminders now more than ever.

As believers, our lives should radiate with the awareness that we are living miracles. The fact that we wake up each morning, breathe, and have another chance to glorify Him is itself a testimony of His grace.

"The steadfast love of the Lord never ceases; His mercies never come to an end; they are new every morning; great is Your faithfulness." Lamentations 3:22–23 (ESV)

When we choose to notice, we begin to recognize how frequently Heaven intersects our ordinary days. A conversation that softens a heart. A check that arrives on the day a bill is due. A Scripture that answers a question we hadn't spoken aloud. These are threads of mercy woven into our stories.

I have also learned that anticipation makes room for miracles. Expectation is not entitlement; it is faith that God is who He says He is. When we gather to pray, when we anoint and agree, when we worship in the face of worry, we are preparing the soil. Unity invites God's power; humility keeps the focus on His glory. And gratitude – before, during, and after – keeps our hearts soft enough to receive and wise enough to remember.

We are stewards of what God has done. Write the stories down. Tell them to your children. Share them in church. Speak of the way God carried you through the midnight hour, how He lifted your head when shame tried to bow it, how He provided when resources ran dry. Your testimony might be the lifeline someone else is praying for today.

"Give thanks in all circumstances; for this is God's will for you in Christ Jesus." 1 Thessalonians 5:18 (NIV)

Gratitude does not minimize pain; it magnifies God. It does not deny reality; it declares a greater reality that God is present, powerful, and purposeful in every season.

Heaven is not silent. God is still speaking. God is still moving. God is still good.

Prayer

Heavenly Father,

Thank You for Your goodness that knows no bounds. Thank You for the miracles seen and unseen – the healings, reconciliations, and divine provisions that remind us of Your love. Lord, for those reading this chapter who are waiting on their miracle, strengthen their faith. Remind them that You are never late and that Your hand is always moving behind the scenes. We thank You for miracles happening in hospital rooms, nursing homes, churches, and homes everywhere. We praise You for every breakthrough, every answered prayer, and every act of grace that draws hearts closer to You. May we live with eyes wide open, recognizing Your goodness in every detail of our lives. And as we testify of Your miracles, let our words bring hope to others.

In the mighty and matchless name of Jesus Christ, Amen.

Anita Sechesky - Visionary Compiler & Publisher

Safe in His Arms
The Goodness of God

Karleen J. Poyser

Chapter Twenty-Two

From Brokenness to Boldness: Discovering Healing and Victory in Christ

It feels amazing to be alive during this season. I have been walking through tremendous changes over the past year that only God Himself could have orchestrated. I've recently come to understand that, no matter what has been lost, taken from your life, derailed, or hidden, God has a way of uncovering and restoring what the enemy has stolen. He has the power to break every chain and free you from the bondage of your past.

I now realize there truly is a time and a season for everything, just as it says in Ecclesiastes 3:1 (NKJV): *"To everything there is a season, a time for every purpose under heaven."*

I love the Lord so deeply because He brought me out of a dark place and into His marvelous light – out of a darkness that clouded both my soul and my mind. Now, I am in a place where I understand His Word more clearly, pray with greater power, and witness tangible results in my life. This enables me to be more effective for His glory.

I see myself as a bird that has been freed from a cage and am now flying into the open blue skies.

Free to soar.

Free to climb.

Free to explore.

Free to live for His glory.

In my past, I failed because I was trying to achieve results in my own strength. But I've come to understand that God does not require us to do anything by our own ability. It is through our faith in His Word and our dependence on the Holy Spirit working in us that we are empowered to succeed.

Right now, I am experiencing a time where God has called me to greater things that I have labored for in prayer. But let me be real. The struggle has been real!

I've battled with follow-through. I've wrestled with letting go of old ideals, rebuilding self-confidence, tearing down mental blocks, managing illness, and overcoming stagnation and delay. I've fought to develop self-discipline while tuning out the negative narratives from people around me who were never called to this assignment.

This has been a difficult time of learning and stretching. I've had to grow through the painful process of overcoming fear and doubt. Deep inside, I knew God had more for me. I knew He was calling me to a higher place, but I kept trying to do it in my own strength. Again and again, I failed because I was still holding on to old mindsets and images of how things had worked in the past.

I've since realized that I had to revamp my thinking and fully surrender. I had to allow God, through His Word, to show me how to rely on Him, not on myself.

In order to move forward in the areas of my life that are divinely connected to my destiny, I had to ask God to take my dreams and goals and reshape them according to His will, so that He alone would receive the glory.

Friendship is such a special thing; I consider it a gift from God. In my life, I've experienced times when friends were abundant, and others when friendships were fewer – yet deeper, closer, and more meaningful. This past year, I had an experience that shocked me but ultimately revealed that God answers prayers.

In a time of being stretched professionally, I realized God was also stretching me in the area of relationships. For many years, I was the type of person who remained quiet when things occurred that I didn't agree with. Past experiences had taught me that speaking up often led to conflict, so I learned to stay silent. I had been praying that God would strengthen me and purify any areas in my heart that were not pleasing to Him. I desired to be more like Jesus, my Lord and Savior.

Unexpectedly, God answered that prayer the very next day by showing me something within myself that needed to change.

I was working at my mobile office when I had an encounter with someone who challenged my ability to speak my truth. Due to existing obligations, I explained that the timing for a discussion wasn't appropriate. However, I was immediately shut down. I felt intimidated, fearful, and unable to advocate for myself. My personal boundaries were compromised, and the respect I extended was not reciprocated.

It was then that I realized something crucial: God does not perpetuate fear or insecurity. Because I had not invited God into every aspect of my relationships, I had unknowingly become a people-pleaser at the expense of my own emotional well-being.

As I continued on this journey of self-discovery, challenge, and change, I experienced both deep spiritual growth and moments of separation from God. I wish I could say the separation was unintentional, but the reality is that it happened because I drifted away from the spiritual disciplines that sustained my closeness to Jehovah.

Over the years, I've learned how to pray, how to fast, how to study and meditate on God's Word, and how to discern His voice.

What has brought the most dramatic transformation in my life has been my commitment to living a consecrated life by staying daily in the Word, remaining in prayer, and depending fully on God.

But during this recent season of stretching, when things became difficult or even stagnated, I started to simply go through the motions. I gradually slipped away from consistent times of dedicated prayer and meditation. In doing so, I unknowingly became spiritually complacent. I was overwhelmed by the personal and family challenges I was facing, and without realizing it, I allowed these circumstances to take precedence over my spiritual well-being.

Eventually, even my faith in God's power to bring breakthrough began to falter. I found it difficult to believe for change because I could no longer see beyond my overwhelming challenges.

I spoke about different situations where I desperately needed God; they were wake-up calls I could no longer ignore. I knew I couldn't allow those three experiences to happen again. I didn't know what to do, but I knew He had to respond. I finally decided to surrender everything, because what I had been doing previously was clearly not working! I began praying earnestly for a breakthrough.

What I had been experiencing in my life was not God's perfect will – it was the exact opposite. It was a time filled with frustration, fear, confusion, and lack in so many areas. There was a lack of truth – God's Word along with a lack of both natural and spiritual resources and a lack of peace. My times of prayer were desperate cries for help. I humbled myself, sincerely asking God for forgiveness for the sins I was aware of, and for those I wasn't yet conscious of – sins that had created separation between us, worsening my circumstances.

I cried out from the depths of my heart, asking for His perfect will to be done in my life. Growing up, we were taught to respect everyone, but I realized I had unknowingly placed people on a pedestal. I believed they had accomplished more than I had, which led me into people-pleasing instead of focusing on pleasing God and walking in my destiny.

Unable to quickly recover from the years of hardship I had endured, I allowed myself to spiral. I somewhat gave up. For years, I believed the lie that I couldn't recover my former abilities, that I had fallen behind, and that I was no longer "as good" as others. But eventually, I cried out to God for clarity and the courage to speak up, to take responsibility, and to make the necessary changes.

Through repentance, I recognized that I had been living in the shadows of who I once was, avoiding the woman God was preparing me to become. I had become like a piñata, battered between the memories of the past and the demands of a new reality. I was barely surviving, resisting the very change God was orchestrating.

I had let intimidation and low self-esteem define my truth. I had to learn to speak up for myself even when trembling, even with a turning stomach. I learned to push through the awkwardness, to assert my confidence, and to speak out against injustice. With that came a shift: I stopped people-pleasing and chose to focus instead on pleasing God and fulfilling the purpose He had for me.

Through these experiences, God exposed the unacceptable patterns I had tolerated in my life. I made a decisive choice to reset, to re-examine how I was living and to pursue a deeper understanding of who God truly is. I began depending on constant prayer and affirmations, focusing on who God said I am. I leaned not on my strength or ideals, but on His Word, His love, and His wisdom.

And God came through for me.

He brought clarity to my heart and mind. I realized He had already given me authority through prayer to shift my circumstances. I started praying differently with greater revelation and understanding of spiritual matters. I learned how to safeguard myself and my family through prayer. I also started changing my associations and raising my expectations for myself. I envisioned a better life and trusted God for greater blessings in the future.

As my identity in Christ became clearer, I noticed shifts in my communication, confidence, and mindset. My confidence was no longer rooted in my abilities but in the goodness of God manifesting in me.

I mentioned that I felt afraid and unable to speak up for myself. What I didn't mention was that I was trembling because of the fear and anxiety I was facing in that situation. I managed to step away and literally locked myself in the ladies' room and prayed. I realized afterward, *"Oh my God, how could I not have seen this? How could I not have seen that I was being disregarded and that the individual had very little respect for me?"*

In that encounter, God clearly showed me that this was something I had tolerated for a long time with many people. In that particular moment, it was exposed to me that I had been belittling myself, putting others on a pedestal because of their achievements. As a result, I was blatantly disregarded. This wasn't something I had been praying about specifically, but because I had asked God to change me for His glory, this issue of always being the underdog was brought into the light.

It was God's way of saying, *"I have not called you to be the tail – holding others in high esteem at the expense of understanding that you are My child, called and chosen in Me before the foundation of the world"* (Ephesians 1:4, NKJV). *"I have put My Spirit in you. You are valuable to Me, and I have a plan for your life."*

God came through for me in that time of challenge and personal attack on my identity by helping me find my voice and establish personal boundaries.

That time of drought, loneliness, and separation from God was not only difficult, it held me back in many ways. But my breakthrough came when I decided to swallow my pride and ask someone for help. I reconnected with a mentor who not only prayed with me and encouraged me but also laid out a God-given plan of action that propelled me into forward motion over the next few months.

I was so grateful that God uses people to help us in our times of need and desperation. He not only brings refreshing through His Holy Spirit and His Word, but also through the lives of those who love and serve Him – essentially becoming His hands and feet on earth.

Today, I can confidently say that God answers prayer, and He truly brings times of refreshing and reestablishes our steps when we earnestly cry out to Him, running back with repentant, open hearts, desiring His will over our own.

I can see the goodness of God in my life today, as my life has been significantly transformed through my understanding of who I am in Him and His faithfulness. I can totally depend on Him. This realization has enabled me to walk in a new level of confidence in my identity in Christ. I now carry myself with boldness and clarity of mind, fully understanding that God chose me in Him before the foundation of the world and that His plans for me are good (Ephesians 1:4, NKJV; Jeremiah 29:11, NKJV).

I truly believe I can do all things through Christ, who gives me strength, as Philippians 4:13 (NKJV) declares. When I rely on the Greater One who lives inside of me, I can face every challenge, whether in my personal life, in business, or in relationships, with the assurance that I will overcome. By depending on God's Word and His Holy Spirit to guide me, I now move with greater authority and unwavering faith through every circumstance.

I freely give of my time and talents, no longer seeking the approval of others. Now that my focus is solely on pleasing God, I don't wait for permission from people. I know that I am already worthy and perfect in His sight, chosen before the foundations of the world, and covered by the precious, legal blood of Jesus Christ, my Savior and Lord.

Friend, God is no respecter of persons, and if He can do this for me, He can do it for you, too! I encourage you: pour out your heart earnestly to God in prayer. Write down your visions and dreams. Move forward in faith, prayerfully, believing for breakthrough, and never give up on your deliverance, dreams, or goals.

Envision your God-given dreams through the eyes of faith. Surround yourself with like-minded believers. Stand on His Word and do not waver.

"A double minded man is unstable in all his ways." (James 1:8, KJV)

Because I have seen the Lord's goodness, His mercies, and His compassion, I can truly encourage you to persevere. Hold on until your change comes because it will come, if you tarry.

Psalm 37:4 (NKJV) tells us, *"Delight yourself also in the Lord, and He shall give you the desires of your heart."* Even though we may walk through storms and challenges, God has promised to be with us, to help us overcome every test. He is faithful to bring His Word to pass in our lives for His glory.

Karleen J. Poyser - Co-Author

Safe in His Arms
The Goodness of God

Kayon Watson

Chapter Twenty-Three

With God All Things Are Possible

When the weight of life's trials presses down on us, it's natural to feel overwhelmed. Financial struggles, broken relationships, sickness, unemployment, or battles with depression can feel all-consuming. However, the Bible reminds us that God's power is greater than anything we face. He is the Creator of the universe – the One who spoke the heavens and earth into existence. If God's spoken word could create the world, how much more can His intervention transform our broken situations?

The Bible assures us of a truth that transcends our circumstances: With God, all things are possible. This powerful promise, found in Mark 10:27 and echoed in Jeremiah 32:27, reminds us that God's power knows no limits and that He is faithful to intervene in our lives when we trust in Him.

I thank God for His blessing and protection throughout my life. He has molded and shaped me over the years so that I was able to overcome the battles of life. By His indwelling Spirit, He has now enabled me to write this inspiring encouragement to His wonderful sons and daughters.

I remember not long ago, I was always worried about materialistic things, or what might happen to me tomorrow, or who loved me, or who didn't. But after a while, I realized that my worries weren't helping solve the issues. Instead, they only added a great amount of stress to my life. So, by learning from my experiences, I understood that I couldn't change the unchangeable. Plus, it doesn't matter how good or honest a person is. Circumstances and unforeseen events will happen to them at some point.

So, I just needed to change my perception of life and know that only in Jesus Christ could I find true rest and liberty from the battles of life.

Mark 10:27 (KJV) declares,

"And Jesus looking upon them saith, 'With men it is impossible, but not with God: for with God all things are possible.'"

This verse speaks directly to the divine ability of our God to accomplish what is beyond human capacity. Similarly, in Jeremiah 32:27 (KJV), God proclaims,

"Behold, I am the Lord, the God of all flesh: is there anything too hard for me?"

These scriptures together form a foundation of hope for those who are overwhelmed by life's hardships.

Before we dive into the specifics of these two powerful verses, let's first explore the circumstances that gave birth to the declarations found within them.

The declaration in Mark 10:27 arises in a profound moment of teaching by Jesus. A wealthy young man had approached Him, asking what he must do to inherit eternal life. Despite his adherence to the commandments, Jesus told him to sell his possessions, give to the poor, and follow Him. The young man left sorrowfully, unwilling to part with his wealth. This encounter astonished the disciples. They wondered who could be saved.

Jesus responded, *"With men it is impossible, but not with God: for with God all things are possible."* Here, Jesus revealed that salvation is not something humans can achieve through their efforts, morality, or wealth. It is entirely a work of God's grace, made possible through faith in Him. Jesus emphasized that the path to eternal life requires complete reliance on God's power, not human capability.

God specializes in doing what humanity cannot. When the world tells us that our situation is hopeless, Jesus assures us that nothing is beyond God's reach. His grace makes all things possible.

On the other hand, Jeremiah 32:27 is set against the backdrop of one of Israel's darkest moments. The nation faced great destruction at the hands of the Babylonian Empire. Jeremiah had been imprisoned for prophesying that Jerusalem would fall. It was during this time of despair and chaos that God instructed Jeremiah to purchase a field. This was a prophetic act symbolizing hope and restoration.

As Jeremiah obeyed, God reaffirmed His sovereignty with the words:

"Behold, I am the Lord, the God of all flesh: is there anything too hard for me?" Jeremiah 32:27 (KJV)

These words declared that even amid destruction and loss, God's plans for His people remained intact. Despite the shame, failure, disappointment, and defeat, God's promise of restoration stood firm.

If you are reading this and feel broken beyond repair, know that these scriptures speak directly to your heart. To those who feel trapped in the ruins of their circumstances, this declaration is a source of hope. Whether it's the ruins of a broken marriage, financial collapse, or shattered dreams, God's question challenges us to consider His power and faithfulness:

Is there anything too hard for Him?

For those burdened by stress, depression, or overwhelming life situations, the declarations in Mark 10:27 and Jeremiah 32:27 offer a lifeline. They remind us that God's power is greater than our weakness. Where we see impossibility, God sees opportunity.

To those who are stressed and broken by situations deemed impossible by human understanding, situations that defy logic or natural order, Abraham and Sarah's story offers hope. The God who brought life to a barren womb is the same God who can breathe life into dead dreams and open doors that no human effort could yield.

If you are carrying the weight of a situation that feels beyond repair, know this: God's power is not bound by anything we use in the world to measure possibility. He is not limited by nature, science, or human understanding. What seems impossible to man is entirely possible for God. The very laws of nature bow to His command. Just as He turned water into wine, walked on the sea, and raised the dead, He can transform your situation no matter how dire it appears.

To the one facing a terminal diagnosis, know that He is Jehovah Rapha, the Healer. To the one whose heart is shattered by loss or betrayal, He is the God who binds up the brokenhearted and restores the soul. No pain, no obstacle, and no circumstance is too great for Him to intervene.

Circumstances are a part of life. They can shape a person into the most beautiful and gentle human being, yet they can also turn people into monsters. It's how people manage their circumstances that defines who they will become. We are living in a world of trouble and turmoil. Sometimes, it may seem like you've been waiting a long time at a crossroad and can't even see the light of day. Life becomes weary and frustrating. But if you look to God and remain resilient, faithful, patient, and enduring, you will walk in the purpose and destiny that God has called you to walk in.

History teaches that every single person must come to a point in life where they have to make a serious decision – will they allow their natural circumstances or the destructive plot of the devil to dictate their lives, or will they look to God for help?

Many of us have faced moments where every option seems closed. We look ahead and see the Red Sea – a barrier too great to cross. Behind us are the armies of our past mistakes, broken dreams, and overwhelming responsibilities. In such moments, depression, stress, and hopelessness can threaten to consume us. But just as God delivered the Israelites, He can deliver us.

God doesn't need favorable circumstances to work a miracle. The same God who parted the sea can provide a way through your financial struggles, heal your emotional wounds, and restore what has been lost. He is the God who makes a way where there is no way. God brings streams in the desert and fights for the oppressed. He sees your pain and hears your cries. God is the God of justice, the One who vindicates and restores.

No matter how impossible your situation appears, with Him, all things are possible.

Have Faith in God

Faith is believing in God for the impossible. It is believing that God can do what no man can do. Faith holds us steady when the storms of life rage.

In Matthew 17:20 (KJV), Jesus proclaims,

"If ye have faith as a grain of mustard seed, ye shall say unto this mountain, Remove hence to yonder place; and it shall remove; and nothing shall be impossible unto you."

Faith does not deny the reality of struggles, but it recognizes that God has the power to transform those struggles into victories. God does not promise that our lives will be without mountains and valleys. Instead, He tells us that our faith in Him can remove them. Faith rescues us from the dark valleys of depression and stress.

Amid failures, disappointments, and battles, it is faith that assures us of God's ability to intervene, restore, and make all things new. When the Israelites endured the pain of exile, their hope was not in their circumstances but in the God who had promised their restoration. They clung to faith and trusted in God's plans for their nation.

Faith also empowers us to face our deepest fears with courage. Isaiah 43:2 (KJV) reminds us,

"When thou passest through the waters, I will be with thee; and through the rivers, they shall not overflow thee: when thou walkest through the fire, thou shalt not be burned; neither shall the flame kindle upon thee."

These words reassure us that no matter how fierce the storm or how high the waves are, God's presence is with us. He promises rescue, provision, and guidance, but it takes faith to trust His methods.

Consider the moments when life feels like a sea of uncertainty, much like the Red Sea before the Israelites. Behind them were Pharaoh's chariots, and before them lay an impossible obstacle. In such moments, despair can feel like the only option. Yet it was their faith in God's command to stand still and see the salvation of the Lord that led to their miraculous deliverance.

Faith is not just about believing in God's existence but actively trusting in His promises. It's about praying with expectation, speaking life over dead situations, and declaring victory even when defeat seems imminent. As you face your own Red Seas, remember that God specializes in making a way where there seems to be none.

In Mark 11:24 (KJV), the Bible declares:

"Therefore I say unto you, What things soever ye desire, when ye pray, believe that ye receive them, and ye shall have them."

Faith in God attracts His power, might, and authority. Just as a mustard seed grows into a mighty tree, so too can the smallest faith lead to great breakthroughs. Therefore, let your faith be unshaken, for it connects you to a God who is faithful. Trust Him in the valleys of despair, the deserts of delay, and the storms of adversity. Hold fast to the belief that the same God who healed the sick and raised the dead is at work in your life today.

Surrender Everything to God

Believing in God's omnipotence is one thing, but living in light of that belief is another. How do we allow the truth of God's limitless power to transform our daily lives?

One critical step is surrendering our worries to God. This involves acknowledging that we are not equipped to solve every problem we face. By casting our burdens upon Him, we invite His divine intervention. This releases the overwhelming weight that comes from trying to handle everything on our own.

Psalm 55:22 (ESV) reminds us:

"Cast your burden on the Lord, and he will sustain you."

When we surrender, we open the door for God to work in ways that surpass human understanding. Surrendering everything to God brings peace to our restless hearts.

Another transformation occurs when we stop trying to fix everything alone. Leaning on our limited abilities often leads to frustration, stress, and a cycle of anxiety. This self-reliance is not only exhausting but also detrimental to our mental and spiritual well-being.

Proverbs 3:5–6 (ESV) urges us:

"Trust in the Lord with all your heart, and do not lean on your own understanding. In all your ways acknowledge him, and he will make straight your paths."

True peace comes when we admit our limitations and allow God to guide us through life's challenges.

Trust in God's Timing

Trusting in God's timing is another essential aspect of living in light of His omnipotence. Sometimes, our impatience can lead to despair, especially when answers to our prayers seem delayed. But God's timing is always perfect, even when it doesn't align with our expectations.

Ecclesiastes 3:11 (ESV) tells us:

"He has made everything beautiful in its time."

When we learn to wait on God, we find peace in knowing that delays are not denials but divine preparations. What feels like a standstill to us may be God planning something far greater than we can imagine.

Seek God Above Everything Else

In moments of pain, sorrow, and hardship, seeking God first becomes a transformative act. Even when life feels like a mess, placing God at the center invites His presence and power into our situations. Seeking God first aligns our hearts with His will and opens the way for restoration and healing.

Consider Job's story as a powerful reminder of this truth. When Job lost everything – his children, wealth, and health – his response was to bow down and worship God.

Job 1:20–21 (ESV) says,

"Then Job arose and tore his robe and shaved his head and fell on the ground and worshiped. And he said, 'Naked I came from my mother's womb, and naked shall I return. The Lord gave, and the Lord has taken away; blessed be the name of the Lord.'"

In his brokenness, Job sought God first, and in the end, God restored everything he had lost. He even blessed him more than before. This teaches us that worship in the midst of trials invites God's blessings, breakthroughs, and provision.

When we seek God first, we allow Him to take His rightful place in our lives as Lord and Savior. This act of faith positions us to experience His power and peace in ways that transform not only our circumstances but also our hearts. He restores what seems lost and gives us new hope. Just as He restored Job's life, He can restore ours. He can mend what has been broken and fill the empty places with His grace. God can deliver us from the snares of the enemy and provide a way out of even the most hopeless situations. And He can provide for our needs, often in ways that defy logic or expectation – because He is Jehovah Jireh.

With God, all things are possible. This truth is not just a comforting idea but a reality that has been proven time and again in Scripture and in the lives of countless believers. I have seen God make the impossible possible in my own life, and I know that He can do the same for you.

When you surrender your worries to God and seek Him even in your pain, you open the door for Him to work miracles in your life. God heals the brokenhearted, restores what is lost, and makes a way where there is none.

Let this truth fill you with hope and strength. Whatever you are facing, take it to Him in prayer, stand firm in faith, and watch as He turns impossibilities into testimonies of His glory.

Pastor Kayon Watson - Co-Author

Safe in His Arms
The Goodness of God

Nasha T. Alexis

Chapter Twenty-Four

Waiting on the Lord

"But if we hope for what we do not yet have, we wait for it patiently."
Romans 8:25 (NIV)

If there is anything about human nature that is common to everyone, it's that we don't like to wait. Every one of us, at one time or another, has been – or is – waiting for something. Some have been praying for years for a husband, while others continue to pray for a friend or family member to come to know our Lord and Savior, Jesus Christ. There are still others who are waiting and believing for healing from an illness or disease. Some are waiting to become pregnant and carry their first child. Then there are those who are praying for their prodigal son or daughter to return home. Others are applying and waiting for that long-anticipated promotion at work.

Waiting carries a lot of weight and, if we are not careful, can lead to discouragement, anger, disappointment, and even walking away from what we know to be true about God. We get so caught up in worrying while we wait that, oftentimes, we lose ourselves in the process. I don't know of anyone who truly likes or enjoys waiting. Even waiting in the grocery store line or the drive-thru can be a problem for some people. Waiting is most definitely not a strong point for most of us.

We are impatient from the moment we leave our mother's womb. Even in the womb, babies are kicking and stretching. Twins are jostling for more space. Think of a newborn baby when he or she is hungry, has a soiled diaper, or wants to be held in a particular way. They may not be able to verbalize what they want or what's causing discomfort, but they will certainly communicate effectively that something is wrong and needs immediate attention.

If that seems familiar, it should. Isn't that the way we sometimes approach God when things are going wrong in our lives and we need a solution right away? I know we can all relate to this.

We must ask: where or when does a newborn learn to do that? To demand attention and trust that someone will step in to fix what's uncomfortable? I don't have all the answers, but I believe it's something we're born with – an innate part of who we are. The only part that tends to fade as we grow older is trust.

A newborn doesn't know any better. They cry, and their needs are met. They're lifted and held the way they want, and the crying stops. Their soiled diaper is changed, and now they are clean and dry – comfortable again. When they're hungry, their cries sound like the world is crashing down. It may have only been one minute since they last fed, but they don't know that. They're convinced the end has come. In reality, you may have simply paused to burp them because they were drinking too fast. You stopped to help them – but they didn't realize it. They just wanted what they wanted.

The moment you start feeding them again, the crying stops – completely unaware of what they were just spared: discomfort and pain. In that moment, they are trusting you, their parent, to meet all their needs, to provide, and to make things right. They don't question it; they just receive.

In the same way, who knows how many times God has stepped in to save us for our own good? How many times has He interrupted our enjoyment or our plans to protect us from the pain that was headed our way? But we, too, often don't realize it. We just want what we want when we want it.

When a child reaches toddler age – commonly known as the "terrible twos" – the demands grow louder. By then, they're better able to express themselves verbally (for a typically developing child) and have no hesitation in doing so. We want what we want when we want it.

As adults, we sometimes behave the same way with God. We become demanding, stomping our feet, and throwing tantrums when we don't get our way. Like a two-year-old, we expect God to drop everything and tend to our immediate desires. We want Him to fix every problem we've created or bless us with what we think we need right away.

Again, waiting is not our strongest suit.

Waiting is one of the hardest things for human beings. However, when we master the skill of waiting, we become more relaxed and less anxious. By disciplining ourselves to wait, we also learn to respect others, develop more patience, and strengthen our self-control. Waiting is a learned skill and not something we are born with. There are no quick fixes.

Just as we teach children to wait with simple phrases like, *"Please wait, I'm coming,"* or *"Just a minute, I'm getting it for you,"* we should remind ourselves that waiting is necessary even as adults. So why is it that when we grow older, we forget those early lessons and want God to solve our problems the moment we open our mouths?

Sometimes, we even attempt to throw His Word back at Him, saying things like, *"You already know my needs, so why do I have to ask You to solve them?"* or *"You already know what I'm going to say, so why can't You just stop this from happening?"* I'll admit, I've been guilty of that myself. We may try to use God's Word to justify our impatience, but we end up twisting it, which is wrong. As it says in Matthew 6:8 (NIV), *"Do not be like them, for your Father knows what you need before you ask Him."*

We've all been in those moments when fear takes over, or guilt from falling into sin, or the weight of life circumstances becomes too much to handle. In those moments, fear and anxiety cloud our vision, and all we see is the problem before us. Waiting becomes the last thing we want to do. We want instant results. We want things to change – immediately. Any form of self-control or decorum we may have possessed goes out the window, and emotionally, we fall apart.

There have been many times when I had to wait on the LORD, and I can tell you; I was not always gracious about it. I threw tantrums. I stopped talking to God, stopped praying, and acted like He didn't exist. I became angry, distant, cold-hearted, silent, and numb. And it wasn't just with God, it was with my family too. I didn't want to speak to anyone or even be around anyone. People's voices irritated me. I just wanted to be left alone.

You might be thinking I was depressed – and perhaps it sounded like that – but I know what depression is, and this wasn't quite it. This was something else. This was a situation where I got myself into trouble trying to help someone with good intentions, but they didn't follow through on their word. Now, I was left holding the burden alone. That kind of disappointment weighs heavily on the heart.

I remember wondering why God didn't stop me from helping that person. After all, He sees the heart and knows all things. He could have prevented it, but He didn't. Now I was left feeling pressured and overwhelmed, while the other person seemed to be living their best life. To me, it didn't seem fair. So, for a "hot minute," I stopped speaking to God.

That feeling of disconnect was very real – and one of the hardest things I've ever experienced. Deep down, I knew God's Spirit was still near, but I was the one keeping the distance. I felt betrayed by God. I thought, *"If He already knows what I need, why do I have to ask? Why wouldn't He stop people from disappointing me – or better yet, stop me from making such a big mistake in the first place?"* I still don't have all the answers to those questions. But what I do know is that He saw me through.

As it says in Proverbs 3:5 (NIV), *"Trust in the LORD with all your heart and lean not on your own understanding."*

I don't know why God allows certain things to happen in our lives, or why He seems silent in some seasons. What I do know is that I'm called to trust Him and wait on His timing.

During seasons of waiting, I've learned to depend on God more than anyone else. I no longer even trust myself to make a decision without checking in with Him first. I've also learned that waiting is not a punishment or a setback – it is a time of growth. It's a space where faith is strengthened and our dependence on God deepens.

People will continue to disappoint us. We will continue to make mistakes. Life will still throw situations at us that feel overwhelming. But we don't have to be shaken by them. We know the God of the Bible—our protector, our helper, our guide. We do not wait in vain or without hope.

Whether we receive the outcome we desire or not, God is and always will be God. We will praise Him and glorify His name, no matter what.

No more will we allow our circumstances to dictate our relationship with our Heavenly Father.

I know I am not where I want to be spiritually, but I also know that He will finish what He started in me. Philippians 1:6 (NIV) says, *"being confident of this, that He who began a good work in you will carry it on to completion until the day of Christ Jesus."* So, I am not fretting or worrying. The tantrums are less frequent as I grow in my faith and as I learn to be still and wait on the LORD. It is not easy, but I've noticed progress in myself. I thank God for His patience with me.

When a person becomes a new believer and follower of Jesus Christ, there are so many things they need to learn and become aware of. We are never to sugarcoat the Christian life or romanticize it – for it is not glamorous. We're told that we will have trials and tribulations. As John 16:33 (NIV) says, *"I have told you these things, so that in me you may have peace. In this world you will have trouble. But take heart! I have overcome the world."*

Being still in the waiting is just one of the many lessons a new believer must learn. The Father wants us to have peace, but that peace can only be experienced when we are in His presence. For years, I had the mentality that God would give me everything I asked for the moment I asked for it. And when that didn't happen, I became angry with God and with myself for believing that He cared about me or my needs. I felt hurt that He didn't give me what I wanted, so I would throw an adult-sized tantrum.

I had this notion that, as a follower of Christ, He was there to meet my every need – and He is – but not in the way I had hoped. I thank God that His ways are not my ways and His thoughts are not my thoughts. As Isaiah 55:8 (NIV) reminds us, *"For my thoughts are not your thoughts, neither are your ways my ways,"* declares the LORD.

I also believed the lie from the enemy that I wasn't praying correctly, and that's why things weren't happening for me. That lie changed my entire perspective on who I thought God was. I didn't want anything to do with Him because I believed He was unfair. I thought He was mean and uncaring and that He didn't want to help me.

But it took the Holy Spirit to begin dispelling those lies and to open my eyes to see the deception and tricks of the enemy of my soul. His goal was to distance me from God – to separate me from the love of Christ.

I started noticing little things: small blessings, confirmations from Scripture, moments of peace. I began reading His Word more consistently and being honest with Him about how I felt. I had to come before the Father stripped of all I thought I knew about Him and surrender my entire self to Him.

It was, and still is, not an easy process. But when a person is serious about being a follower of Christ and is simply tired of running, eventually, they will surrender.

And that moment of giving up became the starting point of my healing journey.

In the waiting period, we must remember who is in control. We must learn to be still in the waiting. God gives us a clear directive on what to do. Psalm 46:10 (NIV) says, *"He says, 'Be still, and know that I am God.'"* We must give the Holy Spirit room to move and work without us throwing tantrums because we don't understand or see what He is doing behind the scenes.

We must learn to release control over whatever situation we may be facing and surrender it to the One who knows best and can truly do something about it. 1 Peter 5:7 (NIV) tells us, *"Cast all your anxiety on Him because He cares for you."* The Father never wants us to be anxious about anything, so He gives us a way out: to cast all – not some, but ALL – of what is bothering us. Think of casting a net out to sea: it is thrown far and wide, with force. So today, let us cast everything to Jesus.

Holy and Mighty God,

I give You thanks and glorify Your name for being Who You are to me – my Heavenly Father. Sovereign God, I give You praise and magnify Your name for the life You have blessed me with. Through it all – whether good or bad – You are still God. You remain the same yesterday, today, and forever. You are the unchanging God with no shifting shadows, and I thank You for that.

I thank You that the plans You have for me are good and that nothing can stop You. LORD, I stand on Your Word that says I must be still and know that You are God. I choose to remain still in You, in Your presence, as I wait patiently. Thank You, Holy Spirit, for guiding me always, and for the blood of Yeshua, which has brought me back into right relationship with my Abba.

Amen.

Nasha T. Alexis - Co-Author

Safe in His Arms
The Goodness of God

Khaimnie Seepersaud

Chapter Twenty-Five

The Arms That Held Me

My name is Khaimnie Seepersaud, but everyone calls me Lorren. I was born in Guyana and currently reside in Toronto. Today, I want to thank the Lord Jesus Christ for what He has done in my life and for everything He has brought me through. I have experienced many encounters and can testify to the goodness of God.

I am a mother of two beautiful girls and have been married to my husband, who is from Sri Lanka, for eleven years. I have witnessed God's powerful hand throughout my life – from childhood to the present. Many of the experiences I've gone through have not only allowed me to reflect on His goodness but have also helped me grow spiritually and understand the purpose He has for me as a believer, a mother, and a wife.

Throughout my journey, life has been bittersweet. It's been a mixture of joy and challenges. Some seasons are filled with happiness, while others bring trials and testing. But it is always God who makes the difference. When we focus on Him, trust in His Word, live by it, and find rest in His promises, we receive the courage through the Holy Spirit to press forward. Over time, we grow to a place where we can pray boldly and overcome whatever circumstances or struggles we face.

Life can be tough at times, especially when faced with unexpected adversities. When I was around eleven years old, in 1996, my aunt hugged me and told me that my dad had died in an accident. I was very emotional because I was close to him, and he was a loving father. The impact on my life as an eleven-year-old was intense. After the funeral, I was tormented by a spirit that appeared every night at midnight. It resembled my dad and had the same look and voice and appeared like a clone of him. I would call for my mom and sister, saying, "Look, it's there." This demon was visible only to me.

One Sunday during the evening sermon, the pastor stopped suddenly and said, *"The Holy Spirit is speaking to me. Someone here is being frightened by a demon. I want you to know it is not your father or loved one. It's an impersonation from the devil, trying to destroy your life. If that's you, come forward to the altar for prayer."* Without hesitation, I went to the altar, allowed the pastor to pray for me, and made a firm decision never to see that spirit again or let it torment me. After that prayer, I no longer saw the image or the clone of my dad.

I thank God for removing that spirit from my vision and completely from my life. It was the pastor's obedience to God's voice, together with my determination and faith, that gave me my breakthrough. Had I entertained that demon or given it space in my life, it could have destroyed me by speaking more, visiting more, and influencing me to respond. I am grateful that, during the sermon, the pastor listened to the Holy Spirit and made that altar call specifically for me. I thank God for His timing and that I was in the right place at the right time to receive deliverance. From that day forward, I was able to walk in victory, knowing I was free.

That was the goodness of God – how He delivered me from a situation that was plaguing my mind and bringing destruction. God used that opportunity to bring me closer to Him. My relationship with Jesus began to grow.

Three years later, when everything seemed like it was getting better, a similar situation occurred again in 1999. It was slightly different;

however, I was more mature in Christ and had more experience in Him. I lost my mom, and when I heard the news that she had passed away, I separated myself from everyone. I walked away and went into the backyard during the early hours of the morning. It was pitch dark, and I stood there, saying only the name, "Jesus."

In that moment, I felt an arm around me. It was so warm and comforting, like a person hugging me. But I knew it was the arms of the Lord. I had never felt so comforted before. That is how I know that God is real and everything about Him is true. Many people doubt the existence of God, but in that moment, I knew it was the arms of Jesus holding and comforting me.

I experienced peace when I thought everything was going to fall apart.

Throughout the journey of my life, it has been one experience after another. Each of them has shaped me into who I am today, and every experience has helped me grow in different ways. Some of them helped me develop emotionally, others drew me into deeper prayer, and still others strengthened my faith – teaching me to trust God, knowing He will come through for me.

During the pandemic, my husband suffered a heart attack and collapsed in the washroom. I heard a noise, ran to check, and realized he had no vitals. Having had first aid training, I quickly went through the ABCs – Airway, Breathing, Circulation – but found nothing. In that moment, many would have immediately reached for the phone to dial 911. But I chose to first exercise my faith in God's healing power.

I laid my hand on my husband and declared, *"Devil, not today. I call you back to life in the name of Jesus!"* I spoke life over him. *"No plan of the enemy will succeed over my husband's life."* I decreed and declared that he would live a long and satisfying life (Psalm 91:16, NKJV). A calmness came over me. Then I picked up the phone and dialed 911 to request emergency medical services, who arrived quickly.

My little daughter, about six years old at the time, stood at the doorway. I said to her, *"Baby, go back to sleep,"* but she replied, *"No, Mom, I want to see the doctors."* I asked, *"Where are they?"* She answered, *"They're right there, Mom, and they have a green light around them."* I asked, *"Doctors?"* She said, *"Yes, they're taking care of my Appa."* That's what she calls her dad. I simply said, *"OK,"* and she replied, *"OK,"* then went back to bed.

She stood there watching until the EMS arrived. When the real paramedics came, those initial "doctors" left. One of the EMS personnel said to my husband, *"Buddy, do you know you were gone for a few minutes?"* When I heard those words and the EMS told me, *"You are lucky,"* I knew how to respond: it was a miracle.

When we call on God, we receive angelic protection.

As I sit back and reflect on the goodness of God, I can say that when my dad passed away, it was an eventful and emotional experience. But through it all, I've grown in God…and grown in Jesus. I've learned to trust Him. I started praying more and reading my Bible more, because I told myself, since I stopped seeing the clone of my dad after just one prayer, there must be power in prayer. That experience ignited a deeper belief in prayer, and I thought that if I continued to pray, perhaps I would see more miracles.

That encounter shaped me as a person and helped build my faith and confidence in Christ from a very young age. It also matured me. When my friends later went through similar losses, I was able to help and encourage them. The death of my mother was a completely different experience, but once again, God showed up in a way I didn't think was possible. I felt the arms of Jesus wrapped around me, and that sense of comfort is something only those who experience it can truly understand. All the negative thoughts that were rushing through my mind just vanished with that one hug. That's when I knew, without a doubt, that I can rely on Jesus. He's going to show up for me.

In my husband's situation, it was no different. By then, my faith had grown even more, especially after my mom's passing. I had started doing ministry, becoming involved in youth ministry, the choir, and various activities in the church. Through this, I gained more exposure and experience. When it came to my husband's life-threatening moment, it was a true test of my faith. Looking back now, I don't even know how I did what I did. It was God who gave me the wisdom, knowledge, and understanding in that moment. I acted as a child of God, putting my faith first instead of reacting in panic. I thank God that my trust in Jesus was strong enough to call on Him without hesitation – and He answered. I give God all the glory.

I want to encourage everyone who is feeling lonely or abandoned: you are not alone.

Losing both parents can make it feel like you're completely isolated, even when others are physically present. If you're struggling with those feelings – wishing your parents were still here – remember that your journey is part of God's plan. When you invite God into your grief and listen for His voice, you'll begin to see purpose in your pain. Every experience, even loss, can lead to growth. Every challenge offers new insight and spiritual maturity. You can trust that God is walking with you through it all.

Everyone grieves differently. Some recover quickly, and others take more time. Both are completely normal. The key is to give your grief to Jesus. Don't remain stuck in sorrow. Let Him turn your mourning into dancing (Psalm 30:11, NKJV). Never believe that no one cares, because Jesus cares deeply. He sends angels and destiny helpers to assist you in your time of need. No circumstance is too hard for Him.

In my own life, I've seen the Lord send the right people, and even angels, at just the right time. Divine intervention is real. If you feel helpless or alone, please remember that God, Jesus, and His angels are fighting for you. Just pray. Seek Him. Even if you've never believed before, just try. Say a simple prayer. God is listening. An answer is waiting. He is always there.

Two scriptures resonate deeply with me and helped carry me through everything.

The first is Psalm 68:5 (NKJV):

"A father of the fatherless, a defender of widows, is God in His holy habitation."

This verse became a living promise after my mother's passing. My teenage years were the time I needed my parents the most. In their absence, this scripture came alive for me. In my loneliest moments, I would declare it out loud, and the assurance that God is a Father to the fatherless brought deep comfort. Though I no longer had my earthly parents, I had the unwavering support of my Heavenly Father and that was more than enough.

The second scripture that sustained me through my darkest seasons is Psalm 46:1 (NKJV):

"God is our refuge and strength, a very present help in trouble."

It was God's strength that kept me from falling apart. Jesus was right there with me, being my safe place and constant helper in times of distress. I ran to His presence and poured out my heart when I couldn't talk to anyone else. Through every trial I endured, I came out victorious – not by my own strength, but because I trusted in God and stayed close to Him.

Prayer

Heavenly Father,

Thank You for being the Father to the fatherless, my refuge, my strength, and my ever-present help in times of trouble. I come to You because You are the only one who truly understands how I feel and what I'm going through. Please give me the courage to keep moving forward. Shine Your light on my path and guide my steps.

Jesus, thank You for paying the price You didn't owe so that I could receive the gift of salvation. Come into my heart and transform my life. Lift every burden of grief that I'm carrying. Turn my mourning into dancing and help me reflect on all that is good and pure. Show me Your way and reveal the purpose You've placed inside me. Help me align with the plans You have for my life.

Lord, filter out anything that is keeping me stuck. Help me rest securely in Your arms, knowing I am safe with You. After You complete the transformation in my life, help me reflect Your goodness to others. As time goes on, make me a blessing to those around me.

In Jesus' name, Amen.

Khaimnie Seepersaud - Co-Author

Safe in His Arms

The Goodness of God

Anita Sechesky

Chapter Twenty-Six

The Goodness of God in Community and Relationships

Community is one of the greatest expressions of God's heart. From the beginning of time, God designed us for relationship – with Him and with one another. In Genesis 2:18 (NKJV), the Lord said, *"It is not good that man should be alone."* Those words echo through eternity, reminding us that connection is part of His divine blueprint. Humanity thrives when relationships are rooted in love, trust, and shared faith. We grow when we are known. We heal when we are seen. We flourish when we are loved.

In today's world, where technology often replaces genuine connection and people hide behind screens instead of seeking heart-to-heart fellowship, building a faith-based community has never been more essential. When believers gather, something divine takes place. The atmosphere shifts. Burdens lighten. Hope is rekindled. That is the power of the Holy Spirit in fellowship, which is a living testimony of the goodness of God manifesting through people.

I have seen this truth unfold time and time again in churches, hospitals, retreats, and community gatherings. I have witnessed humanity in its rawest moments as an RN. In those sterile hospital corridors, strangers often become family, united in prayer and compassion. It's there that I've seen the power of community ignite faith in the hearts of those who had all but lost it. Suffering has a way of stripping life down to what is most important, and again and again, God uses people to carry His goodness to one another.

There was a time when a young mother, barely able to stand, held her child in her arms as doctors fought to save the infant's life. I watched as other mothers in the waiting room came around her – women she had never met – holding her hands and whispering prayers. One woman sang softly, *"Great Is Thy Faithfulness,"* until tears of surrender streamed down the mother's face. When the baby stabilized hours later, the mother turned to those women and said, *"I came in alone, but God sent me a family."* That is the essence of a supportive faith community – the presence of God reflected through love in action.

Scripture reminds us of this sacred truth: *"Bear one another's burdens, and so fulfill the law of Christ"* (Galatians 6:2, NKJV). When we gather in faith, we multiply strength. We transform pain into purpose. We become living testimonies of God's goodness, proving that even in suffering, His mercy and compassion abound. When one heart is heavy, the whole body leans in to lift it. When one voice falters, the chorus of community sings louder.

A supportive faith community is more than a group of people who meet on Sundays. It is a living, breathing organism that mirrors the heart of Christ – a safe space where vulnerability is not met with judgment but with prayer. It's where testimonies are shared and healing begins. It's where practical needs are met alongside spiritual ones. Meals are delivered, rides are offered, and hands are held. When a family rejoices over answered prayer, it becomes a collective victory for the entire body of believers. When someone grieves, tears are shared and hope is spoken tenderly, without rushing the process.

This interconnectedness reflects the early Church described in Acts 2:44–47 (NKJV), where believers *"had all things in common… continu[ing] daily with one accord in the temple, and breaking bread from house to house… praising God and having favor with all the people."* They shared their lives, not just their beliefs. In today's faith communities, this same spirit can still thrive when we choose unity over division, empathy over pride, and prayer over gossip. The goodness of God is magnified through relationships that heal, not harm; that cover, not expose; that restore, not reject.

I've often told those in my mentorship programs and anthologies that "connection is ministry." Whether in leadership meetings, online gatherings, or conferences, when people come together with a shared heart for God, transformation follows. Walls come down. Miracles happen. Healing begins. Faith communities are spiritual ecosystems. When gratitude and encouragement flow freely, the soil becomes fertile for growth. Each person, no matter how broken or weary, can find rest and restoration in the presence of God through the love of others.

Life's most difficult seasons are when we truly witness the goodness of God revealed through others. During storms, community becomes a lifeline and the arms of God extended through human compassion. I remember standing beside a grieving family who had just lost their son in a tragic accident. Their pain was indescribable. Yet within hours, church members arrived at their home with food, prayers, and gentle words of comfort. The mother later said, *"If it wasn't for my church family, I don't think I would have survived that week."* That's the miracle of faith in action when love becomes tangible.

A supportive community doesn't erase pain, but it helps us carry it. When we are too weak to pray, others lift our hands. When our faith wavers, their intercession sustains us. It's through this shared burden-bearing that God's goodness becomes visible. "Rejoice with those who rejoice, and weep with those who weep" (Romans 12:15, NKJV). The same God who heals broken bodies also mends broken hearts through the warmth of fellowship. In the economy of the Kingdom, tears are not wasted; they water seeds of future joy.

Communities built on compassion often birth testimonies of divine intervention. There are countless moments when God has shown His power through the unity of His people – a prayer chain resulting in healing, a fundraiser meeting needs beyond expectation, or an unexpected visitor offering encouragement at the perfect moment. These are not random acts; they are divine appointments orchestrated by the goodness of God working through His children. Where unity is present, the blessing of the Lord flows.

Gratitude is the glue that binds communities together. A thankful heart sees the hand of God in others. When believers gather to give thanks, whether in small groups, family dinners, or corporate worship, gratitude becomes contagious. It spreads joy, shifts atmospheres, and strengthens unity. In my ministry and publishing work, I have seen the power of gratitude transform teams and projects. When authors express thankfulness for one another's gifts, collaboration flourishes. When leaders appreciate their teams publicly, motivation and creativity soar. Gratitude invites God's presence into every partnership and keeps our focus on the Giver rather than our preferences.

When we thank God collectively, it reinforces the truth that His goodness extends beyond individuals to entire families, congregations, and cities. *"Behold, how good and how pleasant it is for brethren to dwell together in unity!"* (Psalm 133:1, NKJV). A grateful community mirrors heaven on earth, which is a reflection of divine harmony where love and humility reign. Gratitude softens speech, tempers opinions, and guards against division. It reminds us that every person is a gift, not a project.

Kindness is one of the purest reflections of God's character. Every act of compassion, no matter how small, carries eternal weight. A smile to a stranger, a prayer for a friend, or a word of encouragement to a weary soul can ignite transformation. These moments often seem simple but are powerful conduits of God's love. I once met an elderly man in a nursing home who told me, *"I used to think God forgot about me. Then one day, a nurse held my hand and prayed for me. I knew then that God still remembered my name."* That one act of kindness renewed his faith after years of bitterness. Kindness is never wasted; it always leaves traces of heaven behind.

Throughout the Gospels, Jesus modeled compassion through action. He touched lepers, spoke to outcasts, fed the hungry, and comforted the brokenhearted. Every act of kindness He performed was a sermon on the goodness of God. When we emulate His example, we become extensions of His ministry on earth. In my years as a coach and mentor, I've seen how one kind word can alter the trajectory of someone's life. A single moment of compassion can breathe courage into someone ready to give up. When we serve others selflessly, we demonstrate the heart of the Father that never tires of loving, forgiving, and restoring.

It's easy to be kind when life is smooth, but the true measure of faith is kindness under pressure. I've seen this firsthand in hospital corridors, where families facing tragedy still take time to comfort others. In those sacred moments, God's goodness is unmistakable. A young nurse once said to me, *"I don't have time to preach, but I can let people feel God's love through how I treat them."* Her words encapsulate what it means to live missionally – to let everyday kindness be an altar of worship.

Kindness often becomes the miracle someone has been praying for. It's the meal delivered to a struggling single parent, the unexpected encouragement sent to a grieving widow, or the friend who listens without judgment. Through these gestures, people encounter the tangible presence of God. Gratitude naturally flows from such experiences. Those who receive kindness often pay it forward, creating a chain of divine goodness that touches countless lives. In this way, community becomes a conduit through which God's goodness keeps moving from heart to heart.

Relationships are sacred spaces where the goodness of God is both tested and revealed. When two people choose forgiveness over bitterness, reconciliation over resentment, they reflect the very heart of God. Healing in relationships is one of the most profound miracles a community can witness. I've seen marriages restored after years of silence, siblings reunited after decades of estrangement, and parents and children reconcile through the power of prayer. These moments don't happen by chance. They happen because of God's relentless pursuit of peace and the willingness of people to say "yes" to His way.

Scripture guides us in how to walk together wisely: *"With all lowliness and gentleness, with longsuffering, bearing with one another in love, endeavoring to keep the unity of the Spirit in the bond of peace"* (Ephesians 4:2–3, NKJV). Unity does not mean uniformity; it means choosing love over winning, and peace over pride. The body of Christ is healthiest when every part is honored, every voice is heard, and every gift is welcomed.

There are times when conflict arises, and even then, God's goodness can be revealed through how we pursue restoration. Jesus taught us, *"If your brother sins against you, go and tell him his fault between you and him alone"* (Matthew 18:15, NKJV). Private conversations, humble hearts, and prayerful motives protect relationships and preserve trust. In community, we do not run from hard conversations. We approach them with grace, believing that reconciliation brings God glory.

We also learn to rejoice in one another's callings without comparison. When one member is honored, we all celebrate; when one member suffers, we all care. *"If one member suffers, all the members suffer with it; or if one member is honored, all the members rejoice with it"* (1 Corinthians 12:26, NKJV). This is the beauty of belonging – victories are multiplied, and sorrows are divided.

Hospitality is another doorway through which God's goodness enters community. A warm table, an open living room, a gathered circle of prayer all become sanctuaries where hearts exhale. *"Do not forget to entertain strangers, for by so doing some have unwittingly entertained angels"* (Hebrews 13:2, NKJV). Hospitality says, "You matter. You are welcome. You are safe here." It is holy work to create spaces where people can encounter God through simple, sincere love.

God also uses community to propel us into purpose. In circles of trust, we discover our gifts, practice leadership, and grow in obedience. Encouragement and accountability walk hand in hand. A friend's timely word can redirect a wandering heart; a leader's wise counsel can protect a budding dream. In community, we learn that calling is not a competition. It is a collaboration with the Holy Spirit and the people He assigns to our journey.

As I look back on my journey through ministry, nursing, publishing, and coaching, one truth remains constant: God's goodness flows most freely through relationships. Whether in an emergency room or at a writer's workshop, His presence fills every space where compassion and gratitude meet. We were never meant to walk this journey alone. The goodness of God is revealed most beautifully when His children gather to weep, to rejoice, to serve, and to believe together.

In community, we find strength; in kindness, we find healing; in gratitude, we find joy.

Together, we reflect the very nature of God Himself.

Prayer

Heavenly Father,

Thank You for the gift of community and the relationships that remind us of Your goodness. Thank You for every act of kindness, every shared prayer, and every moment of compassion that reveals Your love through us. Lord, help us to be vessels of grace to love unconditionally, to forgive freely, and to serve wholeheartedly. Strengthen the faith communities across our cities, nursing homes, hospitals, and churches. Let them be places where Your Spirit dwells richly. Teach us to see Your goodness in one another and to nurture gratitude in every season of life. May our homes become sanctuaries of peace and our words instruments of healing. And as we walk together in faith, may we continue to be reflections of Your boundless love and goodness to a world in need.

In the precious and powerful name of Jesus Christ, Amen.

Anita Sechesky - Visionary Compiler & Publisher

Safe in His Arms
The Goodness of God

Koreen J. Bennett

Chapter Twenty-Seven

The Goodness of God – God Knows the Plan

Have you ever been in a place where God has been so good, you just don't know where, or how, to begin to share? Well, that's exactly where I am. I truly didn't know how to start this chapter, simply because there have been so many trials, so many ups and downs for my family and me over the past six, going on seven, years. And yet, through all of it, God was always there – even when I didn't feel Him or acknowledge His presence.

When you're going through traumatic seasons in life, the dark cloud can seem to overtake and overshadow the light and goodness of God. But He has shown His goodness over and over, both in the big moments and in the smallest details of my life. I'm sure you could say the same.

God's Word says in Isaiah 41:10 (KJV), *"Fear thou not; for I am with thee: be not dismayed; for I am thy God: I will strengthen thee; yea, I will help thee; yea, I will uphold thee with the right hand of my righteousness."*

Can you stop for a moment and reflect on the last thing God did for you? Has God not shown up for you?

God has been a solid foundation in my life since I was a little girl growing up with my grandparents. I always go back to that time because it's where the seed of God's goodness was first revealed to me. Sometimes, we go through difficult seasons and find ourselves asking, *"Why? Why am I facing this? Is this punishment? Is this really my life's journey?"*

But God is not a God who delights in evil or pain. Psalm 5:4 (KJV) says, *"For thou art not a God that hath pleasure in wickedness: neither shall evil dwell with thee."*

It is God's goodness that gives us the grace to endure. It is His mercy that often keeps us from falling into a pit of anguish, pain, and despair.

Isn't it the goodness of God when a single mom of five always has food on the table, a well-furnished home, and her bills paid? As a child, I never once worried about being homeless or going to bed hungry.

But it's fair to question God's goodness when life keeps knocking you down. You're going about your day and suddenly you're hit with news: a diagnosis that your child will need surgery and will be disabled for life. You're told to prepare to give up your nursing career. A routine exam turns into a terminal illness. A close friend or beloved family member dies, leaving behind a space that feels like it will never be filled – an indescribable void.

The goodness of God? What does that look like in moments like these?

And yet, His goodness shows up. It shows up when you're in overdraft and someone unexpectedly arrives with bags of groceries. It shows up when someone sends you the exact amount you need by e-transfer to cover an urgent bill. From the outside, it may seem like coincidence. But we know better. That's the goodness of God in motion.

The goodness of God shows up when you've called everyone you know for help, and out of the blue, a person appears with exactly what you need in that moment. The goodness of God shows up when you have to work, but your elderly parent or parents suddenly require constant supervision. However, within a few phone calls, someone who's been waiting for a job is available to start immediately.

The goodness of God shows up when you've stayed up all night with your sick child, exhausted and worried, and a friend just happens to stop by for a visit, offering to take over so you can rest for two hours. The goodness of God shows up when you're overwhelmed with worry or anxiety about a situation, and as you scroll through your phone or flip through the television channels, every scripture that appears seems to leap out at you, reminding you not to be anxious or afraid.

> *"Be anxious for nothing, but in everything by prayer and supplication, with thanksgiving, let your requests be made known unto God. And the peace of God, which passeth all understanding, shall keep your hearts and minds through Christ Jesus."* Philippians 4:6–7 (KJV)

God's goodness reminds us that even when we don't understand His plan, He already has our blueprint laid out. He gently assures us that He will never allow us to stray toward danger without pulling us back. He is our protector.

There will be times and seasons when things happen that we cannot explain; when nothing seems to make sense. But even in those moments, the goodness of God provides covering, direction, insight, peace, and love.

Jeremiah 29:11 (KJV) declares, *"For I know the thoughts that I think toward you, saith the Lord, thoughts of peace, and not of evil, to give you an expected end."*

I also love how The Message bible translation puts it: "I know what I'm doing. I have it all planned out – plans to take care of you, not abandon you, plans to give you the future you hope for."

God is waiting to pour out His goodness all over you and me.

The goodness of God is seen even in His patience – waiting for us to return when we've tried doing things our own way.

God's Goodness

God's goodness is giving you and me the grace to go through trials that humble us and prepares us for greater positions, increase, and advancement.

God's goodness is shown in His giving of His only begotten Son to die on the cross for our sins. Jesus taking our place on the cross. Now that's a good, good Father.

God's goodness is seen when He advocates for you and me after we've been lied about, manipulated, and targeted. The goodness of God shows us compassion, transforms us, heals us, and delivers us.

"The Lord also will be a refuge for the oppressed, a refuge in times of trouble." Psalm 9:9 (KJV)

"This poor man cried, and the Lord heard him, and saved him out of all his troubles." Psalm 34:6 (KJV)

God's goodness is His guidance, even when you don't understand the route He has you on. Proverbs 3:5–6 (KJV) reminds us to, "Trust in the Lord with all thine heart; and lean not unto thine own understanding. In all thy ways acknowledge him, and he shall direct thy paths."

Know that God is in the details. He knows your seasons. His timing is always perfect – not a second off.

My first book as a visionary author was truly an expression of God's goodness. At the time, I didn't fully understand it. God took one of the most excruciatingly painful moments in my life, a moment that felt unbearable, and used it for His glory. It was a season where I thought the pain would never end, where life itself felt impossible.

This moment came after the passing of my firstborn son, Terell. Through His love, peace, grace, and mercy, the Lord pulled me out of a deep, dark pit into a place where I could finally speak about Him without falling apart. I reached the point where I could drive past our favorite eating spots and not have to pull over in tears – though they still flowed like a waterfall. I was finally able to write about the love and bond between a mother and her son.

It was God's goodness that entrusted me with His precious gems: my sons.

So how does a mother keep going when the womb that carried her child for nine months and two weeks (yes, he wanted to stay longer!) and the arms that cradled him for twenty-five years must now release him, knowing he will no longer be here in the flesh?

God, in all His goodness, allowed me, along with nine other beautiful souls, to share our journeys of crossing over from hurt, pain, and despair to the land of peace, joy, and hope for the future. Together, we wrote a book called *Oil of Joy*, which became a bestseller within twelve hours of its release on Amazon. There it is again – the goodness of God!

A little girl who once dreamed of writing poetry was now authoring books that inspire healing and encouragement for many who read them. God took what was devastating and used it to bring ten people together, not only to heal individually but to heal collectively as we wrote our stories.

Is this not the goodness of God?

As I reflect on the challenges of my younger years to now, I know the Lord has been with me every step of the way – directing me and redirecting me many times. The lessons I've learned along the journey have shown me that everything I've walked through has been preparation to be a vessel to help others facing similar circumstances.

Through it all, the Lord has whispered, *"Everything you are going through, I will use for My glory."*

A Prayer of Gratitude and Reflection on God's Goodness

Heavenly Father,

I thank You for Your divine love toward me. Even when I didn't understand why I was going through trials, You cushioned me and collected my tears. I thank You for Your lovingkindness during the times I was not obedient – when I chose to follow my own way, only to turn around and do it Your way. I thank You, Lord God, for the moments when I only needed that one mark to pass, and You granted me favor.

Thank You for the times I was sitting at a red light, thinking it was taking forever, when in reality, it was only a few minutes because You were protecting me from the accident that happened just two minutes before I would have arrived at the next intersection. Thank You for Your goodness toward me, my family, and my friends. Your grace and Your mercy are new every single morning.

Thank You for Your divine protection over my loved ones – those who are so dear to me. Thank You for delivering my family and me from ancestral curses and bondage. Thank You for waking me up every single day, eyes open, breathing in and out, with the ability to roll out of bed (yes, even for those of us going through pre-menopause!), and for being able to dress myself in the latest trends with strength and confidence.

Heavenly Father, Your goodness shows up every single second, minute, and hour of the day, if we would only pause to notice. Your love, grace, mercy, kindness, holiness, and righteousness are never-ending toward us.

My beloved reader, I challenge you: take a moment. STOP! Yes, wherever you are (please make sure you are in a safe place), close your eyes, listen to the beating of your heart, notice the sounds your ears can hear, feel the thoughts running through your mind (focus only on the good ones), and you will begin to see and hear the goodness of God.

What a privilege it is to be given this gift from God – the opportunity to share my experience of His goodness with you. I hope and pray that these words of encouragement will leave an imprint on your heart and inspire you as you walk your own journey. I hope that my story will encourage you to share your testimony of God's goodness, whether through speaking or, as I've done here, through writing.

I encourage you to journal. Write down your thoughts, your prayers, the scriptures the Lord gives you. I pray that whatever situation you are facing or overcoming, God will show you His love through His lens. May His peace, divine love, kindness, grace, and mercy overtake you. May His goodness be revealed to you even in the smallest of details.

Prayer

Heavenly Father,

I thank You for the readers of this chapter. I pray that the goodness of God will follow them all the days of their lives. I pray they will seek You first, as in Matthew 6:33 (KJV), *"But seek ye first the kingdom of God, and his righteousness; and all these things shall be added unto you."*

I pray that their hearts will be changed and renewed as they call upon You. Thank You, Lord God, that You perfect that which concerns them. Thank You for remembering them, for opening doors of opportunity, and for bringing breakthroughs and miracles into their lives. Thank You for signs and wonders.

Thank You for reminding them that they are the head and not the tail, above and not beneath, and that their lives are precious in Your sight. I declare increase and elevation over them in this season. Favor knows their names. Grace and Mercy know their names. *"The joy of the Lord is their strength"* (Nehemiah 8:10).

I speak Psalm 23:1 (KJV) over you, *"The Lord is my shepherd; I shall not want."*

I pray over you, dear reader, Psalm 23:6 (KJV), *"Surely goodness and mercy shall follow me all the days of my life: and I will dwell in the house of the Lord forever."*

"Every good gift and every perfect gift is from above, and cometh down from the Father of lights." James 1:17 (KJV)

"O give thanks unto the Lord, for he is good: for his mercy endureth forever." Psalm 107:1 (KJV)

"Serve the Lord with gladness: come before his presence with singing." Psalm 100:2 (KJV)

"For the Lord is good; his mercy is everlasting; and his truth endureth to all generations." Psalm 100:5 (KJV)

Koreen J. Bennett - Co-Author

Safe in His Arms
The Goodness of God

Lesa Isaacs

Chapter Twenty-Eight

The Goodness That Found Me in the Storm

Life is filled with many ups and downs, like storms. These ups and downs come to develop godly character within us. Do you know that sometimes God is trying to get our attention? It was an accident that took place at work.

In September of 2019, things felt off. I didn't have the passion or drive. I found myself not caring for those with whom I worked and was getting upset easily at the smallest things. This was not like me at all. The love I had for my job was slowly slipping away. I was told I had compassion fatigue. It was something that I had never heard of. So when I looked it up, this is what the *Merriam-Webster Dictionary* said:

> Compassion Fatigue (noun): *The physical and mental exhaustion and emotional withdrawal experienced by those who care for sick or traumatized people over an extended period of time.*

Knowing all this, it still did not stop me from being at work. I even had a conversation with my principal about how I was feeling, and she told me to take time if that's what I needed. But in the back of my mind, I believed that the kids needed me. To be honest, I was the one who needed them and was depending on them.

My life was caught up in my title of being a Special Needs Assistant (SNA for short). So I continued to push on until the injury happened on November 29. That day, everything came to a screeching halt.

The title that I had wrapped myself in for the previous seven years felt as if it was slipping away. I wouldn't stop until I was forced to stop. I never thought of myself as a workaholic until I was forced to stop working.

But even then, I still had not seen what I see now. My brain went to, If I am unable to do this job, what can I do? That's how I entered the entrepreneurial world – not wanting to stop, to take the time to heal properly, but to continue and push myself.

My life finally came to a real halt when I ended up in the hospital in October of 2020. Over the next year, I was in and out of the hospital four times. I was seeing different doctors, a specialist, and had many tests done, all while losing a significant amount of weight. It was during those hospital stays, when I was all alone, that I began to cry out to the Lord. Like never before, Jeremiah 29:13 became very real to me. It says, *"You will seek me and find me when you seek me with all your heart."*

Over the next couple of years, that is what I did. When the storms in my life seemed like they were raging, and at times, I felt like I was drowning, there were many lessons to learn and character development that would come from these same storms. I learned more about who I was, and my relationship with my Heavenly Father was being strengthened. There was a peace amid all that was happening. It was something I had never experienced before.

> *"Now, may the Lord himself, the Lord of peace, pour into you his peace in every circumstance and in every possible way. The Lord's tangible presence be with you all."* 2 Thessalonians 3:16 (TPT)

As I began to surrender, I found serenity. It was tangible, and it was what was keeping me. As I continued to align with the Father, I felt more consumed by this serenity, which caused me to want to seek Him more.

The *Merriam-Webster Dictionary* describes peace as *"a state of tranquility or quiet, such as freedom from civil disturbance; freedom from disquieting or oppressive thoughts or emotions."* But Christ said in John 14:27 (NIV), *"Peace I leave with you; my peace I give you. I do not give to you as the world gives. Do not let your hearts be troubled and do not be afraid."* This peace Christ is speaking of refers to being complete or whole. No, my circumstances were not changing, but I was changing. I no longer found myself troubled by the things that were happening outside of me. My focus was on what was happening inside of me and what the Lord was doing within me. God was working on me from the inside out. And that's the best kind of work that one should experience.

I stopped asking, *"Why me?"* and *"What did I do to deserve this?"* and started to believe that things were not happening to me but for me. When we believe things are happening for us, we can often learn a lesson from them.

There was a plan that God had. No, I couldn't see it at the time, but I believed it. It was like it says in Jeremiah 29:11 (NLT), *"For I know the plans I have for you, says the LORD. They are plans for good and not for disaster, to give you a future and a hope."* And that is what I would run with.

The first thing the Lord brought to my attention was who I thought I was and what I was believing about myself. He began to show me that my identity was not in my past mistakes or any job title that I had. I had wrapped my identity in being an SNA (Special Needs Assistant). That was all I knew myself to be.

As I started to see the lies I was believing about myself, I was able to see the truth from God's Word. He started reminding me that I was created in His image, that I was more than a title. I would not have believed that if things had not come to a halt. He began to tell me that I am His Child, Forgiven, His Masterpiece, More Than a Conqueror, Fearfully and Wonderfully Made, and His Beloved.

This scripture began to resonate with me more, *"Now, if anyone is enfolded into Christ, he has become an entirely new person. All that is related to the old order has vanished. Behold, everything is fresh and new"* 2 Corinthians 5:17 (TPT). My identity in Christ was much more than any title that I claimed from this world.

The next thing that the Lord began to reveal to me was the pattern of my thoughts. One pattern specifically was the storm of worry. It had been raging in my life from an early age. It carried me into my adult life. Can you fathom having such a mindset? I knew how to ruminate on things of the past and the future, often spinning tales in my mind of what could happen. Let's just say that I was on the worry train, headed for a complete disaster that could ruin one's life.

But Jesus saved me from myself. And He can do the same for you.

God got my attention. In the stillness, He would show me. Sitting in the hospital bed, He would gently guide me. He was showing me the stories that I was creating in my mind based on what I was worried about. If I believed in Him and trusted Him, there was no need for me to continue to worry. He brought me to Matthew 6:25-34 so that I could better understand what He had said about worrying. My prayer was that He would help me not to worry.

Everything about the unknown scared me, but I was learning that the more I surrendered in prayer to Christ, the less worrying took over my life. I wanted to live in the present, and worrying wasn't allowing me to do that. He truly wanted me to. *"Pour out all your worries and stress upon Him and leave them there, for He always tenderly cares for you"* 1 Peter 5:7 (TPT).

Well, Lesa, how can you call yourself a Christian and worry the way you did? You see, I had not allowed my mind to be renewed by the Word of God like it says in Romans 12:2 (NLT), *"Do not copy the behavior or customs of this world, but let God transform you into a new person by changing the way you think. Then you will learn to know God's will for you, which is good and pleasing and perfect."*

I had to surrender my old ways of thinking, beliefs, attitudes, and ideas for the new mindset that Christ was willing to give me. Once I began to do this, my thought life started to change, and I began to worry less. While working with a mindset coach, she allowed me to become more aware of my thoughts by using a tool called the Thought Download. I was learning the process of taking thoughts captive, according to 2 Corinthians 10:5 (ESV), *"We destroy arguments, and every lofty opinion raised against the knowledge of God, and take every thought captive to obey Christ."*

As believers, we are to take those thoughts captive, but not stop there. Our thoughts must align with what God's Word says. Once we take the thought captive, we then have to do as it says in Philippians 4:8, "Brothers and Sisters, continue to think about what is good, and worthy of praise. Think about what is true and honorable and right and pure and beautiful and respected." These are the thoughts we should be thinking about.

As I found myself in my Bible more, I noticed that my heart was changing as well. God wants us to do what He says in Matthew 6:33 (NCV), "Seek first God's Kingdom and what God wants. Then all your other needs will be met as well." His Word was now being hidden in my heart and mind. I began to memorize and meditate on Scripture as well.

"Study this book of Instruction continually. Meditate on it day and night so you will be sure to obey everything written in it. Only then will you prosper and succeed in all you do." Joshua 1:8

As the Lord was beginning to till the ground of my heart, it began to soften so that the seed of God's Word could be planted firmly and begin to take root – which is what should have been happening all along. I was finally getting to know the Lord for myself.

As I continued to surrender to what the Lord was doing in me, it was like His serenity was enveloping me. Sometimes, I am not even sure I can explain it. I will try. It's like sitting at the beach and watching the waves. The waves move gently and bring about a calming effect. It is in this place that I learned that just like those waves, I have no control. But I know the One who controls them.

This is such a great reminder that we should surrender to the Lord all that we are trying to control. He knows the situations. Let's learn to shift our focus from our circumstances to God.

There was another storm where God wanted to show me how I could receive serenity – by allowing myself to let go of people and things, slow down, and take time to grieve losses. I struggled with letting things go or dealing with them as they arose. The tool that I was to use was forgiveness.

You see, 2019–2020 was a rough year. There were multiple deaths, sickness, physical loss, and job loss. I was holding onto too many things that I needed to let go of and forgive. My emotions were all over the place. I would often react instead of responding in situations. In surrender, there came a rest in knowing that my emotions were no longer controlling me. I addressed the emotions as they came up, which led me to allow myself the room to start to let go and forgive.

Unforgiveness is dangerous not only to our spiritual life but to our physical life as well. The more I held onto things, the more it worked its way into my body. I was disregarding the Scripture that says, *"Yes, if you forgive others for the wrongs they do to you, then your Father in heaven will also forgive your wrongs"* Matthew 6:14 (NCV).

If I wanted my Heavenly Father to forgive me, I would have to forgive others and myself as well. Having unforgiveness in our hearts keeps us from God. Too much unforgiveness causes a hardened heart, and I no longer wanted that. Abiding in Christ means we forgive as He forgives us.

Through the surrender of my old self, forgiveness, old patterns of thinking, and things I could not control, God was working. All the storms of life, especially my health, were beginning to heal. The Lord was healing me. The work that I spoke about in the beginning had to happen inside me first. Through surrender, I found serenity.

My mind was now fixed on Christ. I was now seeing that the mustard seed of faith was becoming a tree. The work Christ had done was to uproot what was old to make space for the new. God's Word says that He will give us peace. To know that you can have chaos happening all around you but internally feel at ease is marvelous.

When you come to the end of your rope, or yourself, you have Jesus. In your despair, cry out to Him, and He will respond. Use that mustard seed of faith to ignite that which Christ alone can do. His peace can make you complete and whole. You see, Christ formed your innermost being, shaping your delicate inside and your intricate outside, and wove them all together in your mother's womb (Psalm 139:13, TPT).

Prayer

Heavenly Father,

I thank You for all who will find serenity through surrender. Let them realize that it was Your presence that was with them.

Thank You, Father, for the lessons they learned about who they are and the character that was developed because of this surrender – that they are spiritually stronger for it.

Father, we thank You for showing up on time. We know that You will never leave us nor forsake us. Let us forge forward knowing that You are a very present help in times of trouble.

Help us to guard our thoughts, for it is the wellspring of life.

Father, for those who have not put their trust in You, may they encounter You like never before. Draw them closer to You. Let their minds be renewed so that they can find the peace that only You can give them.

Father, I praise You for the lives that will be encouraged to have a closer walk with You in this season.

Transform us, Lord.

In Jesus' name, Amen.

Lesa Isaacs - Co-Author

Safe in His Arms
The Goodness of God

Lindsay Cesario

Chapter Twenty-Nine

From the Pit to His Presence – A Journey Redeemed

"If He could save me, cleanse me, and pull me out of the pit I dug for myself, then He can do it for anyone."

My journey with Christ truly began about a year ago, though I now realize He had been chasing after me long before I ever noticed Him. I grew up in a Catholic household. We went to church, said our prayers, and repeated our rosaries, but deep inside, I always wondered, *"Who is God, really?"* I was the kind of kid who did what was expected – kneel, stand, repeat the verses – but I never felt anything move inside of me.

Church was something I attended, not something I experienced. I knew there was a God, but He felt far away, like a figure in a story rather than a presence that could change my life. Then, everything shifted on April 5th, 2024. A close friend invited me to hear her testimony at a local church. I didn't expect anything special to happen. I just wanted to support her. But the moment I stepped inside, something felt different – the air, the atmosphere, the music. When she began to share her story, I felt something powerful stirring in my chest, a warmth I couldn't explain. It wasn't just emotion; it was a Presence. It was love itself reaching out to me. For the first time in my life, I felt God grab hold of my heart. From that day forward, I began to seek Him, reading, praying, and listening to sermons online. It wasn't an instant transformation, but step by step, I began walking in His direction. A couple of months later, on June 25th, 2024, I made the decision to be water-baptized. When I came out of that water, I knew I was leaving my old life behind.

Before that night, my life was a whirlwind of chaos and self-destruction. I was trapped in addiction – alcohol, drugs, parties, and a lifestyle that tore my family apart. I was in and out of jail, fighting everyone who loved me, burning every bridge that could have saved me. I remember one night in particular, which was the lowest point of my life. My body was shutting down from the drugs. I was alone, dizzy, barely conscious. I honestly thought I was going to die. That night, I whispered a desperate prayer: *"God, if You let me wake up tomorrow and my family doesn't find me dead, I'll stop. I'll change. I'll walk away from this."*

When morning came, I opened my eyes...and I was alive. I sat up, still shaky, but breathing. In that moment, I knew God had heard me. I promised Him that I would never touch those substances again, and by His mercy, I kept that promise. It wasn't easy. I had to distance myself from people who pulled me back into darkness. There were nights I cried and nights I almost slipped. But something inside me – something divine – kept me going. God's hand held me steady when everything in me wanted to fall apart. It was in those early days of sobriety that I began to understand grace – the unearned, undeserved love of God that reaches into the mess and says, "You still belong to Me."

From Questions to Revelation

Even after that, I still had questions. I used to wonder why a loving God would let me suffer so much; why He would allow pain, addiction, betrayal, and loss. I used to compare myself to others, wondering why their lives looked easier while mine felt like constant struggle. I remember asking, *"If You love me, why am I hurting? Why do I feel forgotten?"* But one night, I came across a verse that changed everything.

"For I know the plans I have for you," says the Lord, *"plans to prosper you and not to harm you, plans to give you a future and a hope."* Jeremiah 29:11 (NKJV).

Those words cut straight to my heart. Suddenly, it all made sense. God wasn't trying to destroy me; He was trying to deliver me. The pain wasn't punishment. It was preparation. He was breaking down my pride, stripping away my false identity, and drawing me into His purpose. Looking back, I see His fingerprints everywhere – in the people He sent, in the moments He protected me, even in the situations that seemed unbearable. Every hardship was an act of mercy, guiding me toward His goodness.

Before I surrendered my life to Christ, my family was my battleground. My parents loved me deeply, but I caused them years of pain. I remember the shouting, the slammed doors, the police lights flashing outside our house as officers took me away. The look of disappointment on my mother's face was something I'll never forget. For years, I blamed them for my problems. I thought they didn't understand me, that they were against me. But the truth is, they never gave up on me. Even when I was impossible to love, they still prayed for me. After giving my life to Christ, God started to rebuild what I had broken. The anger that used to live inside of me began to melt away. Forgiveness started to flow – both ways. For the first time in over a decade, my mom and I could talk without fighting. My dad, though quiet, started to look at me with pride again. The peace in our home now is something I never thought I'd experience. I can feel the difference. It's lighter, warmer. That's what happens when Jesus steps in. What once was shattered becomes whole again.

The Night Everything Changed

April 5th, 2024. That night will forever be written in my story. I walked into the church thinking I was just there to listen, but God had a different plan. As my friend shared her testimony, I saw pieces of myself in her story – the brokenness, the search for meaning, the surrender. Every word she spoke hit my heart. And then, while everyone bowed their heads to pray, I closed my eyes and felt something powerful. It was as if a weight had been lifted from my chest, replaced with warmth, peace, and love. Tears began to stream down my face. I heard a voice deep inside my spirit say, *"My child, you are home. You are safe. I have you."* At that moment, I knew I had encountered the living God. When the pastor invited people to come forward for prayer, I couldn't even move. My body felt numb, overwhelmed by the love of God. The pastor and my friend came to me, prayed over me right where I sat, and I gave my life to Christ that very night. When I woke up the next morning, everything was different. The heaviness I had carried for years – guilt, shame, regret – was gone. I felt light, free, and new. It was as though God Himself had hit the reset button on my life.

Since that night, God has rewritten every chapter of my story. He's delivered me from the addictions that once defined me. The cravings are gone, not because of willpower, but because His Spirit replaced my desires with peace. My anxiety and depression, which used to weigh me down like chains, are no longer in control. Now, when fear rises, I pray. When sadness creeps in, I worship. I talk to God in the car, at work, or sitting quietly at night. He's become my constant companion – a friend who listens, comforts, and reminds me that I'm never alone. Even through trials, like my father's Alzheimer's diagnosis, I've seen His grace. Instead of falling apart, God gave me strength, patience, and compassion I didn't know I had. I no longer rush through life; I rest in Him. The old me – the reckless, angry, lost version – is gone. A new person has emerged, not perfect, but redeemed.

The Power of Testimony

I've learned that our stories aren't just for us. They're bridges for others to find hope. When we share what God has done, it plants faith in hearts that have given up. Never did I imagine that attending my friend's testimony would lead to me standing here, sharing my own. But that's what the Lord does. He transforms our pain into purpose. Now, every morning, the first words out of my mouth are, *"Thank You, Lord, for another day."* I ask Him to prepare my steps, protect my family, and use me to reach someone who's still where I once was. I want my story to be a reminder that no matter how deep the pit, God's hand can still reach you.

Growing up Catholic, I prayed through saints and rituals because that's what I was taught. I didn't realize that God wanted to talk directly to me. Everything felt routine – confess, repeat, pray, and go home. But when I encountered Jesus personally, I realized I didn't need an intermediary. Now, when I pray, I go straight to the Source. If I'm hurting, I call on the Lord. If I'm grateful, I thank Him directly. It's personal now. It's real. And I know that when my time on earth ends and I stand before Heaven's gates, I won't be greeted by anyone else first. It will be Jesus, my Savior, welcoming me home.

When I look back at who I used to be, it feels like remembering a different person entirely. And honestly, I am no longer that person. That's my testimony. Proof that through God's grace, there is change and there is growth. It's okay to hold on to memories of who you used to be, not to live in regret, but to see how far you've come. I'm not the same person I was a year ago, and it's all because of the goodness of God. He took the broken, addicted, and angry version of me and turned me into someone new – someone who loves, forgives, and lives with purpose. Every scar reminds me of His mercy. Every breath is proof of His grace. I am a living testimony that when God steps into your story, He doesn't just change your direction, He changes your identity.

Prayer

Heavenly Father,

Thank You for every reader holding these pages in their hands. If someone is lost, battling addiction, depression, or shame, touch their heart right now. Remind them that You are not distant. You are near, loving, and full of mercy. Lord, heal every wound. Break every chain. Restore every son and daughter who's searching for meaning. Let them feel Your embrace, just as I did. Show them that no sin is too great, no life too broken, and no heart too far for You to redeem. Let their pain become purpose, their struggle become strength, and their story bring glory to Your name.

In Jesus' mighty name, Amen.

"Therefore, if anyone is in Christ, he is a new creation; old things have passed away; behold, all things have become new." 2 Corinthians 5:17 (NKJV)

Lesa Isaacs - Co-Author

Safe in His Arms
The Goodness of God

Nicole Ragguette

Chapter Thirty

Restoration

The journey of restoration is deeply personal and heartfelt. This book was written during a season of my life when I was completely broken. My voice had been silenced, my heart shattered, and I no longer had the strength to pray. I would whisper to God through my tears, asking Him to restore me. I didn't understand how it would happen or what that restoration would look like – I just knew I didn't want to remain in the place I was in.

The testimonies and stories shared in these pages are not just meant to inspire you; they are meant to heal you. Restoration often begins in secret – in the hidden places where God rebuilds our shattered pieces and brings us back to life from the inside out.

This book is for those who've lost their voice, their strength, their confidence, and their identity. It is for the weary believer who wonders, *"Can these dry bones live again?"* (see Ezekiel 37:3).

I want you to know that yes, they can live again. I want to walk with you as you rediscover the power of God's love and healing. Through the Word, the power of testimony, and the presence of the Holy Spirit, you too can experience total restoration.

You may be reading this as a leader, a mother, a husband, a single woman, a pastor, or someone in transition – this message is for you. God is calling you to arise from the ashes. Your testimony will be one of victory, not defeat. The glory of your latter days will be greater than the former. Your story is not over. Restoration is your portion.

Pixel 1 – It Stops Here

I grew up in poverty.

I grew up with what seemed like a hopeless situation.

I grew up with abuse.

I grew up in a family that was broken.

I grew up in a family that only went to church at Christmas and Easter.

I grew up in a family that did not have a relationship with Jesus the Christ.

I grew up in a family that did not pray every day.

I grew up in a family that came from generational poverty.

I grew up in a family that was so broken – and to be honest, it didn't look promising.

I was on the wrong path and spiraling downhill really fast. It looked as if nothing good would come from my life.

My father was an alcoholic. My grandfather was an alcoholic. All my father's brothers were alcoholics. My father was an abuser of children, and a sexual abuser of women and young girls.

There have been generational addictions, strongholds, brokenness, underachievement, wrong mindsets, broken families, sexual abuse, lack, shame, sickness – forces of evil that have prevented my family from thriving for generations.

But one day, I had an encounter with Jesus. And He told me, *"When you become whole, your entire family will become whole." The words that came out of my mouth after that encounter were, "It stops here!"*

It was then that I began the journey orchestrated by God, led by the Holy Spirit. Line upon line, precept upon precept, my life began to change. The trajectory of my life – and the lives of my entire family – would be completely altered. The cycles of pain and demise that marked the generations before me would be broken, and those who came after me would walk in restoration.

This is where transformation begins.

This is where wholeness happens.

This is where the cultivation and activation of the mindset originally planned for me and my family begins to manifest – a return to God's original design.

This is where we take back our power.

This is where we take back our life.

This is where we take back our family.

This is where we take back our relationships.

This is where we take back everything the devil has stolen from us.

This is where we reverse the order of every evil thing that was spoken over us.

This is where we become everything that God said we are.

The Bible says:

"For I know the plans I have for you," declares the Lord, "plans to prosper you and not to harm you, plans to give you hope and a future." Jeremiah 29:11 (NIV)

Pixel 2 – A Journey Through Generations

My biological father, John, was an ironworker, an alcoholic, and a child sex abuser – just as his father had been before him. My mother, on the other hand, was a nurse, a caregiver to thousands, an intercessor for many, and the matriarch of our family. The fact that you are reading this book today is largely due to the consistent and strategic prayers of my beautiful mother, whose faith made it possible for me to share my story.

I often say, *"If it weren't for the Lord, I don't know where I would be."* I've said it so many times because, when I reflect on my life, I realize that if even one thing had been different, I wouldn't be the person I am right now.

We lived in Scarborough, Ontario, in a large apartment complex with five massive buildings in the lush Morningside area. I still have vivid memories of my old neighborhood. I can picture the tennis court that lay along the walkway to the other apartments. I remember the path to Rose Holder's home – the kind lady who took care of my brother and me when our parents were at work. Rose was from Guyana, and I'm amazed at how many little details from my childhood I still remember: what she looked like, the swimming pool beyond the tennis court, even her husband's face.

Now, at nearly 50 years old, I often find myself wondering about revisiting the place where I grew up. I ask myself: Why has it been so important to go back? I've carried the picture of those buildings and memories in my mind for over 40 years. What will I find if I return? How will I feel when I get there? To be honest, I don't remember anything bad happening there – except for one unsettling memory. Why is it so important to me?

I suppose time will tell.

In 1978, my parents decided to leave Scarborough, Ontario, and move to Calgary, drawn by its booming economy and the belief that the West would offer better opportunities than the East. If my memory serves me right, they packed up a trailer, my younger brother, and me, and made the move to Calgary. At the time, there was a lot of work and opportunity in Calgary, and they believed it was the right decision for our family.

When we first arrived in Calgary, we didn't have a house yet, so we lived in the trailer we used for vacations. The trailer park was called Happy Valley, and I remember living there for several months, even through the harsh winter – all four of us in that small space.

It wasn't long before my parents found a basement suite to live in. I recall my mother working two jobs – as a full-time nurse and part-time administrative worker in an office. My father worked as an ironworker with the union. I remember my mother telling me that my father struggled to advance in his career, not only due to his inability to read well, but also because of his addiction to alcohol. His generational addiction prevented him from excelling in any position, and I now understand how this played a major role in limiting his potential.

Pixel 3 – Testimony: October 2019

I couldn't take it anymore. I had decided that I was going to end my life. I had been clean for a while, but then I relapsed – this time, it was the worst. I went out, bought sleeping pills, and when the children left for school, I took as many as I could. I remember feeling my soul leaving my body, thinking everyone would be better off without me. I believed I was going to hell for sure, because that's what happens when you take your own life. I was living a hellish existence already, drowning in addiction. What was the difference?

BUT IF IT WASN'T FOR GOD…

"MOMMY! MOMMY! MOMMY!!! I'M HOME! WHERE'S MY LUNCH?"

Suddenly, I came back. I began to vomit up the pills. It felt surreal – I can't believe I'm here.

I have to be honest – the beginning of this testimony isn't easy to share. It's often easier to share the victory than the pain, but I have to be obedient to God. I keep hearing in my spirit that someone needs to hear this – that God delivers, defends, preserves, transforms, and makes all things new.

BUT IF IT WASN'T FOR GOD...

I didn't hear it at first, but soon, the fog in my mind began to lift, and I heard His voice so clearly: *"I've got you."*

"My sheep hear My voice, and I know them, and they follow Me." John 10:27 (NKJV)

I knew it was His voice, just like the scripture says. I continued to follow Him, even though the road wasn't always smooth. It was the best road for me. The more I spent time with Him, the more clearly I could hear His voice. I remember waking up at 2 a.m. with downloads of all that He was telling me. At that time, I was attending Emmanuel Community Church in Calgary, and our beloved Pastor often told me that those midnight wake-ups were "night school with Master Jesus."

The messages I received weren't always for me. I had so much zeal that I would text people immediately with the word God gave me for them – often not considering the time! During that season, God spoke to me often, through prayer, visions, and revelations of things to come. Many of those things came to pass.

Pixel 4 – The Faithfulness of God: A Journey of Deliverance and Restoration

From a young age, my life was marked by hardship and darkness. I was born into a world where sexual abuse, neglect, and betrayal were daily realities. These early years were marred by experiences I could never have imagined. And yet, through it all, the hand of God was already at work, preparing me for a future I could not comprehend at the time. Despite the weight of abuse, addiction, and rejection, God had a plan for my life that was far greater than the devastation I had endured.

I remember the pain of those early years – seeing my father and relatives perpetuate the cycle of abuse, feeling helpless and trapped in a world I couldn't escape. By the time I was a teenager, I was lost in a world of drugs, promiscuity, and rebellion. At just fifteen years old, I prostituted myself as a way to cope with the unbearable pain inside. I never imagined that God would intervene in my life, but His grace was greater than all my mistakes.

In the years that followed, I found myself in the depths of addiction, struggling to survive each day. I had two children out of wedlock, and my life seemed like a never-ending cycle of brokenness. My marriage, which began with such hope, deteriorated as I fell back into the grips of addiction. I used drugs to numb the guilt, shame, and condemnation that haunted me. My health, relationships, and sense of self-worth were in ruins. I felt like a failure – a broken person who would never be whole again.

But God had a different plan.

One of the darkest moments of my life came when I reached a point of hopelessness. I had relapsed, and the weight of my failure felt like it was too much to bear. I decided to end my life. I took as many sleeping pills as I could, believing everyone would be better off without me. I felt like I had lived a hell on earth, and the thought of going to hell after death seemed like a fitting end. I could feel my soul leaving my body. But then something extraordinary happened. As I drifted into unconsciousness, I heard the voice of my young daughter:

"MOMMY! MOMMY! MOMMY!!! I'M HOME! WHERE'S MY LUNCH?"

In that instant, God intervened. My soul was pulled back into my body, and I began vomiting up the pills I had taken. I couldn't believe I was still alive. It was in that moment that I understood the depth of God's mercy. If it hadn't been for God's intervention, I wouldn't be here today. His grace and mercy reached me when I had given up on myself.

Soon after, I began to hear God's voice more clearly. He spoke to me, saying, "I've got you." In the midst of my pain and confusion, God was assuring me that He had a plan for my life and that I wasn't beyond His reach. He began to restore my soul, heal my wounds, and transform my heart. I realized that God had been with me all along, even when I couldn't see Him. He was always there, leading me out of darkness and into His marvelous light.

As I pressed into God's presence and learned to hear His voice, my life began to change. The more I sought Him, the more I began to understand my purpose. Through the trials and challenges, God was speaking to me, teaching me, and showing me that He had a greater plan for my life.

One of the most profound moments in my journey of healing came when I had the opportunity to travel to Lagos, Nigeria, to work with Feed the Nations. It was a humbling experience to serve the people of Lagos – to do mission work and provide aid to those in need. God had taken me from the depths of despair to a place where I was able to give back to others. It was a reminder that God is not just in the business of restoring lives but also of using those lives to impact others.

In Lagos, I saw firsthand the poverty, the struggles, and the resilience of the people. It was a powerful reminder of God's provision and faithfulness. Through my work with Feed the Nations, I had the privilege of seeing lives transformed by God's love, and I knew that this was part of the purpose He had for me. It was no longer just about my healing – it was about extending God's healing to others.

A few years later, I was blessed with the opportunity to go to Cape Town, South Africa, for an outreach mission. It was an incredibly emotional experience, as I shared my testimony and the healing I had received through God's grace. I was able to speak life into those who felt hopeless, just as I once had.

God had not only restored my life but had equipped me to help restore others. He delivered me from despair, gave me a new identity, and has been faithful through every trial. I'm no longer defined by my past, but by His love, grace, and purpose.

As I continue my journey of restoration, I'm determined to embrace all He has for me. I know God's work in me is far from finished. There are more lives to touch, more people to heal, and more souls to save. I'm committed to walking in the freedom and restoration He's given me, excited for the future He has in store.

Through it all, God has been faithful – delivering, defending, and restoring me, and I continue pressing into all He has for me.

To God be the glory.

Prophetess Nicole Ragguette - Co-Author

Safe in His Arms
The Goodness of God

Anita Sechesky

CHAPTER THIRTY-ONE

Daily Practices for Embracing Gratitude

Gratitude is more than a fleeting emotion or a polite thank-you. It is a divine rhythm of the heart that transforms how we see God, others, and the world around us. To live with a grateful heart is to cultivate awareness of His goodness in all things: in laughter and in tears, in victory and in trial, in the stillness of morning and the busyness of everyday life. Gratitude trains our spiritual eyes to notice the blessings that weave through each day – some obvious, others hidden beneath the surface of hardship or routine. It becomes the lens through which we recognize that God is constantly at work, even when circumstances seem ordinary or uncertain. This awareness deepens our faith, helping us interpret life through the truth of God's character rather than the tension of our circumstances.

When we wake each morning, we have a sacred opportunity to begin again with gratitude. Before the responsibilities of the day press in, before the notifications, calls, and schedules, take one quiet moment to whisper, *"Thank You, Lord, for another day of grace."* That single breath of thanksgiving resets the heart. It redirects focus from worry to worship, from self-reliance to trust. Gratitude draws our attention away from anxiety and toward abundance. It reminds us that the breath in our lungs, the sunlight breaking through the clouds, and the love of those around us are not random occurrences. They are gifts from a faithful God who sustains us daily. This brief intentional pause creates space for the Holy Spirit to settle our thoughts, align our priorities, and prepare our hearts to walk in His peace.

The apostle Paul wrote, *"In everything give thanks; for this is the will of God in Christ Jesus for you"* (1 Thessalonians 5:18, NKJV). Notice that Paul did not say for everything, but in everything. Gratitude is not denial. It's choosing to recognize God's hand even in difficult places. When we give thanks amid the unknown, we declare that our faith is greater than our fear. We begin to hear the quiet whispers of His presence in the moments others might overlook: the small provisions, the timely encouragement, the unexpected strength that appears just when we need it most. Gratitude awakens spiritual sensitivity. It tunes our hearts to the melody of His goodness. Over time, it becomes a spiritual reflex, a way of living that naturally invites God into every moment, both simple and significant.

Gratitude doesn't always rise from joy; sometimes, it is born from pain. It is in life's valleys that we learn what it truly means to trust God. One of the most painful yet sacred valleys of my life came through the loss of my first child – my beautiful daughter, Jasmine Rose, who was born sleeping. That moment shattered my world. I had prayed, planned, and dreamed of holding her, watching her grow, and sharing in her laughter. Instead, I was left with silence – the kind that echoes through the soul and stretches time into stillness. It was a silence so heavy that it pressed against my chest, making it difficult to breathe, difficult to think, difficult to hope. Yet even in that depth of sorrow, there was an undeniable nearness of God that could not be explained…only felt.

There are moments in life when our faith is tested beyond understanding. As I sat in that hospital room, holding my daughter and whispering goodbye, I felt the presence of God wrap around me like a blanket. It was as though Heaven itself leaned close, whispering to my heart, *"She is with Me."* I had no words, only tears. Yet, within those tears was peace, the kind that surpasses all understanding (Philippians 4:7, NKJV). It was a peace that did not erase the pain but held me through it. A peace that did not answer every question but surrounded every ache.

The pain was immeasurable, but so was the peace that came afterward. It was a peace that could only come from the One who *"heals the brokenhearted and binds up their wounds"* (Psalm 147:3, NKJV). Through the grief, I discovered that gratitude and sorrow can coexist. I thanked God for the precious months I carried her, for the joy she brought even before her first breath, and for the assurance that her spirit was safe in His care. I thanked Him for the way her short life deepened my compassion, strengthened my faith, and opened my heart to see the fragility and beauty of life through a new lens.

In that season of mourning, I learned that gratitude does not erase pain…but redeems it. It doesn't silence grief – it sanctifies it. Gratitude became the bridge between heartbreak and healing. It allowed me to see that even loss can hold beauty when it leads us back to the heart of the Father. Each tear became a prayer, each sigh a surrender, and every moment of pain a deeper revelation of His faithfulness. Gratitude became the quiet companion that walked alongside my grief, gently reminding me that God was still with me, still good, still holding every broken piece.

Gratitude taught me that mourning is not a sign of weakness; it is a sacred process through which love finds expression. Even in the valley, God's goodness remains. As Psalm 34:18 (NIV) reminds us, *"The Lord is close to the brokenhearted and saves those who are crushed in spirit."* My gratitude became a way to keep her memory alive, not through sorrow, but through thanksgiving for the short but meaningful miracle that she was. Her life, though brief, left an eternal imprint on my heart – one that continues to remind me that God's goodness meets us even in places we never expected to walk.

Throughout my life and ministry, I have often been misunderstood because of the kindness of my heart. There were seasons when I poured out love, generosity, and compassion, only to be met with rejection or indifference. I've opened my home, prayed for others through their storms, and given freely – sometimes beyond my own strength – only to realize that not everyone values or understands that kind of love. For years, I wrestled with that pain. I asked God, *"Why does kindness sometimes hurt?"* The ache of feeling unseen, unappreciated, or misjudged can settle into the soul like a weight, making us question whether our efforts mattered or if we were simply giving too much. Kind people often carry silent battles, fighting to remain soft in a world that can be harsh, guarding their hearts without growing cold.

In time, He showed me that kindness and wisdom are partners, not opposites. To love deeply is to risk deeply, but to live guarded is to miss the fullness of God's call. Gratitude helped me reframe every painful encounter. It reminded me that every act of service, whether acknowledged or not, was seen by Him. Gratitude transformed disappointment into discernment and bitterness into blessing. It taught me that obedience to God's prompting is never wasted, even when people don't respond the way we hoped. Gratitude became the balm that soothed the sting of rejection, shifting my perspective from *"Why wasn't I valued?"* to *"Thank You, Lord, that You saw every sacrifice."*

I came to understand that not everyone who enters our lives is meant to stay, and not every relationship is meant to mirror our effort. Some people are assignments, others are teachers, and all of them are opportunities for growth. Gratitude helped me thank God not only for the people who stood by me but also for those who walked away. Both played a role in shaping my faith and maturity. Some relationships revealed my strengths; others exposed areas where God wanted to heal and strengthen me. Even the painful exits were divine pruning moments, clearing space for healthier connections, wiser boundaries, and deeper intimacy with God.

Being misunderstood is part of walking closely with God. Jesus Himself was misunderstood, even by those He loved most. He healed lepers, fed thousands, and raised the dead. And yet, many still doubted Him. John 1:11 (NKJV) tells us, *"He came to His own, and His own did not receive Him."* Still, He loved without restraint. That is the challenge for us – to keep loving, even when love is not reciprocated, and to stay grateful that God knows our motives and sees our hearts. Gratitude keeps our hearts tender, preventing offense from poisoning our spirit.

When the world fails to understand you, remember: Heaven does. Gratitude steadies the heart in those moments. It whispers, *"God sees what others overlook."* It reminds us that every seed sown in faith will produce fruit – maybe not where we planted it, but always in God's time and way. Gratitude anchors us in the truth that we love because He loves, we give because He gave, and we continue because He sees.

One of the most powerful ways to nurture a lifestyle of gratitude is through intentional reflection. For me, that comes in the form of a gratitude journal. Each night, before closing my eyes, I take a few moments to write down three things I'm thankful for: moments of kindness, lessons learned, or simple joys. Some entries are monumental: *"A door opened for the ministry."* Others are simple: *"The sunset was beautiful tonight."* Sometimes my list includes things that initially felt painful but later revealed purpose. Other times, it's something as subtle as a moment of peace in the middle of a busy day.

Over time, these small notes became a written testimony of God's faithfulness. When discouragement comes, I flip through the pages and remember. I see how He provided, how He healed, how He turned uncertainty into opportunity. My gratitude journal became my personal altar, much like the Israelites built stones of remembrance after crossing the Jordan River, saying, *"When your children ask… 'What do these stones mean?'… tell them that the flow of the Jordan was cut off before the ark of the covenant of the Lord"* (Joshua 4:6–7, NIV). Just as those stones reminded future generations of God's power, my journal reminds my own heart that God has never left me.

Gratitude records are spiritual memorials and the evidence that God has never failed us. They remind us that we are carried by grace and anchored by His love. Whether written in a journal, spoken aloud in prayer, or shared during fellowship, gratitude keeps our hearts soft. It transforms memory into worship. It teaches us to pause, reflect, and recognize God's fingerprints all around us.

If you struggle to begin, start small. Each morning or evening, write one sentence beginning with, *"Today, I thank God for..."* Over time, your list will grow, and so will your awareness of His goodness. Gratitude is not about perfection. It's about perception. It's learning to see with Heaven's eyes, welcoming God into the details of each day.

Gratitude finds its purest expression in service. Every act of kindness, whether large or small, becomes an offering to the Lord. When we serve with gratitude, we turn ordinary moments into sacred ones. What may look simple to others like holding a hand, offering encouragement, preparing a meal, or listening without judgment becomes worship when done with a grateful heart. Gratitude shifts the intention behind our actions. It transforms "I have to" into "I'm honored to." It reminds us that every moment of service is an invitation to reflect the heart of Jesus.

I have witnessed moments of both human fragility and divine strength. Sometimes, healing did not come through medicine but through compassion: a listening ear, a gentle word, a prayer whispered beside a hospital bed. I remember nights when the weight of responsibility felt overwhelming, when the cries of patients echoed in my spirit long after my shift ended. Yet in those moments, gratitude lifted me. I would pause, take a deep breath, and silently say, *"Thank You, Lord, for trusting me with this moment."* That simple act reframed every challenge into ministry. Gratitude became the lens through which I could see God working through me, even when I felt tired or inadequate.

Serving others with gratitude shifts the focus from what I must do to what I get to do. It reminds us that the ability to serve is a privilege, not a burden – a calling, not an obligation. Jesus modeled this beautifully when He knelt to wash His disciples' feet. *"If I then, your Lord and Teacher, have washed your feet, you also ought to wash one another's feet"* (John 13:14, NKJV). Gratitude makes service joyful, not draining. It transforms duty into delight. It empowers us to go the extra mile without resentment, because our strength flows from God, not from human applause.

Grateful service extends beyond professional roles. It shows up in how we speak to family members, how we forgive others, and how we steward the small opportunities of each day. When we help a neighbor, volunteer, or offer encouragement, we are participating in the goodness of God flowing through us. *"Whatever you do, do it heartily, as to the Lord and not to men"* (Colossians 3:23, NKJV). Gratitude fuels that heart posture. It shapes the way we show up, the way we give, and the way we love.

When we live and serve this way, gratitude becomes contagious. It multiplies across families, workplaces, and ministries. It turns strangers into allies and communities into sanctuaries of grace. It invites others to serve with joy rather than obligation. And as we give, God replenishes. The more we pour out, the more He fills. Gratitude ensures that the overflow never stops flowing.

Prayer

Heavenly Father,

I lift up the person reading this chapter – the one who may be walking through storms, facing uncertainty, or carrying silent pain. You know every detail of their story, every ache of their heart, and every tear that has fallen unseen. Lord, I pray that Your peace would rest upon them right now. Remind them that even when life feels heavy, You are still good, and Your mercy still endures forever.

For the one grieving a loss, bring comfort. For the one feeling forgotten, remind them they are seen. For the one misunderstood or taken for granted, reassure them that You understand completely. Restore their strength, renew their hope, and fill their spirit with gratitude that transcends circumstance. Let this moment mark a new beginning where they find beauty in broken places and purpose in every trial.

Teach them to notice Your hand in the little things, to give thanks even in waiting, and to trust that You are working all things together for their good (Romans 8:28, NKJV). Surround them with love, with faith-filled people, and with the assurance that You are holding them close – safe in Your arms, where peace and healing abide.

In the precious and powerful name of Jesus Christ, Amen.

Anita Sechesky - Visionary Compiler & Publisher

Safe in His Arms
The Goodness of God

Patricia Giron

Chapter Thirty-Two

The Goodness of God – Patty's Story

"Every pain, every struggle, every confusing moment that once broke me apart was really God's way of drawing me closer to His heart."

When I think about the goodness of God, I can't help but marvel at how He already had everything planned from the beginning. Life has a way of unfolding slowly, piece by piece, like a puzzle we never quite understand until we're standing far enough away to see the full picture. And when I pause, look back, and reflect on the steps I've walked, I realize that God's fingerprints were everywhere; from the moments I celebrated to the seasons I grieved, and even in the times I felt completely lost.

There were days I questioned everything:

"Why this?"

"Why now?"

"Why me, Lord?"

Not out of rebellion, but out of pain and confusion. Yet even in those moments, He was near. Quiet. Patient. Steady. Working behind the scenes in ways I didn't understand.

Sometimes I sit quietly and think about how my life has unfolded – the good, the bad, the tears, and the laughter – and I can see now that none of it was random. God's hand was always there, shaping my story even when I didn't realize it. When I look back, I see a God who orchestrated every step, even when I felt like I was stumbling in the dark.

The Bible says in Jeremiah 1:5 (NKJV), *"Before I formed you in the womb I knew you; before you were born I sanctified you."* That verse hits deep for me. It reminds me that my life has always had purpose, even in times when it felt like everything was falling apart. It reminds me that nothing about my story surprised God. He wasn't shocked by the heartbreaks or intimidated by the battles. He had already mapped out every mountain and every valley, every joy and every sorrow.

There were moments when I felt unseen, moments when I felt forgotten, and moments when I wondered if my prayers were reaching Heaven at all. But now I understand something that took years to grasp: God was never absent. He was never silent. He was simply preparing me – gently, lovingly, and wisely – for what was ahead.

He used disappointment to build resilience and delays to cultivate trust.

He used heartbreak to cleanse places of my heart I didn't even know needed healing.

Lastly, He used loss to anchor me in His love.

Every struggle, every disappointment, every loss that once seemed senseless was really part of a greater plan I couldn't see yet. I realize now that He was protecting me from things I prayed for but wasn't ready to receive. And He was preparing blessings I didn't even know to ask for.

The older I get, the more I understand that God often hides His work until we're ready to appreciate it. Seasons of wilderness – the dry, lonely, confusing times – were really the seasons He strengthened my roots the most. When I thought He was silent, He was actually rebuilding me. When I felt forgotten, He was setting the stage for breakthrough. When I felt abandoned, He was closer than my breath.

God was not delaying my blessing; He was designing me to carry it.

God Redirects Out of Love

When we're young, we make plans. We dream big. We map out our lives based on what makes sense to us at the time. I used to imagine how things would turn out, who I would become, what I would achieve, the family I would build, and the happiness I thought I could control. But then life came with twists I never expected.

I learned slowly, and sometimes painfully, that God's plans rarely match our plans, but they are always better. His "no" was never rejection; it was redirection. It was His protection. It was His mercy in disguise. He saw things I couldn't see and shielded me from situations that would have broken me.

I didn't always understand His timing. There were seasons when my waiting felt unbearable. I watched others receive answers quickly while my prayers seemed to linger unanswered. I wondered why certain doors didn't open for me when they opened for others. But looking back, I realize that God was saving me from unnecessary pain while positioning me for something far more meaningful.

Sometimes His plan looked like a delay. Other times, it looked like disappointment.

And sometimes it even looked like heartbreak.

But in every case, it was love.

I often say that God is the Master Weaver of our lives. We only see the threads – some bright, some dark – intertwined in ways we can't understand. But He sees the entire tapestry, and every thread has purpose.

There were times when a door I expected to open shut so fast it stunned me. Opportunities evaporated. Relationships ended. Plans unraveled. But now I understand that God was removing what would have limited me. He was guiding me away from people and places that were never part of His purpose for my life.

A closed door is not God being cruel; it is Him being protective.

We love to praise God for open doors, but some of the greatest blessings are the doors He refuses to let us walk through. What I once called loss was actually deliverance. What I once called disappointment was divine protection.

God's "not this one" was Him saying, *"Daughter, I have better."*

Waiting teaches us patience, cleanses our motives. It transforms our character and exposes our true beliefs. And waiting reveals whether we trust the promise…or the God who made it.

Unexpected Blessings Wrapped in Hard Seasons

One of the greatest revelations in my walk with God is that some of the most beautiful blessings come wrapped in painful seasons. I used to think blessings arrived gently, but now I know many come through breaking, stretching, and surrender.

If I'm honest, many blessings I cherish today were born in places I once cried over. God truly uses pain to birth purpose.

There were seasons when I wondered, "God, why this?" I didn't know that those very moments were preparing me for future strength.

God never wastes anything – not a tear, not a heartbreak, not a silence, not a delay.

Some blessings are loud: breakthroughs, opportunities, answered prayers.

Others are quiet: wisdom, healing, resilience, peace.

But all are God's goodness.

Hard seasons don't just change our circumstances…they change us. They transform our capacity to trust God, to forgive, to endure, and to love.

A closed door positioned me for unexpected favor.

A heartbreak deepened my sensitivity to God's voice.

A wilderness season led me into deeper intimacy with Him.

These were blessings I didn't pray for, but blessings I desperately needed.

Blessings aren't always about what God gives. Sometimes the real blessing is who we become while trusting Him.

One of the most beautiful parts of my story is the miracle of my daughters. Becoming a mother was the deepest desire of my heart. But the journey to motherhood was not easy. It was filled with waiting, tears, hope, disappointment, and prayer.

I carried a longing only God fully understood. I watched others receive what I prayed for. I whispered prayers that only Heaven heard. And then came the long seasons of waiting, which is one of the hardest places to be. It tests faith, exposes fear, and teaches surrender. Some nights I cried, not from unbelief but from the weight of hope deferred.

But every tear was watering a seed God had planted long before.

Every whispered prayer was shaping my future.

Every moment of surrender was strengthening my faith.

When my daughters finally came, they weren't just blessings. They were promises fulfilled. Their arrival reminded me that God wasn't ignoring my prayers. He was aligning everything perfectly. God wasn't delaying the miracle. He was preparing my heart to receive it.

Some blessings are worth the wait because the waiting builds the character needed to hold them.

My journey taught me that:

God is never late.

God is never early.

God is always perfectly on time.

He answers at the moment that brings the most glory to Him and the most growth to us.

A Mother's Blessing & Prayer

Heavenly Father,

Thank You for every precious reader who has found their way to these words. I pray that as they read my story, they will see Your goodness written between every line. Touch their hearts the way You touched mine. Remind them that no tear is wasted, no prayer unheard, and no season forgotten.

To the woman waiting for her miracle – wrap her in Your peace.

To the man who feels lost – shine Your light on his path.

To the person who feels forgotten – whisper Your love into their heart.

Just as You blessed me with daughters after years of prayer, I ask that You open new doors for every person believing for their breakthrough. Breathe life into barren places. Bring peace where there is confusion, joy where there is sorrow, and strength where there is weariness.

Surround every reader with Your presence, Your love, and Your perfect timing.

You are faithful and good.
You are always right on time.
In Jesus' mighty name, Amen.

Patricia Giron - Co-Author

Safe in His Arms
The Goodness of God

Nasha T. Alexis

Chapter Thirty-Three

A Seed of Hope

"For I know the plans I have for you," declares the Lord, "plans to prosper you and not to harm you, plans to give you hope and a future." Jeremiah 29:11 (NIV)

God's plan and purpose for your life will never change. His plans for you and me are pure and good. It may take some of us time to get on the right track, but rest assured, God is pursuing you and will find you. He alone can take what seems unusable and make it useful.

Looking back, I can see there were times when I didn't want to make it, and I'd given up all hope. I was ready to end everything. My life and mind were in shambles, and I was tired of being tired. I suffered in silence and isolation, which the enemy loved. My mind was his playground. I had thoughts about dying and ways to accomplish it.

There were days and nights when I played the "What If" game in my head. It all stemmed from negative words spoken over me during a difficult season of my life. They were those stinging, hurtful words like, *"You're nothing and will never amount to anything,"* or *"How stupid can you be?"*

There were questions and hateful declarations like that – and so much more. From a young age, I always felt invisible and unwanted. Hearing words like that later in my teenage years only solidified what I had already believed to be true: nobody wanted me, loved me, or even cared about me.

Then, in one moment of weakness, I thought, *"What if I died right now?"*

It sounded like a good idea at the time. I figured everyone would be happy, wouldn't have to put up with me anymore, and their lives would be better without me. Those thoughts plagued my mind so often that some nights I would lie in bed as still as possible, holding my breath – just imagining myself dying.

Now, I understand that I was not struggling against flesh and blood, but, as the Word says, *"...against the rulers, against the authorities, against the powers of this dark world and against the spiritual forces of evil in the heavenly realms"* Ephesians 6:12 (NIV). The enemy was able to get into my mind and make me feel worthless and abandoned – not only by people but by God, too.

But now I understand why the Apostle Paul, earlier in Ephesians 6:10–11 (NIV), gives us the means to defend and protect ourselves from such attacks from Satan. Those verses read, *"Finally, be strong in the Lord and in His mighty power. Put on the full armor of God, so that you can take your stand against the devil's schemes."*

We must understand that the devil is always scheming – plotting ways to destroy us. He is not your friend, and his only goal is to harm you and watch you suffer.

Sad to say, so many have lost that battle. I, too, have come closer than I want to admit to losing.

But God.

Time Went On, And So Did Life

Later, having my first child, ten days before I turned twenty-four, was the first seed of hope I held on to when those dark days and thoughts would come. Even then, there were moments when I believed I'd be doing her a favor if I weren't around – afraid I might somehow ruin her life. I felt completely unfit to care for another human being when I could barely take care of myself. It seemed she would be better off with someone else as her mother.

It was a constant internal struggle. To compensate for that guilt, I gave her anything she wanted, as long as I had the money. But I had one rule: never embarrass me or create a scene in public if I said no to something. I would gently remind her, *"You'll get it, just not today."* She was very good and obedient, except for one occasion when she tried, but it didn't go well for her. After that, she never tried again.

Life moved on with highs and many lows, and some of those dark days were very dark. I eventually came to accept it as just "how life was" and settled into that existence. It felt oddly comfortable, familiar, and I had learned how to function in it. In hindsight, I wasn't truly living. If you could call it living, it was on autopilot. I knew what was expected of me, at home and at work, and I did it without giving much thought.

But He said to me, *"My grace is sufficient for you, for my power is made perfect in weakness"* 2 Corinthians 12:9 (NIV).

Then in 2005, I was blessed again with another child – a baby girl. It was a difficult pregnancy, to say the least. By that time, I had been married for five years. That relationship had not been good from the beginning, but I was determined to make it work by any means necessary, even if it meant sacrificing my mental health. At one point, things were so bad that I said, *"I feel like jumping off the building just to get away from you,"* and the cold response I got was, *"Who's stopping you?"* I remembered that I froze in my steps, and thought someone else, besides me, who thought it would be better if I were dead. As I lay in bed that night, I thought, *"Wow, another person to add to the list of people who don't care."* I was used to that, so I just let it slide.

So, as I said, I was blessed with another child that year – my second seed of hope. Despite all the struggles I experienced emotionally, physically, and socially during that pregnancy, I know that God was with me. I can see it clearly now. The previous year, 2004, God had placed me in a church community that He knew I would need – a group of people who would care for me like family. People from that church called and prayed with me over the phone, and they prayed for me and my family at prayer meetings. Some brought food and monetary gifts, while others drove me and my mother to and from appointments. Some kind gentlemen would take us to church and back home, even when I would be throwing up in their vehicles. Who would do that? Again – but God. In His providence and sovereignty, He knew what I would need long before I knew it myself. He had an army to help me, which became an extension of His hands.

Because it was a difficult pregnancy, I spent many long, lonely nights in the hospital with only my thoughts to keep me company. And as they say, old habits die hard. You guessed it…the "what ifs" started again. This time, the emotional weight was heavier, with pregnancy hormones and the realization that the beginning of the end of my marriage had started to unfold. I even began thinking my first child would be better off living with other family members.

There was one night I remember vividly. Like the Apostle Paul, who pleaded with God to take away the thorn in his flesh (2 Corinthians 12:7b, NIV), my plea was for death. But when I would wake up the next morning, I was angry with God, so much so that I didn't even want to acknowledge Him. I was filled with rage, hurt, and deep disappointment, feeling like He had abandoned me again.

Sometime later, still angry and with nothing else to do, I finally opened the drawer next to my hospital bed and found a Bible. As I flipped through and skimmed the pages, I landed in 2 Corinthians 12. After reading verse 9, *"But he said to me, 'My grace is sufficient for you, for my power is made perfect in weakness'"* (2 Corinthians 12:9 NIV), all I could do was cry. I just kept whispering over and over, *"I'm sorry. I'm sorry."*

I don't know how long I stayed like that because the next thing I knew, a nurse was waking me up, telling me that I had to eat my dinner. That was the best sleep I had during that entire pregnancy.

The rest of the pregnancy remained difficult, and there were moments when I would lapse back into dark thoughts. I had to intentionally force myself to think of my two girls – two beautiful lives who needed their mother. I had to fight. If not for myself, then for them.

I am so grateful, eternally thankful, that God didn't listen to my desperate pleas or my begging. And you know what? The most amazing thing about that pregnancy was that the doctors never expressed any concern about the health of my baby. With every check-up, they assured me she was fine. Her heartbeat was strong, and she was growing well. In fact, I think that puzzled them the most. They had never dealt with a pregnancy like mine before – emotionally and physically complicated – yet the baby was thriving.

In the end, I gave birth to a healthy baby girl who weighed over eight pounds.

Despite living with all the shame and guilt of considering suicide as my way out of the painful situation, God's plan and purpose for my life never changed. In all my pain and anguish, He stepped in at the right time and gave me hope when I needed it most. At times, because of the choices we make, we are detoured from the plans God has for us. Other times, it's situations beyond our control that set us back. But we must remember that even during those seasons, God is never late; He is always on time. His plans for you will never fail.

There comes a time when we must surrender and allow Him to do the good He has already planned for us, to accomplish His purpose through us. In Numbers 23:19 (NIV), we are told, *"God is not human, that he should lie, not a human being, that he should change his mind. Does he speak and then not act? Does he promise and not fulfill?"* We can take God at His word, for He also tells us in Isaiah 55:11 (NIV), *"So is my word that goes out from my mouth: It will not return to me empty, but will accomplish what I desire and achieve the purpose for which I sent it."*

This is the hope that we have in God: we were created with a purpose in mind. We only need to be obedient, open, and ready to step into His plan.

"Be alert and of sober mind. Your enemy the devil prowls around like a roaring lion looking for someone to devour." 1 Peter 5:8 (NIV)

God didn't wait for me to clean up my life or my mind first, as some people are led to believe – and as I thought I had to – before working in my life. He called me at a time when I thought I was "not good for anything." In His grace and mercy, He took something that I was already passionate about, something I love to do, and met me there.

Side note: The devil and his minions are out there in the world looking to destroy you. They're not in hell having parties; they are out there roaming the earth, looking to devour you (1 Peter 5:8, NIV). Think of a lion lying in wait, stalking its prey before attacking and killing it. That is the devil, and that's what he attempted to do with me. He used every negative, hate-filled word spoken to me in anger and frustration by others to stop me from fulfilling the plans of God. He used the people closest to me to try to derail me from the purposes of God. He only caused me to go on a detour for a while, but God never gave up on me.

When I least expected anything good to happen through me, God used my love of music and dancing and turned it into a ministry for His purpose and glory. The first time I was asked to participate in dance worship at church, I was apprehensive, but I did it anyway. I was so scared that I barely moved from the spot where I was placed. I just waved the flags as instructed. There were a few times when

I wanted to move, but thought I would embarrass myself if I fell because I had never danced with flags before.

After the service, I was told to come prepared to do it again the following Sunday. I was surprised, but I agreed. The following Sunday, I showed up dressed in white, ready to dance again. I took my same position at the front, faced the congregation, and held tightly to my flags. As the music started and with my stomach in knots, I started to sway to the music, waving my flags as I had the previous Sunday. Then I closed my eyes and imagined myself being carried on the feet of Jesus, like a little child dancing with their feet on top of their father's.

When the worship portion came to an end and I finally opened my eyes again, I found myself on the other side of the sanctuary. I don't remember traveling across the room, but there I was. Most people who know me know that I love to dance, but that wasn't just dancing. It was something different, and I liked it. Without knowing or realizing it at the time, a seed of hope was planted in me.

I reluctantly said yes one day, and God used it as a launching pad for new words to be spoken over me. They were good, kind, encouraging, and healthy words – different from what I knew before. Even now, when the enemy tries to remind me of those negative words, I know they're not true. In worship, I find peace, love, joy, and freedom.

We can come to God anytime, with anything, and give it all to Him. Ask Him to take it – whatever the "it" is – away. In 1 Peter 5:7 (NIV), we are told, *"Cast all your anxiety on him because he cares for you."* Ask Him *"to transform you by the renewing of your mind. Then you will be able to test and approve what God's will is – his good, pleasing and perfect will"* (Romans 12:2 NIV), because after all, His plans *"are good, pleasing and perfect."* Again, *"plans to give you a hope and a future"* (Jeremiah 29:11 NIV).

Finally, at a time when I was suffering in silence and isolation and thought that death was my only way out to end the pain and shame, God stepped in.

He did it for me, and He can and will do it for you.

You only need to ask Jesus Christ.

Nasha T. Alexis - Co-Author

Safe in His Arms
The Goodness of God

Samantha Mills-O'Brien

Chapter Thirty-Four

Redeemed by Grace – The Goodness of God in My Story

"Great is His faithfulness; His mercies begin afresh each morning. I say to myself, 'The Lord is my inheritance; therefore, I will hope in Him!' The Lord is good to those who depend on Him, to those who search for Him." Lamentations 3:23–25 (NLT)

From the moment I gave my heart to Jesus Christ at the tender age of twelve, something within me changed forever. It was as though a quiet light had been turned on inside my soul – a light that could never be extinguished, no matter how dark life would later become. At seventeen, I experienced the infilling of the Holy Spirit alone in my room. I remember the stillness, the peace, and then the overwhelming warmth of God's presence flooding my heart. In that moment, I knew my life would be no ordinary life. I sensed a calling – a divine assignment to live for His glory, even though I could not yet see the path before me.

Over the years, I have experienced the goodness of God in more ways than I can count. His protection has preserved my life and the lives of my family members time and time again. Though there have been moments of danger, hardship, and disobedience, I can look back now and see His hand gently guiding me, even when I didn't deserve it.

The first time I remember God's miraculous protection, I was only seven years old. My family (my parents, my siblings, and I) had been out running errands together. It was an ordinary day, one of those simple outings that fill childhood memories. But in an instant, the ordinary became extraordinary.

As we approached a busy intersection, another vehicle suddenly collided with ours from the right side. The impact sent our car spinning wildly into a 360-degree spiral. I still remember the sound of screeching tires, the smell of burning rubber, and the terrified cries filling the car as everything around us blurred. We had no control; everything seemed to move in slow motion. I didn't know if we would stop, if we would survive, or what would happen next. But then, miraculously, the car came to a stop in the middle of the road, inches away from another oncoming vehicle. We were shaken, trembling, and in shock, but not a single person was injured. Not even a scratch.

That moment marked me deeply. Even at seven years old, I knew it wasn't luck – it was God. He had placed His mighty hand upon us. I remember my mother whispering, "Thank You, Jesus," through her tears, and my father gripping the steering wheel in stunned silence. God had truly covered us under His wings, just as Psalm 91 declares: *"He shall cover you with His feathers, and under His wings you shall take refuge."* That day, I learned firsthand what divine protection feels like. It's a holy shield of love that defies logic, a reminder that His angels encamp around those who trust Him. I have never forgotten His mercy, and that memory continues to anchor my faith even decades later.

Years later, when I was in my twenties, I found myself once again under His divine protection. I had been working, serving faithfully in a local church in London, Ontario, and exploring new career paths. I had just entered the financial industry, earning my license to sell life insurance and attending training programs to advance my career. Life was busy and full of possibilities.

In early 2018, I had the opportunity to attend a large conference in another city. Everyone in my company talked about how transformative these events were; how they inspired, motivated, and connected people across the industry. I was thrilled. But a few days before the trip, my pastor, who had a strong gift of discernment, warned me not to go. He said the Holy Spirit had impressed upon his heart that I should stay home. I remember his words clearly: *"The weather will not be safe. The Lord is telling me to tell you to stay."*

Even as he spoke, I felt that familiar nudge of the Holy Spirit within me, confirming the same warning. But I ignored both. My excitement clouded my obedience. I reasoned with myself, thinking, *"It's just a little winter snow. It's nothing to worry about."* The forecast mentioned freezing rain, but I didn't take it seriously. I was determined to go.

The morning of the trip, our group of agents set out in several vehicles. The roads looked manageable at first, and we were confident that the city had salted them overnight. But about an hour into our journey, the truth became clear. The roads were slick, deceptive, and coated with patches of invisible black ice. We didn't see it until it was too late.

The vehicle in front of us began to slide uncontrollably, veering off the road. As we slowed to help, our own car hit the same black ice and slammed into theirs. Within moments, other vehicles behind us tried to stop and help, only to lose control as well. Six cars collided on that icy highway in what could have been a devastating tragedy.

When our car came to rest, I sat frozen, unable to move. My heart pounded as I looked around at the chaos, expecting to see blood, broken glass, or worse. But miraculously, everyone was safe. Not one person suffered a serious injury. The police later said that given the conditions, it was a miracle no one was killed.

In that moment, I broke down in tears. I knew that even in my disobedience, God's mercy had covered me. He had spared my life once again. My pastor must have been praying fervently for me. That experience taught me a painful but necessary lesson: obedience to the Holy Spirit's voice is not optional. It is life-preserving.

After that season, my faith wavered. I continued serving in ministry, particularly with children and youth, finding joy in teaching them scripture through stories, songs, and creative lessons. Watching young hearts fall in love with Jesus was one of my greatest rewards. But beneath the surface, I was struggling financially and emotionally.

My work in ministry was voluntary, and though fulfilling, it didn't cover my living expenses. I juggled multiple jobs, trying to make ends meet. Slowly, the pressures of daily life began to weigh me down. Instead of depending on God, I leaned on my own understanding. Bills piled up, debts grew, and my spiritual life weakened. I stopped praying as often and began prioritizing survival over service. Each month felt like a race against time, trying to stay afloat while keeping a smile on my face for those I ministered to.

Without realizing it, I drifted from the close relationship I once had with the Lord. I stopped being accountable to my pastor and allowed distractions to take root. My heart became divided – partly devoted to God, but mostly consumed by my own ambitions and desires. I sought companionship, validation, and comfort outside of His will. The enemy used loneliness to lure me into disobedience.

The truth is, sin never shows up in full form. It creeps in gradually, wearing the mask of justification. For me, it began with emotional compromise of making excuses, lowering boundaries, and ignoring conviction. I told myself I deserved happiness, that I needed to take control of my life. But soon, compromise turned into bondage. I found myself caught in cycles of impurity, dishonesty, and guilt. I knew what I was doing was wrong, yet I couldn't seem to stop. I was living a double life: ministering on Sunday, but struggling with temptation through the week, torn between conviction and the comfort of my own desires.

There were nights I would cry silently, knowing I had disappointed God. I missed His voice, the peace that once filled my room during prayer, and the closeness that had defined my early years of faith. But shame built walls between me and the One who longed to restore me. My outward ministry remained intact, but inwardly, I was breaking.

When I got married, I hoped marriage would fix everything – my loneliness would disappear, that love would heal my brokenness. But instead, my hidden struggles followed me. My husband often traveled for work, leaving me home with our two young children. I felt abandoned, isolated, and emotionally drained. I allowed bitterness, resentment, and self-pity to take root in my heart.

Sin thrives in secrecy. The loneliness I refused to surrender to God became an open door for compromise. My habits of impurity continued in private. Shame and guilt consumed me, yet I justified my actions as "normal." People I confided in – even those in the church – told me not to worry, that everyone had flaws and weaknesses. But deep down, I knew better. The Holy Spirit grieved within me.

Years passed in that quiet inner war. My once vibrant faith had become dry and mechanical. I would attend church, smile, and serve, yet feel completely disconnected from God. I no longer sensed His presence or heard His still, small voice. I was spiritually numb. But even in that desert, God's goodness never let me go.

One evening, after another argument with my husband, I sat alone in the dark, feeling unworthy and ashamed. I thought about the promise I had made to God at seventeen. My body and life would belong to Him alone. Tears filled my eyes as I realized how far I had drifted from that vow. I whispered, *"Lord, I don't even know where to begin. I'm so tired of pretending."*

In that moment of surrender, the Holy Spirit began to remind me of God's Word. It wasn't condemnation, but love calling me home. He reminded me of Galatians 2:20: *"I have been crucified with Christ; it is no longer I who live, but Christ who lives in me."* That verse broke something deep within me. I realized that I didn't have to keep living in defeat. Jesus had already paid for my sins. His grace was not an excuse to continue sinning. It was the power to overcome sin.

Over the next several months, I committed to a process of repentance and renewal. I sought accountability, poured myself back into prayer, and filled my heart with worship instead of shame. I began journaling my prayers, confessing openly before God, and reading scripture daily. Slowly, healing began to take root. The addiction that had once chained me lost its grip. My thoughts became clearer, my desires began to change, and I started to feel the presence of the Holy Spirit again.

It wasn't easy. There were relapses, tears, and moments when I questioned whether I could truly be free. Some days I woke up heavy, burdened by guilt, but I chose to worship through the pain. Other days, I felt the warmth of God's presence wash over me like sunlight after a long storm. Through it all, I discovered that grace isn't a moment. It's a journey. God's faithfulness never failed. He reminded me daily that His mercy is new every morning. It's not just for the righteous, but for the repentant. And each day, I felt Him restoring what the enemy had stolen, piece by piece, breath by breath, until joy began to live in me again.

As I looked at my life, I realized that some of my struggles weren't just personal. They were generational. Many in my family had faced similar cycles of compromise and heartbreak. Patterns of premarital pregnancies, broken relationships, and unhealed wounds had traveled down our family line like an uninvited inheritance. But I knew that with God, the curse could end with me.

I began to pray intentionally over my children, declaring that they would walk in purity, righteousness, and favor. I spoke life over my marriage, even when I didn't feel it. I asked God to teach me how to truly love my husband, not from a place of selfish need, but from a place of grace. Gradually, peace entered our home. Forgiveness replaced resentment. Where there was once bitterness, there was now healing.

Each morning, I anointed our home with oil and prayed over every doorway, declaring it as a place of unity and blessing. I broke soul ties from my past and renounced every generational stronghold that had once held my family captive. God began to reveal hidden wounds and showed me how to walk in spiritual authority. Slowly, joy returned to our conversations, laughter filled the rooms again, and the love we had once lost began to flourish under the covering of God's grace. The more I prayed, the stronger the atmosphere of peace became. It transformed our home into a sanctuary of love, faith, and restoration.

Today, I can say with confidence that the goodness of God has covered every chapter of my story – the joyful ones and the painful ones alike. I am not proud of my past, but I am deeply thankful for His mercy that never let me go. I have seen firsthand that even when we fall, God's grace is greater still. His goodness doesn't depend on our perfection; it flows from His unchanging character.

He is faithful to restore what is broken, to renew what has been lost, and to breathe life into the dry bones of our spirit. Like Ezekiel's vision, when God told the prophet to prophesy to the lifeless bones, the Lord spoke to me: *"Breathe again. Live again. Hope again."*

No matter how far we fall, the arms of Jesus are wide enough to catch us. When I reflect on the accidents I survived, the warnings I ignored, and the sins I fell into, I see a common thread: grace. It was God's goodness that kept me alive, His love that called me back, and His mercy that gave me a new beginning. Each scar I carry is now a testimony, a reminder that His purpose always prevails, and that even in my weakest moments, His strength was made perfect in me.

Prayer

Heavenly Father,

Thank You for Your mercy that never fails. Thank You for every moment You saved me from destruction, even when I didn't deserve it. Lord, I lift up every reader of this testimony who feel broken, distant, or unworthy of Your love. Breathe new life into their hearts. Let them feel Your goodness wrap around them like a warm embrace. Remind them that Your grace still covers them and that You are not done writing their story. Restore their faith, renew their strength, and remind them that every valley leads to a mountaintop of victory. Surround them with peace, fill them with hope, and pour out Your everlasting love upon them.

In the mighty and matchless name of Jesus Christ, Amen.

Samantha Mills-O'Brien - Co-Author

Safe in His Arms
The Goodness of God

Sharon Teklu

Chapter Thirty-Five

God's Goodness Found Me When I Let Go

I have been on a journey of walking with God for quite some time – a journey I cherish deeply. It is this journey that gives me life and continues to help me discover who I am and whose I am.

This writing takes place during the autumn season. As the leaves change and fall, I'm reminded that God's goodness is present in every season of change. Just as autumn prepares the earth for renewal, this season in my life reminds me to release what is past, trust His timing, and rest in the beauty of His constant faithfulness.

In this period of my life, I see God's goodness woven through every detail – sometimes boldly, sometimes quietly, but always faithfully. His presence feels like a steady anchor when everything around me shifts. Even when I don't have all the answers, I can sense His hand guiding me, reassuring me that I am never walking alone.

I have come to recognize His goodness not only in the major victories, but also in the small, gentle moments – the peace that calms my heart after a prayer, the unexpected encouragement that arrives just when I need it, the strength that rises in me when I thought I had none left. These are all reminders that He sees me, knows me, and cares deeply for me.

Looking back, I can now see how He used every detour to shape me, to draw me closer, and to help me trust Him more completely.

When I Couldn't See His Goodness

When I couldn't see God's goodness in my challenges, it felt like walking through a fog so thick that even familiar paths seemed unknown.

I remember a time when I was working as a registered nurse in a hospital, pulling twelve-hour shifts, both nights and days, on a rotating schedule, with only two days off between. It was constant, day in and day out. I felt utterly exhausted, spending my days off sleeping and then returning to work again. Life had become a cycle of work and rest, but there was no life beyond work. Emotionally, I started feeling irritable and discontent. Without realizing it, I began to carry the weight of my burdens, hoping for a career change or better working hours. On the outside, I appeared to be coping, but on the inside, I was dissatisfied. I would tell myself I was fine, that I just needed to think more positively. But no amount of self-talk could quiet the dissatisfaction that came from feeling spiritually disconnected.

During a financially challenging time in college, when part-time work and student loans still didn't meet all my needs, I found myself desperately searching for signs of divine care. All I could see were unmet needs. I told myself to keep pushing and keep finding solutions, but beneath all the effort was a deep ache – a quiet sense that I was missing something greater.

When faith feels distant, even the simplest things become heavy. It's as if the weight of every decision, every bill, and every moment of uncertainty presses down harder. I would wake up each morning and feel worry waiting for me like an unwanted companion. I was tired of waiting for evidence of His goodness when life felt like a storm with no break in the clouds. Trying to handle it all on my own seemed like the only option. I told myself I had to be practical, responsible, and composed. Faith began to feel like a luxury I couldn't afford. So,

I busied myself with planning, calculating, and fixing anything that gave me a sense of control. Yet, the more I tried to manage things, the more out of control I felt.

I couldn't sense God's presence. The still, quiet voice I once knew felt muted by the noise of my own worry. There's a particular kind of loneliness that comes when faith feels far away. It's not just being alone in a room; it's feeling unseen by the One who knows you best. Confusion sets in: Why did His goodness seem so visible in others' lives but invisible in mine?

In those seasons, even gratitude felt forced. I knew I should be thankful, but the words caught in my throat. I would write down things I was grateful for in a journal, trying to convince my heart to see the light. It wasn't that God's goodness was gone. It was that my worry had clouded my vision. Yet, at the time, I couldn't see that. I mistook the silence for absence, when, in truth, it was often the space where God waited for me to surrender.

Emotionally, I longed for God but resisted reaching out to Him. I retreated into silence. That silence, however, became heavy. Deep down, I think I knew that my challenge wasn't just financial or emotional, it was spiritual. It was the ache of a heart that needed to be reminded of love when circumstances whispered otherwise.

Looking back now, I can see how much trouble came from trying to navigate those seasons without surrender. But at the time, all I could feel was frustration. Every failed plan chipped away at my confidence. Every delay made me question whether goodness still existed for me. When I could not see His goodness, I mistook the silence for absence.

Yet what I know now is that God's goodness is not always loud. It is often quiet, steady, and hidden beneath the surface of challenge. The emotional toll of living without that awareness is profound. It drains joy, dulls hope, and leaves the heart restless.

In those moments, I discovered how fragile self-sufficiency really is. It is exhausting to play the role of savior in your own story. Until I stopped trying to hold everything together, I couldn't see that His goodness had never left. It had simply been clouded by my struggle to let go.

In those challenging moments of my life, the weight of unseen promises pressed so heavily. It was a season when God's goodness seemed like a story told to others, but not a reality I could touch. That turning point came in the quiet stillness of a night filled with reflection.

I had done everything I knew to do – worked harder, prayed for hope – but nothing seemed to change. I had spent so much time trying to fix things, trying to be strong, trying to make sense of what God was doing. Yet, the more I tried to control, the heavier everything became. My heart felt distant from God, and I reached the point of exhaustion.

I remember sitting in the dark, the silence louder than my thoughts, and whispering, *"God, I cannot do this anymore, but I know You can."* It wasn't a prayer of eloquence or great faith. It was a prayer of surrender.

Surrender, for me, wasn't about giving up. It was about finally letting go of what was never mine to carry alone. It was the kind of surrender that comes when your strength has run out and you have no words left. I admitted that I did not understand His ways. I confessed that I could not see His goodness in the challenge and that I needed Him. That honesty broke something open inside me.

That was the moment surrender became real. It wasn't dramatic or loud – it was quiet. I stopped fighting against what I didn't understand and started trusting that even these challenges were not wasted in His hands. I told Him He could have it all: the worry, the fear, and even the part of me that still doubted.

The Scripture that came to my mind was: *"Casting all your care upon Him, for He cares for you"* 1 Peter 5:7 (NKJV)

In that surrender, peace found me. Not because everything changed, but because I did. My heart softened in the letting go. I began to see that surrender isn't weakness; it's trust in motion. It is the sacred exchange of control for comfort, of striving for stillness. And somehow, in the dark, I began to feel His light again – gentle, steady, enough.

When Goodness Broke Through

When I finally surrendered the two challenges that I was facing – the first being the exhaustion from shift work, and the second, financial hardship while in college. I thought I was letting go into silence. I didn't expect an answer. I had come to the end of myself, weary, whispering prayers that felt like they dissolved into the night.

But in that quiet surrender, something unseen shifted. I didn't know it then, but God was already moving. His goodness was preparing to break through, not with a loud announcement, but with quiet, undeniable grace.

In the mornings that followed, life looked the same. Nothing instantly changed. The struggle with shift work was still real, and the uncertainty of my financial situation still weighed heavily. But my heart was softer. In both cases, I no longer felt the need to fix everything. I simply whispered, *"God, I trust You in these situations."*

I began meditating on this verse day and night: *"Trust in the Lord with all your heart and lean not on your own understanding; in all your ways submit to Him, and He will make your paths straight"* Proverbs 3:5-6 (NIV).

Then the unexpected happened. The institution where I worked as a registered nurse was going through management changes, and they decided to lay off nurses. I was let go from my nursing duties. The saying *"sometimes things get worse before they get better"* proved true in my case.

Within a few days, I started working for an insurance company, and I was excited. It was a daytime job, which meant no more shift work, and I was pleased with that. I got what I wanted, except that it was only part-time.

Shortly after starting that job, I visited a client's home. She happened to be a nurse who worked for the government in a Monday-to-Friday position with better benefits. As we talked, I told her I was also a registered nurse. She mentioned that her department was hiring and encouraged me to apply. That was the beginning of the kind of employment my heart had been aching for.

I didn't waste any time. I applied immediately and was accepted for a full-time, office-based nursing position. It was exactly what I had asked for in the dark: to know that God still saw me. It felt as though God had reached through the silence and touched my heart gently, reminding me, *"You were never unseen."*

The twists and turns that brought me there were all worth it. A door I hadn't even knocked on had opened. An opportunity came that met a need I had laid before Him with trembling faith. It wasn't something I orchestrated. It was clearly His doing. Everything about it felt divinely timed, as if God had been arranging it long before I surrendered. That moment taught me something powerful: His answers don't come when I control. They come when I release.

God also came through in my second challenge: financial hardship while in college. A friend approached me and said a nurse was looking to rent out a room and board, and she offered to introduce me if I was interested. This opportunity turned out to be far more affordable than having my own apartment – and it included meals.

This reminded me that God's response wasn't just in the blessing. It was in the transformation that began inside me. I started to feel lighter, not because my circumstances changed, but because I stopped carrying what was not mine. My prayers became different – less about asking for escape and more about asking for endurance and awareness of His hand at work.

God's goodness broke through in ways I could never have planned: a divine connection, an answered prayer, a new strength that didn't depend on circumstances. But the most beautiful part? Realizing that He had been there all along – working quietly, faithfully – waiting for me to let go so He could step in.

Living in the Light of His Goodness

The light of God's goodness has changed everything for me. It didn't happen overnight, but came through seasons of questioning, waiting, and learning to trust when I couldn't see what He was doing. But as I began to see His hand in places I once thought were failures, my whole perspective shifted. I started to realize that God's goodness is not something that comes and goes with circumstances. It is who He is.

Spiritually, I have grown in ways I never expected. My prayer life is no longer only about asking God to fix things, but about being still with Him, listening and trusting that He knows best. I have learned that His silence does not mean His absence. Prayer has become my security, my conversation of peace and gratitude. My faith feels more alive because I've seen His goodness show up in ways I didn't deserve and in moments I didn't expect.

Trusting in His goodness has taught me surrender – not as giving up, but as giving over. Letting go of my plans to embrace His has brought so much peace. I've seen that His ways, though sometimes mysterious, always lead to something greater. When I stopped trying to control every outcome, I started to experience real freedom – the kind that lifts the weight off your shoulders and lets your soul breathe again.

Walking with God now feels lighter, more joyful, and more bold. I am no longer afraid to dream, to hope, or to step into the unknown because I know His goodness is already there waiting for me. It is a life no longer driven by fear but guided by faith. Each day feels like an invitation to trust Him a little more, to live with gratitude, and to reflect His goodness in the way I love and walk through life.

Living in His light hasn't made everything easy, but it has made everything beautiful, meaningful, and free.

Final Words to the Reader

I want to remind you that God's goodness is not just a story from Scripture. It is alive and active in your life right now, even in the moments when you cannot see it. His goodness is working behind the scenes, bringing purpose out of your challenges and beauty out of your waiting. I have seen His faithfulness turn what I once thought was lost into something redeemed, and I know He can do the same for you.

Trust that His heart toward you is always kind, always loving, always intentional. Do not let fear or disappointment make you doubt the goodness that has never left you.

Be reminded and meditate on this scripture: *"I remain confident of this: I will see the goodness of the Lord in the land of the living"* Psalm 27:13 (NIV).

And declare, *"I believe in the unshakable goodness of God, and I trust that His plans for me are full of hope, joy, and victory."*

Prayer

Thank You, Lord, for opening my eyes to see Your goodness in every season. Let my heart rest in Your faithfulness and let my life shine with unending trust in You.

Amen.

Sharon Teklu - Co-Author

Safe in His Arms
The Goodness of God

Anita Sechesky

Chapter Thirty-Six

The Transformative Power of Gratitude

Gratitude is one of the most powerful spiritual forces in the life of a believer. It has the ability to shift atmospheres, soften hardened hearts, and open our eyes to see the hand of God even in places where pain once blinded us. When we learn to live with a thankful spirit, we begin to interpret life differently. Not through the lens of lack or disappointment, but through the lens of divine purpose. Thankfulness does not mean denying pain or pretending that everything is perfect. Instead, it is a conscious decision to focus on God's faithfulness rather than our frustration. Gratitude reframes our reality, transforming the mundane into the miraculous. It trains us to look beyond what is happening and recognize what God is doing beneath the surface. In gratitude, we become more spiritually alert, more sensitive to His leading, and more aware of His presence in every season.

When we pause long enough to reflect on how far God has brought us, the simple things – like the ability to breathe, to walk, to love, to create, or to serve – suddenly become sacred reminders of His goodness. Each day presents countless opportunities to practice thankfulness: the sunrise that greets us each morning, the laughter of a loved one, the provision of a meal, or the quiet peace of answered prayer. All of these are daily miracles if we choose to see them that way. Gratitude allows us to slow down and recognize the divine fingerprints woven throughout our daily lives. It calls us to notice the beauty in ordinary moments, to honor the present instead of rushing through it, and to celebrate the grace that sustains us breath by breath.

Even in moments of challenge, gratitude invites us to look deeper. It whispers, *"God is still here."* It teaches us that pain is not permanent and that joy can rise from the ashes of broken dreams. When we are grateful, our spiritual vision clears; we begin to discern that what once looked like loss was often a setup for something greater. *"Oh, give thanks to the Lord, for He is good! For His mercy endures forever"* (Psalm 107:1, NKJV). Gratitude helps us recognize that His goodness does not change with our circumstances; it is the foundation we stand on when everything else feels unstable.

When we practice gratitude, we partner with Heaven's perspective. We shift from asking *"Why me?"* to *"What are You showing me through this, Lord?"* This change in outlook does not remove difficulty, but it empowers us to grow through it with faith, patience, and trust. Gratitude transforms trials into testimonies and obstacles into opportunities to witness God's sustaining grace. It becomes a holy habit that steadies us, especially when life feels uncertain or overwhelming. Gratitude is not merely a feeling; it is a spiritual discipline. As we intentionally give thanks – out loud, in prayer, in writing – our minds are renewed, and our hearts are lifted. *"Through Jesus, therefore, let us continually offer to God a sacrifice of praise – the fruit of lips that openly profess his name"* (Hebrews 13:15, NIV). Continual praise forms a new pattern of thinking: instead of rehearsing the problem, we rehearse God's promises. It shifts our internal dialogue from despair to hope, from fear to trust, from worry to worship.

True transformation begins when we allow gratitude to reshape our inner life. Gratitude acts like a key, unlocking the peace and joy that God has already placed within us. It silences fear, weakens bitterness, and nurtures contentment. Consider Job, a man who experienced unimaginable loss and suffering. His children, possessions, and health were stripped away, yet Job declared, *"The Lord gave, and the*

Lord has taken away; blessed be the name of the Lord" (Job 1:21, NKJV). In that moment, Job's gratitude was not based on circumstances but on relationship – a trust in God's character that remained unshaken by adversity. His declaration of praise in the midst of devastation was a spiritual stance, a reminder that gratitude rooted in covenant is stronger than the storms that try to break us.

Gratitude has the same power to refine us. When we choose thankfulness in the face of sorrow, our perspective begins to change. Our spirit grows stronger, our heart grows softer, and our faith becomes rooted in something eternal. Gratitude doesn't ignore the storm. It declares peace in the midst of it. It says, *"God is still in control,"* even when everything around us feels unstable. David modeled this pattern repeatedly. Many of his psalms begin with lament and end with praise. His honest thanksgiving, even through tears, realigned his heart with God's promises. *"Bless the Lord, O my soul, and forget not all His benefits"* (Psalm 103:2, NKJV). Gratitude helped David shift his focus from the giant in front of him to the God who equipped him.

This same spiritual pattern applies to us today. Gratitude becomes the turning point between lament and victory. It draws us closer to God, positioning our hearts to receive the transformation He desires to bring. We begin to notice the quiet miracles: the strength we didn't know we had, the wisdom gained through hardship, the compassion born from our wounds. Transformation is the fruit of a grateful life. Gratitude also changes how we steward what we have. Instead of striving from scarcity, we serve from abundance. We stop comparing and start celebrating. *"Every good gift and every perfect gift is from above and comes down from the Father of lights"* (James 1:17, NKJV). When we recognize every good thing as a gift, our hands open to give, to bless, and to share. Gratitude turns our lives into a continual offering, overflowing with the goodness God has poured into us.

Every believer walks through seasons that test the foundation of their faith – times when prayers seem unanswered, relationships fracture, or dreams fade into disappointment. It's in these wilderness seasons that gratitude becomes both a weapon and a lifeline. Thankfulness, when practiced in pain, is not denial. It is defiance against despair. It says, *"I refuse to let my circumstances define my faith."* Gratitude becomes our spiritual stance; our declaration that God is still sovereign, still faithful, and still working behind the scenes even when we cannot see the full picture.

In my own life, I have faced moments where I had to cling to gratitude through tears. I've experienced deep personal loss, betrayal, misunderstanding, and seasons of waiting where I questioned God's timing. I've walked through days when my heart felt shattered and nights when hope seemed distant. Yet, in those valleys, gratitude became my anchor. It reminded me that even when life felt unstable, God's love remained unmovable. *"The Lord is my strength and my shield; my heart trusted in Him, and I am helped; therefore my heart greatly rejoices, and with my song I will praise Him"* (Psalm 28:7, NKJV). Gratitude restored my footing when everything around me felt like shifting sand.

Gratitude does not require perfection; only surrender. It means letting go of the need to understand everything and trusting that God's ways are higher. It is choosing to praise Him in the hallway before the door opens, to thank Him for the promise even before the manifestation. Through every hardship, I discovered that His goodness is not dependent on outcomes, but on His unchanging nature. Paul's counsel brings this posture into focus: *"Be anxious for nothing, but in everything by prayer and supplication, with thanksgiving, let your requests be made known to God"* (Philippians 4:6, NKJV). Thanksgiving does not minimize our needs; it magnifies our confidence in the One who meets them. Gratitude shifts our eyes from what we lack to the God who supplies. It steadies our hearts and invites peace to rule where anxiety once tried to overwhelm.

Sometimes the miracle is not that the mountain moves, but that our heart does. Gratitude transforms suffering into strength. It teaches us that the very pain we thought would break us can become the place where God rebuilds us stronger, wiser, and more compassionate than before. Gratitude shifts our posture from despair to expectation, allowing faith to rise even when circumstances remain unchanged. And when the answer finally comes, gratitude has already prepared us to steward it with humility and grace, recognizing that every blessing is a gift and every victory a testimony of God's unwavering faithfulness.

Transformation grows in practical soil. Small, consistent practices cultivate a grateful heart:

- **Begin and end with thanksgiving.** Start the day by naming three things you're thankful for; end the day by noting where you saw God's hand.

- **Turn worry into worship.** Each time anxiety rises, speak a Scripture of gratitude. *"This is the day the Lord has made; we will rejoice and be glad in it"* (Psalm 118:24, NKJV).

- **Keep a gratitude journal.** Write brief daily entries. On hard days, re-read what you've recorded. It is a personal archive of God's faithfulness.

- **Practice spoken thanks.** Tell people, *"I appreciate you."* Honor small kindnesses. Bless and do not withhold good words.

- **Offer thanks before the breakthrough.** Jesus gave thanks before multiplying the loaves (John 6:11, NKJV). Thanksgiving invites Heaven's increase.

These rhythms are not about perfection; they are about direction. Over time, gratitude becomes instinct – the reflex of a heart trained to see God.

Gratitude is contagious. When one heart becomes thankful, it inspires others to see God's goodness in their own lives. Communities rooted in gratitude thrive because thankfulness produces humility, unity, and love. When we take time to acknowledge those around us and say, *"I see you," "I appreciate you,"* or *"Thank you for being there,"* we strengthen the bonds of faith and fellowship. These small expressions of gratitude can heal divisions, restore friendships, and build trust. A simple word of appreciation can soften hearts that have grown guarded, rekindle relationships that were strained, and build bridges where walls once stood. Gratitude creates space for vulnerability, reminding us that we are not alone in our journey.

As a faith-based minister, I've seen the power of collective gratitude firsthand. During prayer gatherings, workshops, or conferences, when people begin to share testimonies of what God has done, the atmosphere shifts. Hope rises. Faith grows. Tears turn into praise. Gratitude unites us because it reminds us that we are all recipients of God's grace. In a world filled with comparison and competition, gratitude redirects our hearts toward collaboration and compassion. It reminds us that we don't need to compete for God's favor. His blessings are abundant for all who seek Him. When gratitude fills a room, comparison loses its grip and love becomes the standard.

"Let the peace of God rule in your hearts, to which also you were called in one body; and be thankful." Colossians 3:15 (NKJV)

A grateful community becomes a healing community. Joy becomes its language, generosity becomes its culture, and unity becomes its strength. The testimony of one person's deliverance becomes the prophecy of another person's breakthrough. Gratitude creates an environment where miracles feel possible and where every voice adds strength to the collective faith.

Even beyond the church, gratitude softens the spaces where we work, learn, and live. It affects how we speak to colleagues, how we treat strangers, and how we handle conflict. When thanksgiving shapes our posture, we listen more carefully, forgive more quickly, and serve more joyfully. Gratitude makes room for the Holy Spirit to move in relationships that once felt stuck. It infuses hope into workplaces, compassion into communities, and kindness into everyday encounters, turning ordinary interactions into opportunities for God's love to shine.

Gratitude also trains us to trust the timing of God. We do not always see answers when we want them, yet thanksgiving keeps our hearts open while we wait. *"And we know that all things work together for good to those who love God, to those who are the called according to His purpose"* (Romans 8:28, NKJV). Gratitude does not rush God; it rests in Him. It believes His "not yet" carries the same love as His "yes." A grateful heart learns to surrender the need for control and embrace the mystery of God's process, trusting that He never delays without purpose.

In waiting seasons, gratitude keeps us from shrinking our world to what we lack. Instead, we learn to gather manna – daily grace, present provision, present presence. Gratitude teaches us to notice how God shows up in whispers long before the breakthrough appears. We discover that God is not only the God of outcomes; He is the God of the in-between. Thankfulness keeps our hearts tender until the promise unfolds, shaping us into people who can carry the blessing with maturity and humility when it finally arrives.

Prayer

Heavenly Father,

Thank You for the gift of gratitude, which is the key that unlocks joy and transforms sorrow into strength. I pray for every reader who finds themselves in a season of uncertainty, pain, or change. May they begin to see Your hand even in what they don't understand. Turn their mourning into dancing, their heaviness into praise, and their questions into declarations of faith.

For the one who feels overlooked, remind them that they are seen and cherished. For the one facing loss, comfort their heart with Your peace. For the one struggling to be thankful, open their eyes to the small miracles that surround them daily. Lord, teach us to live with hearts that overflow with gratitude not just for what You do, but for who You are.

Help us to speak words of thanksgiving that shift atmospheres, heal relationships, and draw others closer to Your love. May our lives become living testimonies of Your goodness and vessels of light in a world that desperately needs hope. And as we thank You for all that has been, all that is, and all that is yet to come, may our gratitude be the bridge that keeps us forever safe in Your arms.

In the precious and powerful name of Jesus Christ, Amen.

Anita Sechesky - Visionary Compiler & Publisher

Safe in His Arms
The Goodness of God

Koreen J. Bennett

Chapter Thirty-Seven

When All You Can Do is Pray – GOD is GOOD

Is there any greater love letter than a mother's prayer? What does a mother's prayer mean to you?

I'm sure if I were to pose this question to multiple people, I would receive a few different answers. Can I share what it means to me?

I believe a mother's prayer is a declaration of love. It is filled with joy, protection, intervention, and intercession on behalf of someone very close and important to her. It is asking God to seal her petition for someone with whom she shares a deep connection – someone she longs to see walking in wholeness, purpose, and divine destiny.

Prayer is a sacred moment. It's when you come before the King of Kings – your Heavenly Daddy – and talk. You talk about life, about family, and about His divine purpose. It is the most precious moment when you step into the throne room of heaven. There, in the quiet place, it's just you and God in conversation – listening to each other in the Spirit. You hear God's heart, and God hears yours.

I truly believe that the prayers of others have helped me through many situations. It is those prayers, combined with God's undeniable love, that have carried me through countless battles. Even today, I am surrounded by many motherly figures and praying women, some I know, and some I've never met personally, who continue to cover me. Watching their example has encouraged me to become a prayer warrior, not only for my own children but for others as well, even those I may never meet.

Moms, how many of you have had other mothers – whether biological or spiritual – take on that role of covering in your life? Perhaps you've had a big sister in the faith who has spoken life over you, declared God's protection over you, and pointed you toward divine direction. And for those who haven't had that motherly figure, why not ask God to bring that person into your life? He is faithful to send what we need when we ask.

I go back to 2004, when I was pregnant with my little boy. I can't recall whether we knew the sex of the baby at the time, but months into my pregnancy, it became evident that our little bundle, our miracle baby, was already facing serious challenges before he even entered the world. Many thoughts and emotions flooded me. My womb was supposed to be a safe haven – a place of nourishment, warmth, and protection. Instead, it became a battleground. My safe space for him was fighting against him. On top of that, his little body was going through its own changes. I didn't just need prayer, I needed a miracle.

During those days and months, I realized that prayer would become my lifeline. I needed prayer not only for my unborn child but also for myself, because I was breaking inside.

What do you do when you don't have the answers to a difficult, painful, or frightening situation? I knew I needed the church to pray. It was hard enough processing my child's diagnosis, but even more difficult to talk about it and to share it with others. But I needed our village to intercede on our behalf.

> *"Is any sick among you? Let him call for the elders of the church; and let them pray over him, anointing him with oil in the name of the Lord."*
> James 5:14 (KJV)

I was so grateful that our pastor at the time was a man of prayer – a true prayer warrior. He believed in prayer like it was the very air we breathe.

As a young girl, I dreamed of having children. I dreamed of a husband, a home filled with love, and many children, both boys and girls. I couldn't wait for that season of life to begin. I never once imagined there would be complications. No thought of struggling to conceive, and no thoughts of anything going wrong during pregnancy. But life has a way of writing a different script than the one we imagined. And it is in those moments – the moments of broken expectations, of worry, of fear – that we come to know what it really means to pray. It's then that we discover just how good God truly is.

These concerns were never a part of my thoughts. I just automatically thought, *"I'm a woman, and I will have kids because that's my plan."* And truly, there's nothing wrong with that mindset. After all, one of the reasons we women were created was to fill this earth with beautiful little beings. So, it was never a thought that I would have complications bearing children.

But as we know, life is far from perfect. It doesn't always flow the way we want or unfold the way we imagine. Life doesn't always go according to plan. And so, this particular pregnancy was especially challenging especially because I had been so intentional about caring for my body. I was mindful about what I ate and drank, took my supplements faithfully, and did everything "right." Still, I was challenged – mentally, emotionally, spiritually, and physically.

How do you process it when you're told that something is wrong with your unborn child before they've even entered the world? How do you keep it together?

Prayers. Prayers. Prayers.

Thank God for praying moms, praying women, and sisters in Christ. Prayers came in from everywhere, and they carried me through one of the most difficult seasons of my life.

Earlier in the pregnancy, I was dealing with fibroids which wasn't new to me. I had been dealing with fibroids for many years. But when you're pregnant, fibroids take on a whole different meaning. There was constant monitoring to make sure the hormones from the pregnancy weren't making the fibroids grow larger, which could complicate the pregnancy.

During one of my many doctor visits to check on the fibroids, an ultrasound revealed that something was wrong with our baby. This led to a referral to a specialist at Mount Sinai Hospital. That's when we found out that our little bundle of joy was battling something dangerous to his well-being. He had a hole in the lower part of his back, and his spinal cord was outside of his body. There wasn't enough amniotic fluid, and I wasn't gaining enough weight. My body felt like it was working against us.

It was so hard not to feel stressed, especially when it felt like my own body was the source of the stress. Trying to stay positive was difficult, but deep down, I knew God was going to save my baby and see us through the pregnancy. I believed that if God had started something, He would be faithful to complete it. My Heavenly Father wasn't going to let me – or us – go through this alone. I trusted that.

Proverbs 3:6 (KJV) reminded me, *"In all thy ways acknowledge him, and he shall direct thy paths."* And Proverbs 18:21 (KJV) reminded me that *"Death and life are in the power of the tongue: and they that love it shall eat the fruit thereof."*

Were we going to speak life or death over our situation? Though I didn't know what the outcome would be, I believed that no matter what, my husband and our son Terell were going to be all right. And so was I.

I had a perfect little boy named Eli'jah (middle name Aaron Ledford, after my grandfather). He was going to have surgery within hours of coming into this world – several surgeries, actually. But as a family, we were going to face this together with the total guidance of our Heavenly Father.

Prayer has been, and continues to be, foundational for our family. Prayer carries anointing. Prayer carries healing. It's as if God places His hands on your prayers and when they land, something shifts. Something changes.

Today, at 17 years of age, Eli'jah is speaking clearly and boldly (I often tell him he should be a lawyer!). Yes, he still deals with physical and mental challenges, but he brings joy, laughter, love, and so much light to our family. He is our firecracker, and it was meant to be that way.

Raising a special needs child brings many ups and downs. I had so many moments of crying out, *"Lord, how am I going to do this?"* I remember locking myself in the bathroom and breaking down. I had moments of insecurity wondering if I was going to be a good mom or if I was even the right mom for this little boy.

In all those moments – the *how, why, when, where, what?* – God was there. He never, ever left me, not even in my moments of doubt, anger, frustration, or sadness. He gave me a child who would love me unconditionally. God entrusted him to me and I was not going to let God down.

No way!

We made it through those roller-coaster years. And yes, I have a few gray hairs, but the joy my little man brings me is beyond words.

Eli'jah, Mommy loves you so much.

Women, do we understand how vital you are to your child(ren) and to your family?

Your child(ren) see love through your eyes, Mommy. They feel safe and secure with every hug. They know that every meal you prepare carries your special ingredient – love. They hear your compassion in your words of encouragement and even in discipline. They learn to follow their dreams as they watch you chase and fulfill your own.

God sees your ups and downs. He sees the sacrifices you make daily. You might feel at your lowest in this very moment, but know this: it is the lowest you will ever be. You are increasing. You are elevating. This season is your time to excel and soar into your divine purpose.

We've had powerful biblical examples of praying women:

- Hannah, who prayed for a child.
- Esther, who prayed for the salvation of her people.
- Deborah, the prophetess and judge, who led and prayed a nation through battle.
- Lydia, who gathered women and prayed.
- And there are many more.

Praying Moms, you are blessed, and you are a blessing – to your children, your family, your community, and your neighbors. You will prosper where you are planted.

So, get down on your knees. Yes, it may seem "old school," but you'd be surprised how deeply this posture touches your Daddy's heart. Cast all your cares, concerns, problems, and wounds onto the Lord your God.

I decree you will leave a legacy of worth, integrity, and love to your children.

I decree you will leave generational wealth for your future generations.

I decree you will be a trailblazer for those coming behind you.

Thank you to every mom, grandmother, aunt, sister, and friend who is faithfully praying for her family, friends, neighborhood, and community. God, you have placed a special anointing upon women

– especially moms – who truly understand the assignment of being prayer warriors.

> *"That our sons may be as plants grown up in their youth; that our daughters may be as corner stones, polished after the similitude of a palace."* Psalm 144:12 (KJV)

> *"Don't you see that children are God's best gift? The fruit of the womb, His generous legacy?"* Psalm 127:3 (MSG)

Prayer

Heavenly Father,

I thank You for the mom, daughter, sister, grandmother, aunt, friend – and yes, the dad, granddad, uncle, and brother – who are reading this chapter and this book. I thank You for their lives and how they align with Your divine purpose.

I thank You that as Your sons and daughters walk through life's challenges, they remember who You are – the ultimate Cupbearer, Problem Solver, and Way Maker.

Remind them that life may bring strong winds, thunderstorms, and hailstorms, and it may feel unbearable at times, but show them the sunshine breaking through the clouds, the falling raindrops kissed by sunlight, and the beauty of a rainbow that follows.

Allow them to feel Your comforting presence and Your Shalom peace. Let them sense deep within that even in the heartbreak, the devastating diagnosis, the mental exhaustion, You are near.

God, You are a Sovereign God. You heal, provide, protect, redeem, and transform. Your heart's desire is for Your children to fulfill the dreams and purposes You have set before them. Through every mountaintop and valley experience, reveal Your glory, Lord.

I declare Jeremiah 29:11 (KJV) over the reader, *"For I know the thoughts that I think toward you, saith the Lord, thoughts of peace, and not of evil, to give you an expected end."*

I declare increase and acceleration in every area of your life, according to the will of God. I declare the oil of joy, laughter, gladness, and peace over you and your family. God richly bless you as you continue to bless your children, your family, and your community.

May you and your children prosper in every place you go. May God's uncommon favor follow you and your children every day of your lives. I pray Psalm 23 over your household.

Thank You, Lord, for this person's life and their salvation. May they wholeheartedly profess Matthew 6:33 (KJV), *"But seek ye first the kingdom of God, and his righteousness; and all these things shall be added unto you."*

In Jesus' Name, Amen.

Koreen J. Bennett - Co-Author

Safe in His Arms
The Goodness of God

Nasha T. Alexis

CHAPTER THIRTY-EIGHT

Fighting the Good Fight – Lies from the Enemy

"Let them praise his name with dancing and make music to him with timbrel and harp." Psalm 149:3 (NIV)

Music and dance have always been a part of my life. When I am sad, a good song – the right song – can help lift my spirit. When I am joyful, music sounds and feels even better. We see even in the Bible, where King David danced before the LORD, *"Wearing a linen ephod, David was dancing before the LORD with all his might."* He was dancing because the ark of the LORD was being returned to the City of David. It was a time of celebration, even though his wife, Michal, despised him for it.

2 Samuel 6:16 (NIV) says, *"As the ark of the LORD was entering the City of David, Michal, daughter of Saul, watched from a window. And when she saw King David leaping and dancing before the LORD, she despised him in her heart."* I cannot say I truly understand her reason for despising her husband for dancing before the LORD…but WHAT!?

As for me, I don't need a reason to dance. Just play the music and give me room. I also love to see other people dancing; joy spreads when you see others having fun and expressing freedom through movement. Growing up in the Caribbean, I danced in high school as part of the school's dance ensemble, which I loved. It was great being part of a team, even though I didn't always feel like I belonged (that's a totally different story in itself). I liked it when the whole thing came together, and we got to finally present all the hard work.

Those are good memories.

After migrating to Canada, I stopped dancing. I always thought about it and longed to join a group, but I didn't know where to begin, so it never happened. Some time later, I watched a Christian program on television and saw ladies dancing. Before that, I had never thought about "Christian dance." I didn't even know it was a thing. I immediately became interested and had dreams of myself dancing. Those dreams felt so real at times, like it was actually happening. But again, I didn't know how to go about it.

Fast forward to my adult years and two children later, a senior member at church asked me to flag with her one Sunday. Out of respect for that individual, but still with hesitation, I said yes. So, we danced that Sunday with limited practice. I was given instructions on how to wave the flag, and that was it. It was a good experience, but I was full of fear. Fear was something I had never experienced before when it came to dancing, whether alone or in front of a crowd.

I was asked to flag again the following Sunday, and truthfully, it was still only out of respect that I continued. But then something shifted. I started looking forward to Sundays because I wanted to dance. Then I had an encounter with the Holy Spirit. I can't explain to you what happened that particular Sunday, but I knew it was good. I felt like I could dance all day. I didn't want to stop. I couldn't stop. Something in me opened up, and all I wanted to do was dance. For the first time, it felt like this was what I was meant to be doing.

Sometime later, I attended a workshop and participated in a conference. I was still new to the concept of Christian dance and learning how to work with flags. At this workshop, we were taught choreography that we had to present one of the nights at the church's conference. For whatever reason, I was having a hard time picking up the choreography. A few of us were struggling, so we were given time to practice on our own. I wrote out the choreography and lyrics of the song where I was having difficulty. I practiced the movements physically, visualized them in my mind, and went back to observe the others and practice on the sidelines.

The instructor didn't know all that I had done. She condemned the group of us who had been struggling earlier. I was sitting at the time, tired. But someone else was still practicing. The issue wasn't just what she said; it was her body language, tone, and facial expression. I felt discouraged and humiliated. I wanted to quit. I even prayed for an injury so I could gracefully bow out without lying. I felt like I was wasting everyone's time. I wanted to disappear.

On the way home, silent tears ran down my face. That entire week, I felt invisible, insignificant, and like I didn't belong. I thought I had nothing to contribute; that I was a burden. I was numb. On the final night of practice, I let my anger and frustration out on God. I asked Him why I was even there, why I was struggling, and why He made me so stupid that I couldn't follow simple choreography. All of this while tears streamed down my face as I drove home.

Then, whether in my imagination or spirit, I heard, *"I am your teacher. Everything you will do, I will teach you."*

It was as if my soul had been waiting for that moment. My tears stopped, I dried my face, and said, *"Okay."* I prayed for His help – for me and the group – that I wouldn't mess up the presentation. I didn't want to embarrass myself, the group, or the director. The relief when it was all over was immense. That was only one week, but it felt like a lifetime. Without realizing it, a seed had been planted.

The following Sunday, back at my church, I stayed at the back to dance – out of sight. When prompted by others to come to the front, I would excuse it by saying there was more space at the back. That wasn't true. Eventually, I did return to the front. Many people were blessed, and I thank God and give Him the glory for using me in that way. People would tell me how certain movements ministered to them – movements I didn't even remember making. I would politely respond, *"Thank God,"* or *"Praise the Lord,"* but I still wanted to hide.

Despite my doubts, I continued dancing. It became my ministry – my gifting from the Holy Spirit. I've learned that persevering even when you're uncertain is part of the journey. If I had done this in my own strength, I would've quit long ago.

As I continued ministering at church, I found freedom in dancing. At times, it felt like I could fly. Other times, the heaviness was unbearable. I knew what often followed – deep depression and backlash from the Enemy. Whether one caused the other, I don't know. But I continued to minister alongside two other amazing, faith-filled women for a few years. We weren't just individuals; we were a team.

Then, COVID happened, and everything changed.

I also had the opportunity to dance with another well-known ministry, which was a powerful experience. Later, I joined the ministry I'm still part of today. Even after more than thirteen years, I hadn't realized that the seed God planted all those years ago was still there, growing despite the fog and lies from the Enemy.

I know and have experienced the joy and freedom that comes with dancing in the Spirit. When I'm at my lowest, music soothes my soul. Dancing allows me to process, clear my mind, and make better decisions. In those low moments, there's nowhere to look but up.

Psalm 121:1–3 (NIV) tells us, *"I lift up my eyes to the mountains – where does my help come from? My help comes from the Lord, the Maker of heaven and earth. He will not let your foot slip – He who watches over you will not slumber."*

In those moments of weakness, I pray more earnestly. When I dance and pray, I go deeper in the Spirit. Nothing is held back. Everything is laid at the feet of Jesus. Sometimes, the best place to be is flat on our faces before Almighty God. Our perspectives shift when we're in the valley. We stop focusing on ourselves and our situation. Our eyes become fixed on the One who can turn things around.

The Spirit of the Living God brings the healing and anointing our souls desperately need. He is the soothing balm for every wound.

I thank God that despite the words spoken against me then, they did not stop me from pursuing Him and participating in His divine plan. Even when doubt crept in and I could hear the voice of the Enemy whispering in my ear, I stood firm and fought the good fight. Ephesians 6:11 (NIV) says, *"Put on the full armor of God, so that you can take your stand against the devil's schemes."*

There were many times when that was my only saving grace – being clothed in the armor of God. The truth is, the Enemy will come against you in all sorts of ways and through various forms, but we have the confidence that God is greater and bigger than anything he can throw at us. So, we go forth with courage to do what we are called to do – WE MUST – because we are not going in our own strength. We have angel armies surrounding us, watching our front, sides, and back at all times.

I thank God that His promises are true. They are never delayed; they are always on time. We may slip and fall along the way, but He is patient and willing to wait for us. His plans can never be altered, changed, modified, or stopped. Isaiah 55:11 (NIV) confirms this promise: *"So is my word that goes out from my mouth: It will not return to me empty but will accomplish what I desire and achieve the purpose for which I sent it."*

THANK YOU, MOST HIGH FATHER. I love knowing that God is God all by Himself, and whatever He says, goes. The only challenge is that we, as humans, are included in His plan…and we tend to mess things up. We can be stubborn. We don't always listen well, and we often try to take the lead, dragging God along with us just in case we need Him. But we need to recognize that He alone knows the beginning from the end – and back again. We are the ones who must follow His lead, go where He sends us, and do what He tells us to do.

Stubbornness can be a blessing in some situations, but in others, it can lead us astray – down rabbit holes we never intended to enter. Still, I am grateful for the stubbornness in me that refused to give up or walk away when things got unbearably difficult. I thank God that the words spoken over me didn't destroy me. In fact, they pushed me further, deeper, and nearer to the cross.

Whenever I dance or wave my flags, I know something is happening for someone. A change is taking place. Hearts are being mended. Minds are being transformed. Spirits are being lifted. Hope is being restored. And I know the power is not in the flags or in me, but in the One who is in me. 1 John 4:4 (NIV) declares: *"The one who is in you is greater than the one who is in the world."*

Dear Reader,

I want you to know that you are not alone and that you are loved – unconditionally and without apology. God created you to be exactly who you are, and you must never let the world tell you otherwise. You are here for a purpose. The Enemy may have already whispered lies to you, and maybe that's all you've been hearing lately, but you must not give up; you must not give in.

Stand firm on the Word of God – not in your own strength – and fight the good fight. The beauty of this fight is that you are not the one doing it. God is fighting on your behalf. Continue walking in your purpose by yielding to the Holy Spirit, who will guide you. And when the Enemy rises against you, all you have to do is be still and watch God work.

Take heart.

Be encouraged.

Walk straight and in confidence, knowing that the LORD is on your side.

Nasha T. Alexis - Co-Author

Safe in His Arms
The Goodness of God

Tricia Marcellin

CHAPTER THIRTY-NINE

Forgiving What I Can't Forget

I was raised in a church-going family, so when I moved to Canada, one of my first priorities was to find a local church to attend. Initially, I joined a church, but I quickly realized that the service felt unfamiliar and disconnected from the worship style I had grown up with. After some time, I decided to explore other churches, eventually finding one where the service resonated with me. The music was uplifting, and I felt a stronger sense of connection to the congregation and to God.

About a year after settling in at this new church, I met a man who was significantly older than me. Our relationship progressed, and five years later, I found myself pregnant with my first daughter. Just six months after her birth, I discovered I was pregnant again. Despite the challenges, I was blessed with two beautiful daughters. Two years later, I had a third child. My life was busy and overwhelming, but I held onto hope that things would improve. My life was a whirlwind of diaper changes, late-night feedings, and endless responsibilities, but amidst the chaos, my children became the anchors that kept me grounded. They were the light in my darkest moments, their innocent smiles and laughter reminding me that I had a reason to keep going, no matter how difficult things became.

Motherhood brought with it a profound shift in my faith. As I looked into the eyes of my daughters, I saw the purity and love that only God could create. Each time I held them close, I was reminded of the incredible responsibility God had entrusted to me. I wasn't just living for myself anymore; I was living for them. Every decision I made was with their future in mind, and this realization deepened my relationship with God.

Before the birth of my first child, this man had helped me with my immigration paperwork to secure my status in Canada. He owned a house and had a deep passion for cricket, even sponsoring players from Trinidad and St. Lucia. However, as time went on, his life began to unravel. He lost nearly everything, and as his circumstances deteriorated, I became the target of his frustration. I endured mental, physical, financial, and emotional abuse during this period. The weight of it all left me feeling isolated, stressed, and deeply depressed.

Being alone in a foreign country with no family to turn to, I felt trapped and uncertain about my future. I was young, vulnerable, and didn't know where to turn. One day, things reached a breaking point. He came home and told me that I had to leave and that I could no longer use his address. I was devastated and confused.

Desperate, I reached out to my doctor, who listened to my situation with compassion. He gave me a phone number for a shelter, and without hesitation, I called them. They advised me to come in, so I hastily packed a few clothes and left. At that time, I was already a mother and pregnant with my second child. The situation felt unbearable, and I cried often, questioning why I had to endure such hardship. I kept everything to myself, not telling anyone about the turmoil I was going through.

One day, a friend called me and told me she had received a letter from immigration. I asked her to open it, and as she read the contents to me, I felt a wave of despair wash over me. In that moment of darkness, I remembered the comforting words of Proverbs 3:5-6 (ESV): *"Trust in the Lord with all your heart, and do not lean on your own understanding. In all your ways acknowledge Him, and He will make your paths straight."*

I learned that this man had canceled my immigration papers, and it seemed like I had no choice but to return to my home country. However, I made a firm decision not to go back. I turned to prayer, seeking God's guidance and strength as I prepared to give birth to my second daughter.

Through this experience, I've realized that I cannot carry the broken pieces of my past into my future. Understanding my identity in Christ has empowered me to step out in faith and build a deeper connection with Him. We are God's most precious creations, perfected in His eyes. While others may see cars, homes, and material possessions as investments, I see myself differently. I am a survivor, and I know that in God's eyes, I am valued and cherished. He has promised never to leave me nor forsake me.

In life's darkest moments, it may feel as though God is distant or even absent. Yet, I've learned that His presence is always with us, even when we cannot perceive it. The world often bombards us with challenges, leading us to question God's involvement in our lives. However, Psalm 46:1 (KJV) reassures us: *"God is our refuge and strength, a very present help in trouble."* Even when we don't feel His presence, God is actively working on our behalf. As Matthew 19:26 (KJV) says, *"With God, all things are possible."* This truth has become the foundation of my faith, teaching me the importance of patience and trust in God's timing.

Balancing the demands of work, family, and other responsibilities often makes it difficult to see God's hand in our lives. However, I've come to recognize that God often works quietly, without fanfare. Have you ever noticed a problem resolving itself or a bad habit slowly fading away? These are signs that God is at work, even if we don't immediately recognize it. The Bible teaches that there is a season and a purpose for everything under the sun. Sometimes, God intervenes in our lives in ways that are subtle but significant, making changes that we may only fully understand in hindsight.

Surprisingly, after some time, this man and I reconciled. He helped me find an apartment and even sent someone to meet me at the hospital when I needed support. Eventually, I moved back into his apartment. But soon after, he left for Trinidad, leaving me alone once again. I sought legal advice, but the lawyer advised me to return to my home country. Despite the difficulties, I remained determined not to leave. I chose to place my trust in God and His plan for my life.

The trials didn't end there. I continued to face verbal abuse, being belittled and called names, my character constantly questioned. Despite the pain, I forced myself to smile and laugh, trying to please those around me. I felt incredibly isolated, often contemplating giving up. But after a year, I reapplied for my permanent resident status in Canada, and to my relief, I was successful.

I had hoped that this man's behavior would change, but it only worsened. However, instead of breaking me, these challenges strengthened my resolve. I started attending a new church where my spiritual eyes were opened even wider to the truths of God. I learned that true worshipers worship God in spirit and in truth. I began preaching to myself, declaring and decreeing God's promises over my life.

All I ever wanted was a simple life: to get married, live for Jesus, and find happiness. I realized that God is always on our side, and we should speak to Him as a friend.

One day, as I stood in front of the mirror, I began talking to God. Suddenly, the Spirit spoke to me, clearly and boldly, saying, *"It's not your season. Wait on Me."* I was taken aback, even looking around to see if someone else was in the room. I felt a chill, and deep down, I knew that this was indeed the voice of God.

That moment marked a significant shift in my life. I realized that this man needed to leave my home for me to move forward. I was already managing to pay the rent and bills on my own, so I didn't need the added burden of this relationship. It became clear that I needed to pray more fervently.

When I confronted him, telling him that he had to leave, he refused and even hid my keys. Then, on July 9, 2023, a friend from church came over to drop something off. I had just returned from work and was downstairs doing laundry when my friend arrived. Within minutes, my children's father came downstairs and began insulting me, even throwing water on me. This happened in front of my friend, and I felt a deep sense of shame. I had to call another friend who knew him, and she was shocked by his behavior.

It was then that I realized it was time to move on to the next chapter of my life. On August 8, 2023, he left my home, and I finally found peace.

Often in life, we become comfortable in our circumstances, even when they're harmful, because change is daunting. But our health and well-being are paramount. When we take the necessary steps to move forward, we open ourselves to the blessings that God has in store for us. Letting go and allowing God to take control of our problems is crucial for healing.

Though the experience was painful, I allowed God to heal my wounds. The scars remain, but they are victory scars – proof that I have overcome. Isaiah 41:10 has become a cornerstone in my life, reminding me not to fear because God is with me. It encourages me not to be dismayed, for He is my God. He promises to strengthen and help me, upholding me with His righteous right hand. This scripture gives me the confidence to face my struggles, knowing that I am never alone and that God is constantly by my side.

It's true that we often become comfortable in situations that are detrimental to us, and it takes immense courage to move forward. My journey has taught me the importance of letting go and letting God handle my problems. My scars are a testament to my strength and the victory I've achieved over difficult circumstances. I'm not fully healed or completely delivered yet, but I believe that God Himself is healing me. There are moments when tears fill my eyes, especially when I'm alone and old memories resurface. But I remind myself that the joy of the Lord is my strength.

Fear is a spirit, not a reality, and it seeks to torment us. When the spirit of fear rises up within me, I call upon the name of the Lord and place my faith in Him. I remember that God has not given me a spirit of fear, but of power, love, and a sound mind (2 Timothy 1:7). I've also learned the importance of acknowledging my pain, processing my emotions, and allowing myself to grow in love. Instead of seeking revenge or holding onto bitterness, I choose to free myself and find peace. I practice compassion, set healthy boundaries, and protect myself from repeating past mistakes.

Psalm 34:4 (KJV) says, *"I sought the Lord, and he heard me, and delivered me from all my fears."* Psalm 27:14 (KJV) encourages us to *"Wait on the Lord: be of good courage, and he shall strengthen thine heart: wait, I say, on the Lord."* Through every trial and triumph, I have learned that surrendering to God's will and embracing His promises is the path to true healing and enduring peace.

Nasha T. Alexis - Co-Author

Safe in His Arms
The Goodness of God

Anita Sechesky

Chapter Forty

Forgiving What I Can't Forget

Everyone longs to believe that there is still hope in this life despite the circumstances we may face. Deep down, we all want to know that the answers to our most painful and complex questions exist somewhere, even if we can't yet understand them. Life, as beautiful as it is, can often feel like an uphill climb. The trials we face sometimes strip away our sense of control, leaving us feeling powerless, broken, and uncertain about what tomorrow may hold. Yet within those very valleys, when we least expect it, the goodness of God has a way of revealing itself – often through unseen hands, whispered encouragements, or supernatural reminders that Heaven is closer than we think.

There are moments in life that challenge our very belief systems – times when faith is tested, and we wrestle with questions that pierce the soul: *Why did this happen? Where was God? Could He really love me after this?* For many, the thought that divine beings, angels of the Lord, might still move among us seems far-fetched or even imaginary. But Scripture is clear that from the beginning of time, God has sent His heavenly messengers to protect, to comfort, and to guide His people.

"For He shall give His angels charge over you, to keep you in all your ways." Psalm 91:11 (NKJV)

These words are not poetic symbolism; they are promises from a God who is deeply invested in His children's protection and care. Angels are not mythical; they are real, divine servants sent to carry out God's will and to minister to those who are heirs of salvation. Even in today's modern world, these divine encounters still occur, often in the quiet moments when our hearts are shattered and Heaven draws near.

As someone who has worked in healthcare for more than twenty-five years, I have witnessed the fragility of life and the miraculous ways God steps into the ordinary. Over the years, I've heard stories of hope, faith, and unexplainable encounters that defy the boundaries of human understanding. Nurses, patients, and even seasoned doctors have shared experiences of divine presence – moments where an unseen peace filled the room, where the dying smiled at something no one else could see, or where comfort came through a gentle whisper that no human voice had spoken.

In hospital corridors where fear and faith often meet, there have been stories of angels standing near operating tables, glowing figures seen by patients moments before recovery, and mysterious strangers who vanished after offering words of comfort. These stories remind us that the supernatural is not confined to Scripture's pages. It still unfolds in our world today. But even with all those testimonies, I never imagined that one day I would personally encounter that same divine presence.

My own story began with heartbreak – the kind that changes you forever. It was the loss of my first child, my precious daughter, Jasmine Rose. She was full-term, perfect, and beautiful. Yet, she was born sleeping. There are no words strong enough to capture the anguish of expecting life and being met with death instead. I remember the cold stillness of that hospital room, the sound of distant laughter from other families welcoming their newborns, and the unbearable silence that filled the space where her cries should have been.

It was the Christmas season, a time when the world was wrapped in lights and joy, but my heart was buried under a mountain of grief so heavy that even breathing felt impossible. Every decoration, every carol, every sparkle of celebration around me became a painful reminder of what I had lost.

When Heaven Drew Near

In those days, I could not pray. I could not speak. I could barely exist. My husband and my mother prayed for me because I had no words left to give. The pain was raw, deep, and unrelenting. I felt like I was living in a dream from which I desperately wanted to wake. I would lie awake for hours, replaying the moment in my mind, wondering what I could have done differently. The questions were endless, but the silence of Heaven felt louder than anything I'd ever known.

Long hours turned into lonely days, which turned into empty weeks without my beautiful Jasmine Rose in my arms. The unbearable grief settled into my very being. Every maternal instinct within me screamed for the baby girl I could no longer celebrate life with. The crying turned to numbness, and numbness turned into a silent void.

Then, one night not long after her funeral, my faith was challenged immediately after I saw a disturbing vision of a tunnel of flames leading from my bedroom door into the hallway. There was a man wearing a dark suit standing at the entrance to the tunnel.

I jumped slightly from the position I was in, reading my Bible in bed. Then, as I turned away from the doorway, something caught the corner of my eye – something that would change the course of my life forever. Even though the bedroom lighting was dim, I was able to clearly see every detail of the warrior angel that visually appeared before my eyes. At first, I thought I was imagining it. But then, in an instant, the veil between Heaven and Earth lifted and the spiritual realm was more real than reality itself.

Standing before me at the foot of my bed was the most magnificent being I had ever seen. It was an angel of the Lord as tall as the ceiling with a cherub face and soft, light-colored curly hair that brought comfort to me. His presence filled the room with a peace that words could never capture. His wings were vast and lush with huge plumes that spread across the entire floor. His arms were massively muscular and folded across his broad and enormous chest, and he wore a leather-pleated skirt and sandals with straps wrapped around his calves. On his left side was strapped an immense sword of great weight shimmering of silver-like metal that did not seem to exist on earth.

It was the face of calmness – a guardian who had carried Heaven's peaceful presence. He didn't need to speak. The atmosphere itself spoke for him. Every fear, every dark thought, every weight of grief that had held me captive seemed to dissolve in that instantaneous moment. I felt wrapped – cocooned – in the love of God Himself.

From that time onward, I have never had another disturbing vision concerning my daughter. When I awoke, I felt lighter, as if Heaven had breathed life back into my weary soul. That night marked the beginning of my healing journey. Though the ache of losing Jasmine Rose would always remain, the despair was replaced by something eternal – the assurance that I was not alone. My daughter was safe in God's presence in the eternal realm and I was safe in God's presence in the earthly realm.

In the years that followed, I often thought about that encounter. I realized that angels do not appear to glorify themselves but to remind us of who God is: faithful, present, and endlessly compassionate. That visitation was not just about comfort; it was about restoration. It reminded me that God's goodness doesn't always prevent pain, but it does promise His presence through it.

People often ask how I can still believe in a good God after such loss. My answer is simple: because I met Him in the middle of my sorrow. I discovered that His love is not fragile; it is fierce. His mercy doesn't evaporate in tragedy; it manifests through it. Sometimes the miracle isn't that the storm ends, but that you survive it with your faith intact.

Through every tear and every quiet night of remembering, God was writing redemption into my story. Over time, He used that experience to shape my purpose. My nursing career became a ministry of compassion. I found myself comforting families who had lost loved ones, offering the same words of hope that had once been spoken over me. My writing and ministry grew from that deep well of empathy, reminding others that even shattered hearts can still shine with His glory.

"The Lord is close to the brokenhearted and saves those who are crushed in spirit." Psalm 34:18 (NIV)

God's closeness in our brokenness is one of the most profound demonstrations of His goodness. He doesn't always take away the pain, but He transforms it into purpose. My pain became a bridge for someone else's healing – proof that Heaven can redeem even the darkest stories.

The God Who Still Sends Angels

When I recall first sharing these profound thoughts, the Easter season was quickly approaching. It is a time when we reflect on the ultimate act of love. The world may see it as a holiday or a long weekend, but for me, Easter represents hope reborn. I often think of Jesus as the gentle storyteller, the healer, the peacemaker, the one who saw the unseen, and loved the unlovable. He was perfect in every way: kind, humble, faithful, and full of grace. Yet He was betrayed, mocked, and crucified for sins He never committed.

He bore the pain of humanity, including mine, including yours.

"Greater love has no one than this: to lay down one's life for one's friends." John 15:13 (NIV)

At the cross, love was not just spoken. It was demonstrated. The blood of Jesus became the eternal bridge between Heaven and Earth. His sacrifice made room for our redemption, healing, and hope. Every drop that fell from His body declared victory over death, darkness, and despair. And because of that sacrifice, we can live with confidence that God's goodness is not a distant promise but a present reality.

The same God who sent angels to guard prophets, deliver messages, and defend His people still sends them today. Some appear visibly, while others move unseen, whispering peace to the anxious, guiding the lost, and comforting the brokenhearted. We may never know how many times we've been protected by unseen hands or spared from danger by divine intervention. *"Do not forget to entertain strangers, for by so doing some have unwittingly entertained angels"* (Hebrews 13:2, NKJV).

Through every season since that loss, I have seen God redeem my pain in unexpected ways. My story is not one of tragedy but of transformation. I once thought my greatest heartbreak was losing my daughter, but now I see that even in death, God was birthing new life within me; one of deeper faith, stronger compassion, and greater trust in His promises. What once felt like the end of my world became the very place where God began rewriting my story with His healing power.

Loss will either break you or build you. For a long time, I didn't know which side I would fall on. The grief was heavy, the silence was deafening, and the ache in my heart felt unending. But even in the darkness, there were small, quiet, and even sacred moments when I felt the unmistakable closeness of God. It wasn't loud. It wasn't dramatic. It was gentle, like a warm hand resting on my shoulder reminding me, *"I am here."*

People often assume that healing comes in grand gestures, but mine came slowly, like sunlight inching its way through the curtains after a long night. Little by little, I began to notice how God was carrying me: through nights of uncontrollable tears, through days when I felt numb, and through moments when memories surfaced unexpectedly. He carried me when I had no strength of my own. And He carried me until I could stand again – not in my own power, but in His.

There is a kind of pain that doesn't destroy you, but it reshapes you. It opens your eyes to what truly matters. It softens your heart toward others who suffer. It humbles you, refines you, and brings you to a place of complete surrender.

Losing my daughter forced me to confront the depths of my faith. Did I believe God was still good? Could I trust Him with the parts of my heart I feared would never heal? Could I believe that something beautiful could come from something so devastating?

Slowly, I learned the answer was yes.

God didn't cause my pain, but He refused to waste it. He took the shattered pieces of my heart and rebuilt them into something stronger, softer, and more compassionate. I began to look at people differently. I could recognize the silent pain in others' eyes because I had lived it. I could pray with a depth I didn't know before. I could extend comfort because I had first been comforted by God Himself.

There are moments of joy, triumph, and decision that shape us.

There are moments of loss, disappointment, and unanswered questions that break us.

And there are moments that reveal who God truly is; sacred encounters where His presence becomes undeniable.

I had all three.

The shaping moments gave me vision.

The breaking moments gave me depth.

But the revealing moments gave me intimacy with God that I never would have found without the valley I walked through.

People sometimes ask me how I can speak of God's goodness after such a painful chapter. My answer is simple: because I met Him there. I didn't just hear about His comfort. I felt it. I didn't just read about His peace. I experienced it in the middle of nights when my heart was trembling. I didn't just believe He was near. I lived moments where I knew I would not have survived if He hadn't been.

You Are Safe in His Arms

If you take nothing else from this chapter, remember this: God's goodness is not fragile. It is fierce, constant, and unstoppable. His love for you is greater than your pain, your past, or your fears. His love is not shaken by your questions, your grief, or your doubts. He is not intimidated by your tears or disappointed by your weakness.

Whether through an angel's wings, a gentle dream, a timely word, or the quiet whisper of the Holy Spirit, He will always find a way to remind you that you are safe in His arms.

Sometimes He speaks through Scripture.

Sometimes through a memory.

Sometimes through a friend or a moment of unexpected peace

But He always speaks because love always speaks.

And to the one reading this who still carries silent sorrow, hear me clearly:

God has not forgotten you.

He is not finished with you.

He is not withholding healing from you.

He is holding you – carefully, completely, and compassionately.

You are not surviving because you are strong.

You are surviving because He is strong.

And just as He carried me, He will carry you.

Just as He restored me, He will restore you.

You are safe, protected, and fiercely loved in the arms of the One who turns grief into glory and heartbreak into healing.

Prayer

Heavenly Father,

I lift up every reader walking through sorrow, uncertainty, or loss. Wrap them in the comfort of Your presence. Remind them that You are near to the brokenhearted and faithful to restore those who have been crushed by life's pain. Let Your angels, your messengers of peace, healing, and hope, surround them.

Lord, where there is fear, bring courage. Where there is despair, bring renewal. Where there is loneliness, bring the assurance of Your love. Heal every wound that grief has opened, and replace anxiety with Your perfect peace. Renew their faith, strengthen their hearts, and remind them that they are never forgotten by Heaven.

Thank You, Lord, for sending Your angels to protect us, for sending Your Son to redeem us, and for sending Your Spirit to dwell within us. May we rest daily in the truth that Your love will never leave nor forsake us.

In the precious and powerful name of Jesus Christ, Amen.

Anita Sechesky - Visionary Compiler & Publisher

Conclusion

As we come to the end of this anthology, we arrive at its most profound culmination – the final chapter Angels Among Us – Safe in His Love. This closing chapter serves as the heartbeat of the entire book, reminding us that every story of redemption, healing, and divine goodness shared within these pages ultimately points to the limitless, unwavering love of God. It's a love so deep, so personal, and so eternal that it surrounds every reader with the assurance that they are truly safe in His arms.

Throughout this anthology, we have journeyed through testimonies of faith, resilience, gratitude, and healing. Each chapter reveals a different facet of God's goodness. Yet, as these reflections draw to a close, the message that rises above them all is that God's goodness is born out of His perfect love. His love is not passive or abstract; it is alive, active, and personal- reaching into the very depths of our human experience and transforming even our pain into purpose. The stories shared here have shown us that God's love is not confined to the pages of history or the words of Scripture alone; it is present and powerful in our everyday lives. His love meets us in our darkest valleys, steadies us in life's storms, and celebrates with us in moments of triumph. It is a love that restores the broken, forgives the fallen, and uplifts the weary. Truly, there is no greater love than the love that flows from the heart of our Heavenly Father.

"Greater love has no one than this, than to lay down one's life for his friends." John 15:13 (NKJV)

Through Jesus Christ, we see the full expression of God's goodness manifested in perfect love. His sacrifice on the cross was not only an act of redemption but an eternal declaration of affection. It is a promise that no matter what we face, we are never alone. His love secures our salvation, restores our identity, and anchors our hope. This is the love that calls us out of fear and into faith, out of shame and into grace, out of darkness and into light. And yet, this divine love does even more. It empowers us. It gives us strength to overcome, courage to stand firm, and faith to keep moving forward even when the road is uncertain. God's goodness doesn't merely comfort us; it equips us to face every challenge with confidence in His promises.

When we walk in awareness of His love, we become unshakable – covered, protected, and filled with supernatural peace that cannot be taken away. Being part of the family of God is an all-encompassing experience. Just as a loving father provides for and protects his children, God's love surrounds every aspect of our lives. He is attentive to our needs, compassionate toward our struggles, and faithful to His Word. Yet even the purest love we find on earth cannot compare to the safety and completeness found in His divine embrace. His love covers our minds with peace, guards our hearts with strength, and shields our spirits from the forces of darkness.

The goodness of God calls us closer not just to witness His blessings, but to dwell in His presence. For it is there, in His presence, that we find both refuge and renewal. His love becomes our armor, His Word our defense, and His Spirit our constant guide. Through every trial and triumph, His love whispers, *"You are not alone. You are Mine."*

God's love is not limited by time, circumstance, or human understanding. It is a love that pursues, redeems, and restores. A love that reaches the individual heart – your heart – and assures you that no matter what life has brought you through, His arms remain open, strong, and safe. *"The eternal God is your refuge, and underneath are the everlasting arms"* Deuteronomy 33:27 (NKJV). If you have ever doubted your worth or questioned God's care, may these final words bring peace to your soul. You are loved beyond measure. You are seen, valued, and chosen by the One who holds the universe yet still calls you, His child. His goodness has carried you this far, and His love will sustain you forever.

As this anthology concludes, let your heart be still and your spirit open. Feel the gentle presence of the Father surrounding you – guiding, healing, and embracing you. May you come to know that to be safe in His arms is to live in the fullness of His love. Indeed, there is no greater love than the love of our God that redeems the past, secures the present, and promises a future filled with peace, purpose, and eternal safety in His embrace.

Sinner's Prayer

Dear Jesus,

I humbly come before You today and ask You to be the Savior and Lord of my life. I seek Your forgiveness for all I have done wrong. Please help me to become the person You created me to be. Restore every broken place within me and fill me with Your peace, love, and truth. May I walk in Your salvation and live for You all the days of my life.

In Your precious name, I pray. Amen.

"For God so loved the world that he gave his one and only Son, that whoever believes in him shall not perish but have eternal life." John 3:16 (NIV)

About The Authors

CHAPTERS 1, 6, 11, 16, 21, 26, 31, 36, 40

Minister Anita Sechesky is an award-winning author who has received the Amazon Gold Ribbon designation in Christian Counselling and Christian Faith for her latest anthology, *Safe in His Arms – The Goodness of God*. She is the CEO, Founder, and Best-Selling Publisher of Faith-Inspird Books, a division of LWL Publishing House, where she has successfully published over 733 authors worldwide.

Anita is the author of multiple #1 Best-Selling books in the genres of Faith, Inspirational Healing, and Positive Psychology, and she also writes and publishes children's literature. Through her 1-to-1 and group coaching programs, she empowers Christian authors and leaders to rise in their divine calling with confidence and purpose.

As the host of the *INSPIRED TO WRITE* podcast and facilitator of transformative Masterclasses for the Body of Christ, Anita's message centers on "Living Without Limitations" as a powerful and successful Child of God.

With a background as an Emergency Room Registered Nurse who has served in numerous healthcare facilities across Ontario, Canada, Anita has witnessed firsthand how spiritual well-being profoundly affects health, relationships, and personal destiny. It is her heart's greatest desire to promote healing – not only of the body, but also of the mind and spirit – through her God-given vision.

A Motivational Keynote Speaker, Graduate of the 5-Fold Minister Academy (Impact University) under Apostle John Eckhardt, and Certified Emotional Healing & Deliverance Minister, Anita also holds a Certificate in Religious Education (Deliverance Ministry & School of Theology, Principles of Spiritual Warfare) under Bishop Robin Dinnanauth. She is an ICF-Certified Professional Coach, Past President of the Holistic Chamber of Commerce (Brampton, ON Chapter, 2019), Kingdom Life Strategist, Mentor, Holistic Book Writing Coach, Ghostwriter, Workshop Facilitator, Conference Host, and Founder & Moderator of the FAITH-INSPIRED LIVING Clubhouse Group.

Her life and ministry continue to inspire countless individuals to discover their voice, walk in faith, and fulfill their Kingdom purpose.

- **Email:** lwlclienthelp@gmail.com
- **Website:** www.lwlpublishinghouse.com
- **Facebook:** LIVING WITHOUT LIMITATIONS in Print - LWL PUBLISHING HOUSE
- **LinkedIn:** asechesky
- **CLUBHOUSE:** FAITH INSPIRED LIVING
- **Instagram:** lwl_publishing_house
- **YouTube:** Faith-Inspired Lifestyle Studio

CHAPTER 2 – Abigail Khan

Abigail Khan is a resilient woman of unwavering faith who has served as a counselor, mentor, and special needs educational resource facilitator for over 30 years. A single mother of three successful adult children, she is passionate about fulfilling her God-given purpose by discipling others and advancing the Kingdom of God. Abigail is active in local church ministry, small group leadership, and international missions, as well as organizing community outreach initiatives. She is currently completing her Christian counseling certification and writing her first solo book entitled *Indestructible – A Testimony of Victories Over Trauma*. She gives all glory to God for her transformation.

Email: Irieservices.ca

LinkedIn: Abigail Khan

YouTube: Spiritual Growth with Abigail

Facebook: Spiritual Growth with Abigail

CHAPTERS 3, 9, 18, 24, 33, 38 – Nasha T. Alexis

Nasha T. Alexis is featured as a co-author of the Best-Selling anthology *Empowered Transformations – Real Stories of Hope*, compiled by Jasmine E. Clarke. She was born in Grenada, also known as the Spice Island, migrated to Canada at the age of 16, and made Brampton, Ontario, her new home. Nasha is the proud parent of two beautiful adult daughters. She loves music and is privileged to use the gifts of dance and flagging to minister and lead others in worship before our Lord and Savior, Jesus Christ. Nasha prays that every reader will find encouragement to keep holding on to the One who is always faithful.

Email: nasha.alexis@gmail.com

Instagram: Empress4love

Facebook: Nasha Alexis

CHAPTER 4 – Brian David Fuller

Brian David Fuller is an award-winning speaker and published co-author who lives by the mantra, "Faith it 'til you make it." His mission is to help individuals achieve greater fulfillment through faith-based mindset mastery. With a bachelor's degree in religious studies and a graduate certificate in public relations, Brian combines education, communication expertise, and powerful testimony to connect with audiences of all ages. His heart-centered style and ability to tell stories of hope and resilience empower people to get unstuck and realize their potential. Brian is available for booking to inspire your congregation, conference, or workforce.

- **X:** @BFullerspeaks
- **Instagram:** @BFullerspeaks
- **LinkedIn:** Brian Fuller
- **Facebook:** Brian Fuller

CHAPTER 5 – Chanroutie Superville

Evangelist Chanroutie Superville is the Founder and Visionary of Divine Freedom Church International. Born in Rio Claro, Trinidad and Tobago, West Indies, she is a devoted mother, grandmother, and mother-in-law whose life reflects unwavering faith and perseverance. A passionate prayer warrior and dedicated evangelist, Chanroutie has devoted her ministry to sharing the love of Jesus Christ and bringing deliverance, healing, and restoration to God's people. Through her leadership and intercessory calling, she continues to inspire many to walk in divine purpose, freedom, and faith, empowering others to experience the transforming power of God in their daily lives.

CHAPTER 7 – Cheryl Gardner

Cheryl Gardner is a first-generation Canadian, born to Guyanese parents. This mother of two and grandmother of two resides in Newmarket, Ontario, Canada. Cheryl wholeheartedly loves the Lord and has had the privilege and honor of using prophetic dance and flags to minister the Gospel to many. She has worked in Corporate Canada for over 30 years, is an ordained Deaconess, and recently attained her license as a Financial Advisor. Cheryl loves to travel and takes great pleasure in writing. She is excited to add "author" to her list of accomplishments and prays to one day write and publish her own book.

- **TikTok:** Sistah_C
- **Instagram:** Sistah_C
- **Facebook:** Cheryl Gardner
- **Email:** tahousi@yahoo.ca

CHAPTER 8 – Cindy Dawkins

Cindy Dawkins, originally from Jamaica, has lived in Canada since the age of fourteen. With over twenty-five years in the fashion industry, she has held senior roles in marketing, buying, and brand development for leading Canadian retailers, including Hudson's Bay. Cindy is also a certified announcer and MC. For nearly a decade, she has worked as an instructor-therapist supporting children and young adults on the autism spectrum. A mental health advocate and financial education campaigner, she also volunteers with youth ministries and gender-based violence survivors. Cindy proudly serves on non-profit boards and is a devoted mother of two young adults.

CHAPTER 10 – Dhanmatie Persaud

Pastor Dhanmatie Persaud (Pastor Gloria) is the Co-Founder and Pastor of *Church in the Fields Ministry*, where she has faithfully served alongside her husband since its founding. A graduate of Faith Theology Seminary and Destiny Dominion Bible Training Centre, she leads Sunday School, intercessory prayer, and Bible study sessions. Passionate about children's ministry, as well as youth and seniors counseling, Pastor Gloria plays a vital role in the spiritual and administrative life of the church. She is a devoted wife, mother of two sons, grandmother of three, and enjoys spending time with her family and caring for her two dogs.

CHAPTER 12 – Harrichand Persaud

Pastor Harrichand Persaud (Pastor Harry) is the Founder and Senior Pastor of *Church in the Fields Ministry*. He began the ministry as a Sunday School in 1994, expanded it into a cell group in 1998, and formally established the church in 2006. While leading the ministry full-time, he also maintains outside employment. Pastor Harry organizes baptisms, weddings, counseling sessions, community events, and outreach initiatives. Known for his servant leadership, he ministers to people of all ages. Outside the pulpit, he enjoys spending time with his grandchildren, tending to his garden, and remaining dedicated to both his faith and his professional commitments.

CHAPTER 13 – Jasmine E. Clarke

Jasmine E. Clarke is the Visionary Compiler of the Best-Selling anthology *Empowered Transformations* and an 8x Best-Selling Co-Author featured in *Stronger Resilience* (Patricia Russell), *Soul Sister Letters* (Anita Sechesky), and *Rise UP!* (Anita Sechesky). She holds a Bachelor's Degree in Worship Leadership, held positions as Choir Director and Assistant Choir Director in various ministries. Jasmine's life mission is to glorify God and proclaim the Gospel of Jesus Christ through every platform entrusted to her. She helps individuals discover and cultivate the God-given gifts within them – reminding others that no matter their past, God has the power to transform their lives for His glory.

Email: youhavemanystoriestotell@gmail.com

Facebook: jasmine.clarke.5815

Instagram: specialinhiseyes

CHAPTER 14 – Jean Lawrence-Scotland

Jean Lawrence-Scotland is a registered social worker, family therapist with over 30 years of frontline experience. She is featured as a co-author of the Best-Selling anthology *Empowered Transformations – Real Stories of Hope*, compiled by Jasmine E. Clarke. Jean specializes in mental health, supporting individuals, youth, and families facing challenges such as anxiety, depression, grief, addiction, and relational conflict. Her client-centered, strength-based approach is rooted in brief therapy and cultural sensitivity, particularly within diverse and racialized communities. A strong advocate for social justice, Jean also consults on equity, diversity, and inclusion in community systems. and founder of JLS Just Listen & Support Counselling Services.

CHAPTER 15 – Joan M. Steward

Joan M. Steward is a Holy Ghost-filled Christian, entrepreneur, and emerging writer with a background in computer science. She is featured as a co-author of the Best-Selling anthology *Empowered Transformations – Real Stories of Hope*, compiled by Jasmine E. Clarke.

Passionate about both faith and innovation, she blends her technical expertise with a heart for ministry and storytelling. Joan's writing is inspired by her spiritual journey, life experiences to uplift and encourage others through the Word of God. This anthology marks her second published work. As Joan continues to grow as a writer and entrepreneur, she remains committed to using her gifts for God's glory and to impacting lives with purpose and authenticity.

Email: jstewa3@hotmail.com

Facebook: Joan Steward

Instagram: jstewa3

CHAPTER 17 – Joshua Otabor

Joshua Otabor is a trained Civil Engineer, passionate pastor, visionary leader, and emerging voice at the intersection of faith, data, and societal transformation. With over 20 years of ministry across Nigeria, Africa, and now Canada, he leads Supernatural Life Center in Toronto. He is committed to raising believers as the Ekklesia – God's governing force in society. A prolific author, his book *7 Mountain Strategy for Discipling Nations* offers prophetic insight for this generation. Joshua is joyfully married to Titilayo, and together they are raising two daughters, Agape and Delight. He lives to see God's Kingdom come on earth.

CHAPTER 19 – Judy Brown

Judy Brown is a university graduate with a Bachelor's degree in Biology. Over the years, she has held various leadership positions in Christian groups at both university and church. Judy is a featured co-author in the Best-Selling anthology *Empowered Transformations – Real Stories of Hope*, compiled by Jasmine E. Clarke. Her primary mission is to build, connect, and inspire people to live with purpose, passion, and freedom – to show that, with God's help, one can freely and authentically be who He created them to be, living the abundant life God established for them.

📧 **Email:** judybrown3808@gmail.com

📷 **Instagram:** @walkinginpower.ca

CHAPTER 20 – Karen Jiron

Karen Jiron is a Registered Nurse, devoted daughter, sister, and aunt who attends Peel Pentecostal Tabernacle, where she has worshiped for the past three years. During her time there, she has grown deeply in her faith under the mentorship of dedicated pastors and leaders who have poured wisdom and spiritual guidance into her life. Karen feels a strong calling from God to serve women and support victims of domestic violence. With compassion and purpose, she is preparing to pursue this mission, using her faith and professional background to bring healing, hope, and restoration to those in need.

CHAPTER 22 – Karleen J. Poyser

Karleen J. Poyser is a 6x Best-Selling author with LWL Publishing House, a compiler, authorpreneur, inspirational speaker, and gospel singer/songwriter. Passionate about music and ministry, she shares the love of Christ through word and song. Karleen empowers others to find hope in God, even through life's toughest challenges. With a background as a financial consultant and legal advocate, she brings both compassion and strategy to her work. Her vision is to establish a wellness center for young adults and women, offering mentorship and skill development to help them grow in confidence, faith, and purpose.

Email: 1kpcconsulting@gmail.com

LinkedIn: kpoyser

CHAPTER 23 – Kayon Watson

As Senior Pastor at *Kingdom Alignment Ministries*, Pastor Kayon Watson demonstrates unwavering dedication to spreading the gospel and empowering others through his expertise in the Hebrew language and spiritual foundation. With a strong emphasis on community outreach and mentorship, his mission fosters a vibrant, faith-driven community. Through his work as an author, Pastor Watson furthers his commitment to inspiring others through the gospel. By leveraging motivational speaking, he innovatively expands his ministry's impact, spreading a message of hope, faith, and spiritual growth that resonates deeply with individuals worldwide.

Website: https://kingdomalignmentministries.com/media-shop

Facebook: Kingdomalignmentministry

Instagram: kingdomalignmentministries

CHAPTER 25 – Khaimnie Seepersaud

Khaimnie "Lorren" Seepersaud was born in Guyana, South America, and now resides in Toronto, Canada. She is a devoted wife, mother of two beautiful daughters, and a prayer warrior who loves to minister the Gospel of Jesus Christ. Through many life-changing experiences, Lorren has witnessed the miraculous power and goodness of God. Her journey – from childhood encounters with grief to divine moments of healing – has strengthened her faith and deepened her faith. Lorren's story is one of courage, restoration, and unwavering belief in God's promises. She continues to inspire others by testifying to His faithfulness and reminding them that no matter the trial, they are never beyond the reach of God's loving arms.

CHAPTERS 27, 37 – Koreen J. Bennett

Koreen J. Bennett is a wife, mother, grandmother, and Registered Nurse with 20 years of experience. She is the Visionary Compiler of the Best-Selling anthology *Oil of Joy*, a 4x Best-Selling co-author of other anthologies published with Faith-Inspired Books, a division of LWL Publishing House. A devoted follower of Jesus Christ and an entrepreneur, Koreen loves to praise and worship through singing and prophetic dancing. Her purpose is to inspire, encourage, and empower others to impact the lives of those they encounter.

Email: koko.bennett@yahoo.ca

Instagram: Kokonnection

Facebook: KokoBennett

CHAPTER 28 – Lesa Isaacs

Lesa Isaacs is a devoted woman of God, wife, mother, and grandmother. With over a decade of experience in education as a Special Needs Assistant, she has also worked in the medical and fitness fields. In 2020, Lesa became an entrepreneur and now serves as a pedicurist. A co-author in the Best-Selling anthology, *Empowered Transformations – Real Stories of Hope* (compiled by Jasmine E. Clarke in 2023), she continues to inspire others through service and leadership. Having volunteered as a girls' club leader and women's group co-facilitator, Lesa now leads a women's life group at her church and is pursuing her calling as a Spiritual Wellness Coach.

Instagram: @LesaRoseBB

Facebook: @LesaRoseBB

CHAPTER 29 – Lindsay Cesario

Lindsay Cesario is a living testimony of God's transforming grace. Once trapped in addiction, anger, and despair, she encountered the redeeming love of Jesus Christ on April 5th, 2024 – a night that forever changed her life. Through faith, baptism, and the power of the Holy Spirit, Lindsay was delivered, restored, and set free. Now walking in purpose and peace, she shares her story to bring hope to others who feel too broken to be healed. Lindsay's message is simple yet powerful: no pit is too deep for God's love to reach.

CHAPTER 30 – Nicole Ragguette

Prophetess Nicole Ragguette is the Lead Pastor of *Supernatural Life Centre Calgary* and a passionate ambassador for breaking the global cycle of generational poverty. As an international public speaker and advocate, she champions the cause of vulnerable populations and ethnic minorities worldwide. Nicole is also the visionary founder of The Rise Project, a dynamic initiative that empowers youth to discover their destiny and equips them to walk boldly in purpose. Her prophetic voice and leadership continue to transform communities both locally and globally.

Facebook: Nicole Ragguette

Instagram: @iamnicoleragguette

CHAPTER 32 – Patricia Giron

Patricia Giron is a devoted follower of Christ, philanthropist, joyful storyteller, and mother of two who finds beauty and humor in everyday moments. With a heart full of faith and a love for laughter, she writes to inspire others to recognize God's hand in every chapter of their lives. Patricia treasures meaningful connections and views communication as a powerful gift. Known for her kind spirit and playful personality, she prioritizes loyalty, compassion, and generosity in her daily life. Through her words, she reminds readers that grace can be found even in the chaos of motherhood through life's simplest blessings.

CHAPTER 34 – Samantha Mills-O'Brien

Samantha Mills-O'Brien was born and raised in Ottawa, Ontario. She is a devoted wife, mother of four, and caregiver to her mother. Samantha holds a Bachelor's Degree in Theology from the International Bible College and certificates in Business Accounting and Marketing from Thames Valley College. She has faithfully served in children's ministry and is passionate about sharing God's love through outreach to children, youth, and the homeless. An entrepreneur, Samantha co-owns Exodus Drywall Sanders Inc. with her husband and continues to live out her calling to serve others in faith and compassion.

Facebook: samantha.mills.509

Instagram: samanthamills672

Email: seekingprayer.srmo@gmail.com

CHAPTER 35 – Sharon Teklu

Sharon Teklu, author of the upcoming devotional-journal *Speak Life & Meditate on the Word*, was born in Ethiopia and has made Canada her home. A Registered Nurse and medical adjudicator with the Federal Government of Canada, Sharon's career spans hospital care, home IV therapy, and insurance assessments. She co-founded the Professional Association of Ethio-Canadians in Ottawa and volunteers with programs like the Oasis Program for Aging Well. Deeply rooted in faith and service, Sharon is passionate about helping others nurture their spiritual and emotional well-being through God's Word and the power of faith in everyday life.

CHAPTER 39 – Tricia Marcellin

Tricia Marcellin is a devoted single mother and a child of the Most High King. Originally from St. Lucia, she moved to Canada in 2004 and now resides there with her three beloved children. Her faith and family are at the center of her life. Tricia believes in walking in God's power and purpose, knowing He is always by her side. She is also an Early Childhood Assistant, passionate about nurturing young minds and committed to making a difference in the lives of children.

Instagram: triciafaithwalk

Facebook: Tricia Marcellin

Email: tmarcellin96@gmail.com

A Special Invitation

Dear Sir/Madam,

Thank you for supporting the authors of *Safe In His Arms – The Goodness of God* and for choosing to partner with LWL Publishing House through your purchase. We trust that the heartfelt testimonies within these pages have blessed you and encouraged your faith journey.

If you are newly discovering our company and have ever considered becoming a published author, here is a brief introduction to who we are:

Since 2013, under the leadership of Anita Sechesky, LWL Publishing House has coached and published more than 730 men and women of all ages, backgrounds, and nationalities. Our mission is to help individuals build confidence, find their voice, and express their story with clarity and purpose. Many of our authors begin as first-time or novice writers, and through our professional coaching, support, and guidance, they go on to become best-selling authors.

We specialize in drawing out the strength and authenticity of each writer's unique vision. By helping authors identify emotional barriers, release past trauma, and write from a place of healed expression, we empower them to produce their most powerful and transformative work. Those who work closely with our Publisher, Anita Sechesky, often surpass their own expectations and step boldly into new levels of creativity and confidence.

Our goal is to produce books that inspire the human spirit – stories that awaken purpose, strengthen hope, and ignite courage in every reader.

Every person carries a story. What's your vision? Let's bring it to life!

- Ready to become a published author by sharing your powerful testimony? Join one of our active anthologies as a co-author.

- Ready to elevate your portfolio and step into leadership? Compile your own visionary anthology with full professional coaching and support from Anita Sechesky.

- Ready to write and publish your own book? Contact us to schedule your personalized coaching session and begin your journey to Best-Seller success with Anita Sechesky.

Please visit our website for more information:

https://lwlpublishinghouse.com

Contact Anita Sechesky: lwlclienthelp@gmail.com

Write Your Book With Us!

www.lwlpublishinghouse.com

lwlclienthelp@gmail.com

www.ingramcontent.com/pod-product-compliance
Lightning Source LLC
Chambersburg PA
CBHW071223230426
43668CB00011B/1280